The Nature of the Mystical Body
Vol. I

Praise for *The Nature of the Mystical Body*

"The notion of the Church as the "Mystical Body of Christ" was developed during the Middle Ages, especially by St. Thomas Aquinas (1225–1274), and appears to be used for the first time in a magisterial document in 1302, namely, the Papal bull *Unam Sanctam*. After this, its most significant treatment can be credited to St. Robert Bellarmine (1542–1621) who advanced the notion in response to Protestant attacks on the Church's institution and emphasis on the invisibility of the Church. It received great attention after the First Vatican Council by theologians until becoming the subject of an entire encyclical by Pope Pius XII, appropriately titled *Mystici Corporis*. Consequently, the doctrine was very important in the lead up to the Second Vatican Council, and so it remains vital both for understanding the Council and for asserting the doctrine of the Church today. In 1934, this work by Ernest Mura stood out, seeing translation from French into German and English. What sets it apart is its spiritual vibrancy, its accessibility, and its illuminating treatment of the theme both in Sacred Scripture and its Thomistic synthesis. The great achievement of the work is the way in which it exposes the deep unity of Christ with His members as an outworking of His multifaceted mediatorship and efficient causality. If that sounds dry and abstract, I assure readers the work is anything but. As conversations about the nature of the Church intensify, this work remains relevant and reliable."

—DR. JAMES R. A. MERRICK, Benedictine College, Atchison, KS

"Faithful Catholics will rejoice in this new edition of a theological masterpiece! In this marvelous book, Ernest Mura masterfully treats the essence of St. Paul's and St. Thomas Aquinas's teaching on the Church, the Mystical Body of Christ. He inculcates a profoundly theological apprehension of the Church and he draws "interior souls" (as Fr. Garrigou-Lagrange calls them in the newly translated foreword) into a living and fruitful contemplation of Christ's Mystical Body as experienced most profoundly in the holy Sacrifice of the Mass. In this book, we see the theological propaedeutic to Pius XII's *Mystici Corporis* and to all subsequent, legitimate magisterial teaching on the Church."

—DR. MICHAEL SIRILLA, Professor of Theology,
Franciscan University of Steubenville

The Nature of the Mystical Body
Volume I

ERNEST MURA
RELIGIOUS OF ST. VINCENT DE PAUL

Translated by
M. Angeline Bouchard

Foreword by
Réginald Garrigou-Lagrange, O.P.

AROUCA
PRESS

Translated from the first volume of *Le Corps Mystique du Christ*, by Ernest Mura, R.S.V., published by André Blot, Paris in 1934. Originally published and adapted for the English edition in 1963 by B. Herder. Pages 235-244 were not included in the original French edition.

The foreword by Réginald Garrigou-Lagrange, O.P., translated by Matthew K. Minerd, Ph.D., appears here for the first time in English. The translation for the second volume of *Le Corps Mystique du Christ* is forthcoming from Arouca Press.

Imprimatur ✠ Joseph Cardinal Ritter
Archbishop of St. Louis, October 17, 1963

Second English Edition © Arouca Press 2023

ISBN: 978-1-990685-67-5 (pbk)
ISBN: 978-1-990685-68-2 (hc)

Cover design and layout by Allison Merrick

Arouca Press
PO Box 55003
Bridgeport PO
Waterloo, ON N2J 0A5
Canada
www.aroucapress.com
Send inquiries to info@aroucapress.com

DICO OPERA MEA REGI

To Christ Jesus
King, Prophet, and Eternal Pontiff
Adorable Head of the Mystical Body,
through Mary
His Immaculate Mother
Queen of the Universe
I dedicate and consecrate
this work
as a testimony
of fidelity, obedience,
And love.

CONTENTS

FOREWORD

Fr. Réginald Garrigou-Lagrange, O.P.
Rome, Angelicum

A book devoted to the Mystical Body of Christ can only be received with true spiritual joy, especially when such a work is, like the present volume, the fruit of many years of study and meditation on the letters of St. Paul and the works of St. Thomas. Indeed, it synthetically presents to the reader everything of the greatest interest for our souls that is contained in the mystery of Christ's Church.

"God," as St. Paul states, "*has made Christ the Head of the whole Church; the Church is the Body of Christ and His fullness*" (see Eph. 1:22–23). These words of the Apostle contain, in concentrated form, the entire doctrine of the Mystical Body of Jesus Christ. Through the ages, this most profound doctrine occupied the thought of the Fathers, was the subject of attentive reflection by great theologians, and has nourished the piety of the faithful. Today more than ever, the Spirit of God invites the Bride of Christ to make this beautiful mystery the subject of her contemplation and the vigorous source of her very life.

St. Thomas was not unaware of the importance of this central dogma of Christianity. One could say that the whole *Summa theologiae* is steeped in this mystery. For a mind that was so permeated with the teaching of St. Paul and St. Augustine and animated by so perceptive a genius, it could not have been otherwise. Like the Apostle to the Gentiles and the Doctor from Hippo, St. Thomas draws all things back to Christ so that they might all be brought back to God: *Vos estis Christi, Christus autem Dei*; You are Christ's, and Christ is God's (1 Cor. 3:23). He who wrote such extensive commentaries on the Gospel of St. John and the Letters of St. Paul could not relegate this teaching concerning the *totus Christus*, the Whole Christ, to a secondary place. The entire mystery of predestination and the distribution of graces find their principle in Jesus, the Mystical Head of the Church, in accord with the words of St. Paul: *Praedestinavit nos in adoptionem filiorum per Jesum Christum*; He predestined us unto the adoption of sons through Christ Jesus (Eph. 1:5; cf. *ST* III, q. 24, a. 3 and 4).

Indeed, in the present order of Providence, every grace bestowed upon men, all the supernatural life given to him, is a fruit of the Redemption. Now, Saint Thomas conceives of our Redemption in relation to the divine solidarity uniting the Mystical Body, which makes Jesus our Head and our surety. "Jesus received grace," says Saint Thomas, "not personally and as a private endowment, but rather, as Head, so that He might pour it forth upon all men. Thus, through his works Christ merited for Himself and for all His members, as any other man [in a state of grace] does for himself alone" (*ST* III, q. 48, a. 48, a. 1).

It is sometimes objected that Our Lord could not suffer for us, nor expiate for faults that He had not committed, since reparation must come from the person who committed the offence in question. Saint Thomas was aware of this objection, and the doctrine of the Mystical Body is what furnishes him with a response: "The Head and members together form *one, single mystical person*. And this is why Christ's satisfaction belongs to all the faithful as to the members of Jesus Christ" (*ST* III, q. 48, a. 2, ad 1). Thus, thanks to this mysterious and divine solidarity, all the Savior's bounty, the infinite merits of His Passion, belong to us, and we can present them as a superabundant ransom to God the Father for all the sins of men. "Christ's Passion," says St. Thomas once more, "Causes the remission of sins according to the manner of Redemption. For since He is our Head, He has delivered us from sin as His members, at the cost of His Passion, which He endured out of charity and obedience. . .This is all because the whole Church, the Mystical Body of Christ, is considered as one person with Christ, its Head" (*ST* III, q. 49, a. 1).

These texts are of the greatest importance, for they cast light upon St. Thomas's entire teaching concerning grace and the Redemption, as the radiance of first principles illuminates all the conclusions drawn therefrom..

In light of these general points regarding the unity of the Mystical Body, our Holy Doctor then descends to the consideration of particular applications. At times, he studies Jesus Christ's role as Head, enumerating, with his customary precision, the functions and prerogatives of this headship. At other times, he considers the diversity of the members in this Body, and explains to us the nature of their supernatural unity.

The whole of *ST* III, q. 8 is devoted to Christ's *capital grace*, shedding light on his quality as the *Mystical Head* of men and angels. Here, we will content ourselves with reporting the essential part of *ST* III, q. 8, a. 1:

The whole Church is one, single Mystical Body, . . . and Christ is its Head. Now, we can consider three things about the head: the place it occupies, its perfection, and its influence. Its place: it is man's most eminent part . . . Its perfection: it contains all the internal and external senses. . . . Its influence: the strength and movement of the other bodily members, and the governance of their activity, all proceed from it. Now, this threefold preeminence belongs to Christ in a spiritual way.

First, through His proximity to God, He received a grace that surpasses the grace had by any creature whatsoever . . . , for all others have received the gift of grace in view of Christ's, in accord with what the Apostle writes to the Romans (8:29, RSV): "For those whom he foreknew he also predestined to be conformed to the image of his Son, in order that he might be the first-born among many brethren." Second, Christ has the greatest perfection because he possesses the fullness of all graces, according to the words of Saint John (cf. John 1:14): "We beheld Him, full of grace and truth." And, thirdly, he has the power to influence and produce grace in all the members of the Church, in accord with the words of Saint John (ibid., 1:16): "And from His fulness have we all received." Therefore, Christ is fittingly said to be the Head of the Church.

Every line, not to say every word, of this incomparable article could justly call for commentary. The threefold preeminence that the holy Doctor attributes to Christ in relation to the Church contains, in substance, nearly the entire doctrine of the Mystical Body. Saint Thomas himself provided for us an ample explanation of this important article, in everything that follows in his treatise on the Incarnate Word and the Sacraments. What he tells us later on concerning the ineffable perfections of the Son of God made man bears witness to Christ's primacy of perfection. The question devoted to Christ's predestination, which is the cause and exemplar of our own, highlights, above all, His primacy of order. And as regards his primacy of influence, Saint Thomas reveals this to us in all the mysteries of the life, death, and resurrection of Jesus Christ: "*Omnes actiones et passiones Christi, instrumentaliter operantur, in virtute divinitatis, ad salutem humanam.* All that Christ did and suffered act instrumentally, by virtue of his divinity, to bring about man's salvation" (*ST* III, q. 48, a. 6).

In a lengthy series of articles and questions, whose dogmatic riches and practical significance for the Christian life are often overlooked, Saint Thomas applies this universal principle and shows us the mysteries of life and sanctification found in all the actions of our Savior, who is worthy of adoration, presenting in particular the principal facts of His time on earth. His birth in Bethlehem (*ST* III, q. 35), His circumcision so full of humility

(q. 37, a. 1), His baptism in the Jordan (q. 39), His temptation in the desert (q. 41), His divine preaching (q. 42), His simple and familiar way of life (q. 40), His glorious transfiguration (q. 45)—all of these are sources of grace, examples of holiness, and principles of divine life for us. Through the power of His Passion and death we die to sin (q. 48–50). Through the mystery of His divine burial we are, in Holy Baptism, buried with Christ and hidden in God (q. 51). Through His triumphant resurrection from the dead we too find a new life, one that is altogether heavenly and supernatural (q. 56). And finally, through His ascension, we enter heaven following Jesus as members united to their Head (q. 57).

Saint Thomas so readily dwells on all these mysteries at length, in a way that is all the more noteworthy in light of how most theological textbooks nowadays pass over them in complete silence, with the exception of the mystery of Our Lord's Passion and death. But our Holy Doctor lingered over all these because he understood how these mysteries of Christ are of interest, in the work of our salvation and our sanctification, each mystery in its own way, according to its own particular grace.[1]

In his treatise on the Sacraments in the *Summa theologiae*, St. Thomas sheds even greater light on how Jesus's Sacred Humanity exercises this vital influence and sanctifying power over the whole Mystical Body. To his eyes, these admirable instruments of grace are nothing other than the means used by the divine Goodness for establishing and strengthening more and more the organic bonds and spiritual union between Jesus and our souls, subjecting us to the beneficent action of our Mystical Head. "For it is manifest," Saint Thomas writes, "that *through the sacraments of the New Law man is incorporated into Christ*, as Saint Paul says about baptism (Gal. 3:27, RSV): 'For as many of you as were baptized into Christ have put on Christ.' Now, man becomes a member of Christ only by grace . . . (And in this way, the causality of grace by the sacraments is a proven fact.)" (*ST* III, q. 62, a. 1).

Therefore, the entire doctrine concerning the Sacraments depends upon the dogma of our incorporation into Jesus Christ. Baptism sanctifies us only because it establishes between Jesus and us this vital bond, thanks to which the holiness of our divine Head flows into us, His members. And if confirmation confers the Holy Spirit on us, this is because it makes us a mystical extension of Christ, upon whom the fullness of the Holy Spirit rests, abiding in Him. But Saint Thomas particularly insists on this life-giving union

---

[1]   Trans. note: Along these lines, the reader should consider meditating on Bl. Columba Marmion, *Christ in His Mysteries*, trans. Mother M. St. Thomas (Dublin: The Cenacle Press at Silverstream Priory, 2022).

with Jesus Christ when he discusses the sacrament *par excellence*, the Holy Eucharist. Indeed, according to him, "the proper grace of this sacrament, the *res sacramenti*, is the unity of the Mystical Body" (*ST* III, q. 73, a. 4).

In addition to this very clear doctrine of Saint Thomas concerning this Headship that belongs to Christ, we must add what he teaches regarding the diversity of the members who constitute the Mystical Body of Jesus Christ. Unity in multiplicity is the law that presides over the harmony of the world. We find it no less beautifully in this supernatural organism which is the Mystical Body. As the holy Doctor tells us in *ST* II-II, q. 183, a. 2:

> For as in the natural order the perfection which is found in God in a simple and uniform way can be found in the created universe only in a divided and multiplied manner, so too *the fullness of grace that is wholly united in Christ, as in the Head, is spread out in various ways in the members so that the Body of the Church may be perfect.* This is what Saint Paul teaches in his letter to the Ephesians (cf. 4:11–12): "Christ established some as apostles, others as prophets, others as evangelists, and still others as pastors and teachers, for the consummation or completion of the saints."

Is the unity of the Church compromised by this diversity of functions? Quite the opposite. The multiplicity of organs in the human body makes its vital cohesion and the interdependence of all its parts all the clearer. The same is true of the Mystical Body: "Such diversity of states and offices," says Saint Thomas, "does not destroy the Church's unity, which is guaranteed through unity of faith and charity and through mutual service, in accord with what Saint Paul teaches to the Ephesians (4:16)" (*ST* II-II, q. 183, a. 2, ad 1).

Nonetheless, faith and charity, and this hierarchical subordination by which "some are applied to the service of others" [cf. 1 Cor. 16:15][2] do not constitute the ultimate principles of the unity of the Whole Christ. According to Saint Thomas, the primary source of this supernatural unity is the Holy Spirit, who is the soul of the Mystical Body, in accordance with the teaching of the Apostle: *Unum Corpus, unus Spiritus* (Eph. 4:4).

"Just as," writes our holy Doctor, "the various members of a natural body are held in unity by the power of its vivifying spirit and disintegrate as soon as the soul departs from it, so too, in the Body of the Church, peace is ensured among its various members by the power of the Holy Spirit, who gives life to the Body of the Church, as Saint Paul teaches to the Ephesians

---

[2] Trans. note: Fr. Garrigou-Lagrange cites Ephesians 4:16.

(Eph. 4:3): 'Strive to maintain the unity of the Spirit in the bond of peace'" (*ST* II-II, q. 183, a. 2, ad 3).

Thus, as is clear, Saint Thomas furnishes us with a precise and quite extensive doctrine concerning the beautiful mystery of the Whole Christ. However, we have only indicated its main lines. What he teaches elsewhere at greater length concerning the nature of grace and the theological virtues and concerning the indwelling of the Holy Spirit in the souls of the just must all be connected to what he has just told us concerning the role of faith and charity, and above all the influence of the Holy Spirit, in maintaining the unity of the Mystical Body. In this way, one will find in the *Summa theologiae* and the Angelic Doctor's other works, no longer merely a simple sketch, but a complete theology concerning the nature and life of the Mystical Body of Jesus Christ.

In the work to which these pages serve as a preface, the reader will find an exposition of this theology, in conformity with St. Thomas's own teaching and in accord with the inspired teaching of St. John and St. Paul. We believe that this is a timely and providential work, for it responds to a need that is felt with particular strength in our days, namely, the desire to understand more fully and to live more profoundly the mystery of our vital union with Jesus, our Head, in the unity of the Mystical Body.

For some time now, this important and truly central dogma of the Catholic faith has received greater consideration from various authors. Many articles have touched on the subject. Various works have appeared in recent years studying the Mystical Body from this or that perspective: from the perspective of Scripture or the Fathers, from the dogmatic point of view, or from the practical perspective of the spiritual life. However, no work, it seems, has yet embraced these different points of view in a theological synthesis, presenting at once the intimate nature of this mystical unity of the Whole Christ and the divine life that animates this supernatural organism. In his beautiful work, *La Doctrine du Corps mystique de Jésus-Christ*, Father Anger laid the foundations for these labors and gathered together the necessary materials. He would have liked to "recast and expand upon his first study"; unfortunately, however, pressing occupations left him no time to do so. With noble disinterestedness, the author expressed the wish to see a theologian arise who would engage more deeply in studying this beautiful doctrine (cf. Anger, "Introduction," *La Doctrine du Corps mystique de Jésus-Christ*, 15).

Responding to these wishes, the present work takes up the subject in a methodical and thorough manner. Considering the Mystical Body in its being and its activity, it divides the matter into two parts: the first studies what pertains to its being, that is to say, the nature and constitution of the Mystical Body in its organic unity and in the diversity of its members; the second discusses what pertains to the activity or life of the Whole Christ. First, it considers the life of the Head, in the threefold manifestation of His redemptive mediation: His divine priesthood, His universal kingship, and His prophetic and doctrinal mission. Next, the work turns to the life of the members of the mystical body: the life of each believer, which is nothing other than the development of baptismal grace, with all its attendant virtues and gifts; as well as the life of the Mystical Body as a whole, manifesting itself through the course of the Church's liturgical worship, in the exercise of her authority through governance, and by the teaching of her infallible magisterium. The study ends by considering the life of the Mystical Body in its full flowering in heaven, what Saint Paul calls "the fullness of the age of Christ" and "the consummation of the saints" (see Eph. 4:12–13) and what Saint John, in Revelation, presents to us as the celebration of the Wedding-Feast of the Lamb with the Church, His Bride.

Mary has a place of prominence in this doctrinal synthesis. Her eminent role as Mother of all the redeemed and Universal Mediatrix is studied here in dependence upon the priestly mediation of Christ the Head, especially according to the remarkable and now-classic doctrine of [St.] Louis Grignion de Montfort.

Those souls who meditate deeply upon this doctrinal whole will certainly draw great benefit for themselves. In this work, dogma and morality, speculative and practical theology, and ascetic and mystical science are all fused together into the unity of the one formal object that belongs properly to sacred science. In this doctrine of the Mystical Body, theology truly shows itself to be a science of life and holiness, placing within the reach of all souls the purest substance of the Gospel and the Apostolic Letters.

More than any other dogma, this doctrine places in the highest relief the role of Mediator belonging to Christ, who is King, Priest, and Teacher of the truth. As King, Jesus rules our activity and guides our steps towards God, who is Supreme Beatitude, for the proper function of kingship is to direct all the members of a society upon the paths of the good, toward the end that is the ultimate aim of their activity. As the infallible Teacher of supernatural truth, Christ nourishes our intellects with the bread of the divine word. And, finally, as eternal priest, Jesus communicates to us the divine life that He acquired for us through His sacrifice upon Calvary, conveying this life to us each day, upon the altar, through "the wondrous sacrament of the Passion" (Collect of *Corpus Christi*).

These truths, which are filled with such salvific power, will lead generous souls in particular to understand more fully the sacrifice of the Mass, which, according to Saint Thomas's teaching, is substantially the same as that of the Cross: *Non est aliud a sacrificio quod ipse Christus obtulit*; this sacrifice does not differ from that which Christ Himself offered (*ST* III, q. 22, a. 3, ad 2). Yes, it is the same, the author rightly insists, because the Eucharist is the sacrament of the Passion, as Saint Thomas repeats, following Saint Augustine: *Sacramentum perfectum Passionis*, the perfect sacrament of the Passion (*ST* III, q. 73, a. 5, ad 2; Augustine, *City of God*, 10.20).

Thus understood, Holy Mass, with Holy Communion made in the same spirit, will lead believers to unite the sacrifice of their whole life to Jesus's own immolation, to truly incorporate themselves into the immolated Christ, and to live the grace of their baptism to the full. In this way, they will complete in themselves "what is lacking in the sufferings of Christ" (Col 1:24) and will realize on their own behalf what Saint Catherine of Siena asked of God in this beautiful prayer: "O eternal God, receive the sacrifice of my life for the Mystical Body of the Holy Church. I can only give you what you yourself have given me. Take this, my heart, and press it upon the face of the Bride!" (Letter to Bl. Raymond of Capua, Feb. 16, 1380, written a few days before her death).

———•———

This work has shed bright light upon these truths. By avoiding both overly technical language and superficial simplification, it makes them accessible to all, without sacrificing any of their elevation and radiance. In this way, it disposes interior souls for the contemplation of these lofty truths, and it invites them always to live upon them and to lead others to do so as well. It is a realization of the maxim dear to Saint Thomas: "*Contemplari et contemplata aliis tradere per doctrinam et praedicationem*. To contemplate and, through teaching and preaching, to hand on to others what one has contemplated" (*ST* III, q. 188, a. 6).

Translated by Matthew K. Minerd, Ph.D.

INTRODUCTION

In his Encyclical *Mystici Corporis Christi*, Pope Pius XII cast a significant light on the dogma of the Mystical Body, corroborating with the weight of his apostolic authority a dogma that is held in high regard and that is studied and preached today. The Pope promulgated this solemn document "to throw an added ray of glory on the supreme beauty of the Church; to bring out into duller light the exalted supernatural nobility of the faithful who in the Body of Christ are united with their Head; and finally, to exclude definitively the many errors current with regard to this matter."[1]

The papal pronouncement proved a stimulant and a valuable encouragement to Catholic theologians to delve deeper into and to make better known to the faithful this mystery of Christ, which is the heart and wellspring of Christian doctrine, the food of faith, and the substantial nourishment of a solid and fruitful piety. Indeed, Pope Pius XII invited "all those who are drawn by the Holy Spirit to study [this dogma],"[2] and expressed the hope that a deeper study of this mystery would "bring forth abundant fruit"[3] of perfection and of holiness in the souls of the faithful.

Further, everything at this tragic juncture in which our poor world finds itself, surrounded as it is by the material and moral ruins of the cultural and spiritual patrimony of so many nations and anxiously searching for a firm foundation on which to build the social and spiritual unity of peoples, invites us to turn with burning faith toward the One who is our peace and who has destroyed in his flesh the enmity among peoples (cf. Eph. 2:14), toward him who is the Head of regenerated humanity, the cornerstone on whom the whole structure rises and grows into a holy temple in the Lord (cf. Eph. 2:20–21).

Not only on the spiritual level, but even on the level of temporal realities, we can assert without mental reservation that there is salvation only in Christ. Because human nature has been wounded by original sin, it does not have within itself the light or the strength to establish a human order

---

[1] Encyclical *Mystici Corporis*, Vatican Translation (National Catholic Welfare Conference, Washington, D.C., 1943), Introduction, par. II.

[2] Ibid., par. 1.

[3] Ibid., par. 4.

that will guarantee the protection of the rights of each man, the growth of a virtuous life, and the maintenance of social peace. Man is saved only by Christ; he cannot with impunity close himself off from redemptive grace and reject the gentle and salutary yoke of the law of the Gospel. He will learn at his own expense that he who does not gather up with Christ, squanders his moral riches and becomes a pauper.

For this reason His Holiness Pope John XXIII, at the conclusion of his new charter of Catholic social action, the Encyclical *Mater et Magistra*, invited all his sons to imbue their souls with the dogma of the Mystical Body so that man's labors may be filled with its life-giving power:

> We cannot conclude our encyclical without recalling another sublime truth and reality, namely that we are living members of the Mystical Body of Christ, which is his Church: . . .
>
> We invite with paternal urgency all our sons belonging to either the clergy or the laity to be deeply conscious of this dignity and nobility owing to the fact that they are grafted onto Christ as shoots on a vine: "I am the vine and you are the branches." And they are thus called to live by his very life. Hence, when one carries on one's proper activity, even if it be of temporal nature, in union with Jesus the divine Redeemer, every work becomes a continuation of his work and penetrated with redemptive power: "He that abideth in me, and I in him, the same beareth much fruit."[4]

We are happy, therefore, to comply with the desires of Holy Mother Church in bringing out an American edition of this work concerning the total Christ.

The doctrine of the Mystical Body, embracing in its supernatural reality the person of the Word made flesh, our Lord Jesus Christ and all his brothers or members through grace, is a sublime doctrine, and one that is most fruitful for the life of souls and of human society. Indeed, this doctrine is not new, for it is at least as ancient as Christianity. It can be found already fully developed in the epistles of St. Paul. Yes, we must seek the doctrine of the Mystical Body in the apostolic letters to the Romans, to the Corinthians, and to the faithful of Galatia, of Ephesus, and of Colossus. We find it set down there, not implicitly or merely in outline form, as are so many other revealed doctrines contained in Holy Scripture, but presented in its fullest development and in its diverse constitutive elements. The Apostle had a

---

[4] Encyclical *Mater et Magistra*, given at Rome, at St. Peter's, May 15, 1961. English translation published in the Special Encyclical Supplement of *The Register*, July 23, 1961, pars. 258–59.

clear conception of the doctrine, and delineated its essential features for us. He even indicated its detailed elements and practical conclusions.

The writings of St. Paul, however, do not present the doctrine to us in a didactic, orderly, and consecutive manner. Fragments of it are scattered throughout all of his principal letters to the churches. In his epistles, the Apostle did not intend to give a complete and methodical teaching; rather he wished to remind the faithful, according to their needs and to the circumstances of time and of place, of what his oral magisterium had already taught them. He laid stress on his past teaching, depending on the progress the various Christian communities had made in the interior knowledge and love of Christ Jesus.

St. Paul did not translate his sublime doctrine into theological formulas or into scholastic terms. He spoke in a concrete, direct style, intelligible to the faithful whom he had instructed. He did this for the very good reason that he was writing at a time when the technical form of theological language neither existed nor would have been understood.

Because of these two facts—the dispersion of Paul's doctrine among several epistles and in the context of various teachings, and the absence of a specific terminology expressing the truths in question in rigorously precise formulas—theologians of today still have a useful and necessary work to accomplish. They must gather the various elements of the teaching of St. Paul on the Mystical Body into a single body of doctrine and explain the doctrine according to the principles and methods of theology. Once this task has been finished, practical applications to the spiritual life will be easy, and a teaching that abounds with the fruits of holiness will be available to interior souls.

The doctrine of the Mystical Body is, as it were, the central point of all Revelation, the supreme mystery of Christianity; St. Paul calls it "the mystery which has been hidden from eternity in God" (Eph. 3:9), "but now is clearly shown to his saints" (Col. 1:26). It is the mystery of our incorporation into Christ, of our life in Christ, of our perfection and spiritual consummation through Christ Jesus.[5]

---

[5] When the doctrine of the Mystical Body is called "the central point of all Revelation," or "the central dogma of Christianity" there is no question of indicating the *formal object* of theology. The specific formality of theology is God himself supernaturally known; it is the Godhead in all that is strictly attributable to it. The various *material objects* which theology attains, outside of God (among them the total Christ which includes the Head and the members), are considered by this science only in their relation to God—so says St. Thomas (*Summa theologiae*, Ia, q. 1, a.7). But precisely among these various objects which sacred science treats, the Mystical Body holds a sort of primacy. This doctrine groups all the other dogmas around itself; it throws light on them; it complements and completes them. And even if the very dogma of the Trinity

Even though the faithful do not need to know the profundities of scholastic teaching, or the degrees and distinctions that theology discerns in the dogma of our life in God and of our union to Jesus Christ, nevertheless it is useful and necessary for shepherds of souls to be familiar with these notions in order to be able to dispense wisely to their flock the spiritual food that is suited to them. Directors of conscience must understand clearly the exact meaning of St. Paul's formulas, in order to forewarn those under their direction against improper or even totally false interpretations of the doctrine of the great Apostle.

Because of such exaggerations certain persons, including many devoted to the interior life, show some apprehension with regard to the doctrine of the Mystical Body. They suspect formulas such as this one: "It is Jesus who acts in me, who suffers in me." These words, which should be used only with discretion, seem to savor of pantheism, as if they expressed a *substantial* identification of our person with that of our Lord.

Obviously we must be on our guard against any exaggeration of this sort, but it is equally dangerous to fall into the opposite extreme and voluntarily ignore a doctrine which is profitable to souls. The golden mean is to present the truth in a light that reveals all its excellence and dispels possible ambiguities and confusion.

This we shall attempt to do, with God's help, by relating the deposit of Revelation to the teachings of theology. Following the method the Church has always used of breaking the bread of divine Scripture for her children, we shall explain the words of eternal Wisdom in the language of human wisdom. This *rapprochement* will have the twofold advantage of making us penetrate the profound meaning of the sacred books with the help of theology, and conversely of enriching a theology, sometimes dry and abstract, with the unction of the Holy Spirit that permeates the pages of Scripture.

Today more than ever before these two currents of sacred science must flow together into the soul of the priest to combat two contrary perils. For if the study of Sacred Scripture without a theological foundation can be a peril for the faith (as the aberrations of modernism bear witness), speculative theology without the science of Scripture can render charity anemic and remain inoperative. On the other hand, together the two constitute

does not enter directly into the theology of the Mystical Body, it is considered indirectly in this dogma as the term and the object of the life of the whole Christ. For fuller treatment of this subject, see the author's *Le Corps Mystique du Christ*, Volume II, Chapter 15.

a wonderful resource, a powerhouse of light and strength (*ad omne opus bonum*) for every salutary work of the apostolate and of the spiritual life.

In exploiting the treasures of Holy Scripture, we have turned principally to the doctrine of St. Paul as being the most explicit and complete on the dogma of our incorporation into Christ, and we have thought it best to set it forth in its entirety. This does not mean that we have excluded other sources of the inspired Book: St. John's teachings on the subject, in his Gospel, in his epistles, and in the Apocalypse, are filled with riches.

We shall likewise use, as occasion offers, the precious contribution made by the Fathers of the Church to the doctrine of the Mystical Body. For a more complete presentation of patristic teaching, however, reference should be had to the specialists in positive theology, and especially to the work of Father Mersch.[6]

The doctrine of the Mystical Body has always occupied a place of honor in the teaching of the Church. Following St. Paul, ecclesiastical writers and Catholic doctors have striven to make known to the faithful the ineffable mystery of our incorporation into Christ. The Fathers of the Church, with St. Augustine, St. Gregory Nazianzen, St. John Chrysostom, St. Cyril of Alexandria, and St. Hilary of Poitiers in the forefront, constantly come back to this central dogma of the faith as the inexhaustible theme of their theological dissertations and of their exhortations to the people. The scholastics in their turn frequently exploit this rich mine of doctrine.[7] And the prince of scholasticism, St. Thomas Aquinas, is so deeply imbued with this doctrine that he continually borrows from it, both in the *Summa* and in his commentaries on Scripture, arguments that solve difficulties, throw light on problems, or settle questions.

The admirable "French School" of the 17th century, following Cardinal de Bérulle, Monsieur Olier, Fathers Condren and Bourgoing, St. Louis de Montfort, St. John Eudes, and many others, has done very well by the doctrine of the Mystical Body. It has studied the doctrine not only with the mind but with the heart, and has drawn from it beautiful practical conclusions, sublime rules of Christian living, and valuable directives for the ascetical and mystical life.

---

[6] Cf. Emile Mersch. S.J., *Le Corps Mystique de Jésus-Christ*, Étude de théologie historique (Louvain: Museum Lessianum, 2nd ed., 1936).

[7] Cf. among others: Piolanti, *Il Corpo Mistico e le sue relazioni con l'Eucaristia in S. Alberto Magno* (Rome, 1939). This work contains numerous references to thirteenth-century scholastics.

At last, today, after a period of partial oblivion and of a relegation to the background that coincided with the worldwide promulgation of the individualist error, Catholic thinkers are again giving more attention to the dogma of the total Christ, of the organic, supernatural, and divine unity that we form together with Jesus. Treatises of theology once again assign a place to this doctrine among their series of propositions. Periodicals of theological, liturgical, and spiritual science study at length one or another of its aspects. Several fine works have stressed, either from the theoretical or practical point of view, the teaching of St. Paul concerning our union with Christ.

We shall not pause to discuss the excellent works of Dom Columba Marmion, the monk of Maredsous who was such a pioneer in this field. In *Christ the Life of the Soul* and in *Christ in His Mysteries*, while he did not treat the dogma of the total Christ in a didactic manner, he contributed significantly to restoring Christian devotion to the great Pauline doctrine. Under his tutelage, souls have learned once again to live their incorporation into Christ, and theologians have found in his teaching a climate of thought favorable to a more thorough explanation of the Mystical Body.

Among the studies that treat our subject *ex professo*, we must first of all point to Abbé Anger's *La Doctrine du Corps Mystique de Jésus Christ*, published in 1929. A few years later, in 1934, appeared the first edition of our own study, and in 1936, the valuable study of historical theology by Father Mersch mentioned above. Father Mersch exploited with patient erudition the principal treasures of the Old and New Testament, of the Greek and Latin Fathers, and of the princes of theology from the earliest days to our own time, providing us with a magnificent panoramic view of Catholic doctrine on this central dogma of our faith. It makes known to us the riches that Christian spirituality was once able to draw from the admirable mystery of our incorporation into Christ. It convinces us that it is impossible to exaggerate the importance of the doctrine of the Mystical Body, whether in the exposition of dogma or in the practice of the interior life—in short, in every phase of Christian life.

Father Mersch's *La Théologie du Corps Mystique*, published in 1946 after his tragic death in June, 1940, a victim of the wartime bombing, is a less successful attempt at speculative synthesis. The author was not able to put the finishing touches to it, and it contains many controversial and inaccurate statements.[8] However his earlier work, *Morale et Corps Mystique*, published in 1937, is excellent from every point of view. This is a collection of articles applying the dogma of the total Christ to the most diverse conditions of Christian life: marriage, the priesthood, social action, the religious life, and so forth.

Father Sebastian Tromp, S.J, professor at the Gregorian University, has contributed several studies, some before and some after Pope Pius XII's Encyclical *Mystici Corporis* of 1943. In 1937 he published *Corpus Mysticum quod est Ecclesia*, a textbook for theology courses of great doctrinal content and rich in bibliographical references. After this general introduction which was re-edited in 1946, he brought out a second and third part under the same title but with the following subtitles: "De Christo Capite" and "De Spiritu Christi Anima." The doctrine set forth is solid, drawn from the Fathers and from the great theologians. In 1948 Father Tromp published an annotated edition of *Mystici Corporis* entitled *Litterae Encyclicae de Mystico Jesu Christi Corpore*. The author has written many tracts on the same subject. *De Spiritu Sancto, Anima Corporis Mystici* consists of two tracts, the first presenting the teaching of the Greek Fathers, and the second the doctrine of the Latin Fathers.

Special consideration should be given to two impressive works that have appeared since the Encyclical: Monsignor Charles Journet's *L'Église du Verbe Incarné*, a two-volume work; and the work of Father Emilio Sauras, O.P., *El Cuerpo Mistico de Christo*.

In the first volume of his work, Monsignor Journet studies the exterior and juridical aspect of the Church under the subtitle *Hiérarchie apostolique*. (An English edition of the work: *The Church of the Word Incarnate, The Apostolic Hierarchy*, was published by Sheed & Ward, New York, in 1954.) The second volume, published in 1951, with the subtitle *Sa Structure et son unité catholique*, delves into the internal aspect of the Church as a mystical organism quickened by the Holy Spirit. It is impossible to sum up in a few lines a work of such great importance. We should note in passing the section devoted to Mary, who exercises the functions of the heart in the Mystical Body and who is also the prototype of the Church.

Father Sauras's work, published in Madrid in 1952, covers the following subjects: (1) the doctrine of the Mystical Body in Holy Scripture; (2) Christ

---

[8] Cf. our article, "La Dottrina del Corpo Mistico," in a work published by a group of theologians, *Problemi e Orientamonti di teologia dommatica* (Milan: Marzorati), II, 379–98, An English translation of Father Mersch's work, *The Theology of the Mystical Body*, was published by the B. Herder Book Company, St. Louis, in 1951.

the Head of the Mystical Body and his vital influence on the members; (3) the divine life of the Head; (4) the members of the Mystical Body; (5) the soul of the Mystical Body;[9] (6) the unity of the Mystical Body; (7) the Mystical Person of the total Christ.

Many studies on the Mystical Body have appeared in Germany. including the following: Thaddeus Soiron's *Die Kirche als Leib Christi*, which has the advantage of placing the theological presentation in the total context of the concepts advanced. The author reduces all explanations proposed to three classes. The first, which Soiron calls *realistico-somatic*, is completely erroneous and it is scarcely believable that lucid minds could have imagined it.

This theory takes the words of St. Paul on the unity of the Mystical Body, composed of Christ and of his members, in the sense of a natural, physical unity: Christ and Christians form a single organism, numerically one. Such is also the view of Kastner, *Marianische Christus-Gestaltung der Welt* (1936), Haugg, *Wir sind dein Leib* (1937), Massmann, *Der König und sein Opfer*, and even more crudely. Pelz, in *Der Christ als Christus* (1939), which means "the Christian as Christ." This last work affirms the identity of the physical body and the Mystical Body of Christ, saying without flinching that all efforts to separate them are useless!

These are the aberrations to which Pius XII alluded in the third part of the Encyclical *Mystici Corporis*, and which show the importance of the work we undertook in 1934 to set forth the true nature of the mysterious unity of the Mystical Body of Christ.

The second series of authors whom Soiron studies in a work entitled *Bildiche Lösung*, sin by default in the opposite direction. For them the unity of the Mystical Body is purely figurative. The Mystical Body, as they see it, is only a symbol, an image that has no relation to reality: thus Deimel in *Leib Christi* (1960).

Between these two extremes there is a third approach that Soiron calls *bildlich-reale*—"figurative-real" which is the one he himself defends. Under the veil of symbol are hidden profound mysterious realities which the theologian must explain by analogy with natural realities. Also in German, the work of Mitterer, *Geheimnis-svollev Leib Christi* (1950), makes a comparison between the doctrine of Pope Pius XII's Encyclical *Mystici Corporis* and the teaching of St. Thomas Aquinas, only to reach an inadmissible conclusion:

---

[9]   In the view of Father Sauras, the Mystical Body has an uncreated soul, namely, the Holy Spirit, and also a created soul, consisting of grace and all the gifts that accompany it, This point is certainly controversial and finds no support in the Encyclical *Mystici Corporis*. For a more detailed discussion cf. below, Chapter II, 211 ff.

namely, that St. Thomas is in contradiction with Pius XII. Even a superficial perusal of the work quickly shows how flimsy is the demonstration that he claims to make of this opposition. Thus, according to Mitterer, the Angelic Doctor would consider the Mystical Body as expressing only the invisible aspect of the Church. We need read only the *Summa*, IIIa, q. 8, a. 3, to see that St. Thomas includes both the body and soul of the Church, both her visible and invisible aspect, in the mystical Body.

An author more deserving of attention is Jürgensmeir. His work *Der Mystische Leib Christi als Grundprinzip der Aszetic* (*The Mystical Body of Christ as the Fundamental Principle of Ascesis*), whose title tells the subject matter, is limited to one aspect of the spiritual life. Two other good works are *Das Mysterium der hl. Kirche* (*The Mystery of Holy Church*), and a commentary on the Encyclical *Mystici Corporis* entitled *Die Kirche als Herrenleib* (*The Church as the Body of the Lord* (1949),[10] both of which were written by Feckes.

Among these works on the mystery of our union in Christ, what is the purpose and orientation of the present work? It has been our purpose, even as early as 1932–1934 when no study—apart from Abbé Anger's first outline—had yet attempted a methodical explanation of the "Mystery of Christ" (Eph. 3:4; cf. Col. 2:2), to investigate with the help of theological principles, the inner nature of this divine organism.

First of all, we had to set forth the constitutive principles of this unity peculiar to the Mystical Christ. Once these were established, there remained to be studied in its entirety the supernatural activity of the Body in its Head and in its members. It was an attempt to set up a sort of supernatural metaphysics of the being of the total Christ, and a supernatural psychology of its faculties of action; or rather an organic theology, both speculative and practical, dogmatic and moral, of the Mystical Body of Christ.

---

[10] In this rapid glance at the works devoted to the study of the Mystical Body, we could also cite others of secondary importance or that deal with our subject only in an indirect manner, that is from the practical point of view, which is also rich in significance for the spiritual life. Let us cite in passing: Mgr. Duperray, *Le Christ dans la Vie Chretienne* (1922); Mgr. Ceriani, *Dottrina e Vita del Corpo Mistico* (1939); R. Plus, *Dans le Christ Jesus*, and *Le Christ dans nos Frères*; Gasque, *L'Eucharistie et le Corps Mystique;* Msgr. Piolanti, *Il Corpo Mistico et le sue relazione con l'Eucaristia in S. Alberto Magno* (1939); Cardinal Mendoza, *De naturali cum Christo unione* (edited in 1947 by Msgr. Piolanti at the Lateran); Daniel Culhane, *De Corpore Mystico Doctrina Seraphici* (Mundelein, 1935).

Culhane's treatise could have provided an interesting monograph. We regret that it is marred by inaccuracies and even by serious theological errors. According to the author, to be part of the Mystical Body one must be in the state of grace! Whence the logical conclusion: "Sinners are not members of the Mystical Body." No one will accept such an assertion in our own day.

The years have sped by since the first edition of our study. The Encyclical of Pope Pius XII, *Mystici Corporis*, has thrown new light on the dogma of man's unity in Christ, confirming most of the positions we had taken. Far from rendering useless and out of date the work then undertaken, it seems to us that it has made the need for a theological synthesis of this great dogma more strongly felt. The American edition which we are presenting fills a great need. Although it is true that professional theologians easily make use of foreign language works, the fact remains that educated laymen and laywomen, whom Pope John XXIII invites to study this dogma, and souls seeking food to nourish their interior life are frustrated in their need to know the great mystery. And yet St. Paul earnestly wished that his faithful should have knowledge of the Gift of God and besought the Father of our Lord Jesus Christ to give them the spirit of wisdom and of revelation, the eyes of their minds being enlightened (cf. Eph. 1:17–18), so that they might know the riches for them contained in Christ and in their union with him (cf. Eph. 3: 14–19; Col. 1:25–28).

The unity of the total Christ and his supernatural activity are the two aspects of the theology of the Mystical Body. The present study limits itself to the first aspect,[11] which is the most delicate problem of all: "*Vos estis Corpus Christi!*"—"You are the Body of Christ!" (I Cor. 12:27). How are we to understand this bold assertion made by St. Paul? The question has been asked by a number of persons who have not attempted to answer it, perhaps through fear of marring with overly human explanations the transcendent beauty of the dogma of our incorporation into Christ Jesus. They do not tell us wherein consists the organic and vital cohesion that makes of Jesus and ourselves a single "total Christ."

Bishop Duperray asks himself:

> How can we define this union according to St. Paul? Is it an essential (*informativa*) union, as the scholastics say, such as the substantial union of soul and body in the human being? Evidently not. Is it a personal union like the hypostatic union of Christ[12] with the Word? Again no. Is it a moral or a physical union? When St. Paul compares the union of the Christian to Christ with the moral union of husband and wife in marriage, he says that the union of the faithful to Christ is still closer than that of two spouses.[13]

---

[11] Namely, the problem of the unity of the Mystical Body of Christ. It is the author's hope that Volume II of his work, *Le Corps Mystique du Christ*, on the activity of the Mystical Body will be published in English at a later date. (This will be forthcoming from Arouca Press—Ed.)

[12] The author means the union of the human nature of Christ with the Word. It is through a slip of the pen that this Nestorian expression has slipped into the author's text.

[13] *Le Christ dans la vie chrétienne*, Chapter 1, par. 2. This interesting monograph by Bishop Duperray was written in 1922 and deals with Christian life in the context of the Mystical Christ.

Father Plus in his turn discreetly tries to determine the nature of our incorporation into Christ. He says: "We are one with him in every sense of the word. It is not a simple imputation, or a pure abstraction. It is a reality [and here he cites Father Prat], because it is the subject of attributions, of properties, and of rights . . ."

He goes on to say: "It is not a physical union rather than a moral union, at least in the sense habitually given to this word. It is an organic and living union, absolutely *sui generis*, for which we possess no analogous term. Such is the nature of our mystical union with our Lord."[14]

Father Prat, in his invaluable work on the theology of St. Paul to which Father Plus was referring, expresses himself in this way: "It is a reality of the moral order indeed, but a genuine reality. . . Mystical is not the opposite of real, and there are realities outside of what can be touched and weighed. Let us remark, however, that this reality is expressed by a metaphor, like all immaterial and transcendental objects."[15] Then the author clarifies his thought by showing how the analogy of the human body is verified in the mystical Christ.

Father Mersch proposes as equally good two explanations of the unity of the Mystical Body: the Mystical Body as a purely moral union or as a union of the ontological order. His personal preference leans toward the latter more difficult but more profound explanation.[16]

As we can see, this supernatural reality of the Mystical Body is situated in an order apart, and theological authors hesitate to give a precise formula and an adequate expression of its nature. Moreover, the various explanations put forward, which we have barely outlined, do not seem at first sight to agree.

In reality, all the solutions sketched above contain a portion of truth. Their differences stem from the complex nature of the unity of the total Christ which we form in union with Jesus. It is a unity both moral and physical, and even the physical unity, as we shall see, is of several sorts. There is not just one principle of unity between Jesus and man. As many as seven distinct principles of unity exist, which, like mysterious ligaments and mystical arteries. bind the members of the total Christ to one another and to their divine Head, and cause a single stream of supernatural and divine life to flow throughout the organism.

---

[14] Raoul Plus, S.J., *Dans le Christ Jesus*, Chapter 2, par. 1.
[15] *The Theology of Saint Paul* (Westminster, Md.: The Newman Press, 1952), 300–1.
[16] Emile Mersch, S.J, *Le Corps mystique du Christ: étude de théologie historique*, Introduction, p. xxiii ff.

The presentation of these seven principles of unity is the purpose of this work. Fully aware of our weakness and limitations, we shall faithfully follow the teaching of the Doctors of the faith, and primarily the doctrine of the great Apostle of the Gentiles and the very luminous principles of St. Thomas Aquinas. In order to carry out our plan, conceived for the greater glory of the Most Blessed Trinity, we implore the grace and light of the Holy Spirit, the help of Jesus, our divine Head, and the assistance of Mary our Mother.

We would like to give an overall view from the start of the whole doctrine that we are about to present, in order to reveal more clearly its order and structure. To this end, the Table of Contents, which is a condensation of the doctrine, should be studied. It will facilitate the understanding of the subject matter and help in assimilating the ideas to be presented, by showing the place of each one in the total doctrinal picture.

When viewed from this vantage point of synthesis, the building up of the Mystical Body will appear to us as the great recapitulation in Christ (cf. Eph. 1:10), to which all the works of God are ordered for the salvation of the human race. Once they are seen in their relationship to this total doctrine, the revealed truths that are most familiar to us take on a breadth, a supernatural beauty, and a practical significance that we did not suspect. A few examples will illustrate what I mean.

The notion of grace, considered in itself as a supernatural entity and a participation in the divine nature, is certainly not lacking in grandeur. But when it is considered in its relationship to the doctrine of the Mystical Body, does it not become more comprehensive, more intelligible? It is not only the life of God but the life of the first-born Son that we receive in participation; for the eternal plan of the Father has been to incorporate us into the Word Incarnate, into his only-begotten Son, so that he might make us his adopted sons through this union: "*He predestined us to be adopted through Jesus Christ as his sons*" (Eph. 1:5). And he has made of us as it were "*joint partakers of the promise in Christ Jesus*" (Eph. 3:6)[17] Thus, our sanctifying grace becomes the fullness of Christ in us his members, and our Christian life, the blossoming of this grace, is nothing but the manifestation of the life of Jesus in our fragile nature, "*that the life . . . of Jesus may be made manifest in our mortal flesh*" (2 Cor. 4:11).

Baptism likewise, when considered in the context of the Mystical Body, appears not only as the sacrament of our supernatural regeneration, an

---

[17] According to the Greek, the sense is: "Grativicavit nos in Dilecto suo."

individual and personal matter, but also as our entrance into this divine Body of the mystical Christ, the act of our incorporation into the total Christ, and the point of departure of our life in Jesus and in his grace. How great is the Christian when seen in this light, and how important is what we may call "the science of his baptism," for it is the science of Christian and eternal life! *Quicumque in Christo baptizati estis, Christum induistis!*

Finally, the dogma of the spiritual motherhood of Mary shines brilliantly when considered in the context of the doctrine of the Mystical Body. As proof of this we need only meditate upon the theologically sound statement of Father Bainvel: "As long as we hold fast to the theology of St. Paul on the Mystical Body of Christ and on our incorporation into Jesus Christ, we shall find in Mary's consent to and cooperation in the Incarnation, the consent to and cooperation in our rebirth in Jesus which constitute her spiritual motherhood."[18] The reason for this is that Jesus was not born for himself alone but for us, so that he might become "the firstborn among many brethren" (Rom. 8:29), the Head of the redeemed human race. Father Bainvel goes on to say: "This is the explanation of Mary's motherhood in relation to men. As the mother of Christ, of God-made-man, she is by that very fact the mother of Christ the Head of the human race, the mother of Christ in his members, the mother of all who possess supernatural being only in virtue of their union with Christ."[19]

May the divine heart of Jesus, the fountain of life and holiness, bestow his blessing upon this humble work, so that every page, every line, every word of it, may inspire souls, by showing them the wonders of his divine charity, to a livelier faith, a more ardent love, and thus contribute to the perfection of his Mystical Body, for the greater glory of the Most Blessed Trinity.

---

[18] *Marie, Mere de grace*, Part II, par. 6.
[19] Bainvel, *loc. cit.*

THE NATURE OF
THE MYSTICAL BODY

"Now you are the body of Christ,
member for member" (1 Cor. 12:27).

This astonishing assertion of St. Paul transports us directly into the
world of supernatural realities, and contains, in spite of its brevity,
the whole doctrine of our incorporation into Christ Jesus. It expresses in
the boldest terms the truth concerning our vital union with our divine
Savior, and concerning the intimate bonds that unite us to one another
in Jesus Christ.

"You are the body of Christ!" These words disconcert our poor human
reason, which might be tempted to refuse assent to them or to see in them
merely a pious verbal exaggeration. But faith enlightened from above
reveals to us in these words of the Apostle an ineffable mystery of love, a
divine reality, the mystery of the predilections of the heavenly Father who
calls rational creatures to become his adopted sons and daughters through
their union with his beloved Son. Thus we glimpse the profound truth of
our divine sonship through grace, which communicates to us a share in the
Sonship of Jesus, the Son of God by nature.

And yet faith is not satisfied with a simple assertion. Stimulated by
love, aroused at the sight of so much mercy, it strives to know more, to
search further into the secrets of the hidden mystery (cf. Eph. 3:9), and "to

1

comprehend with all the saints what is the breadth and length and height and depth" (Eph. 3:18) of God's inconceivable charity for men.

In answer to the aspirations of faith, and obeying the impulsion of the love that the Holy Spirit kindles in the hearts of his faithful, we shall seek to know the dogma of our incorporation into Christ and to understand better the nature of the mysterious unity that makes of Jesus and of all the faithful a single supernatural organism. Only then shall we be in a position to study and understand the life of the Mystical Body.[1] For the life and the operations of every being are according to its nature.

In this volume, which deals with the nature or constitution of the Mystical Body, we shall proceed in two stages. First, we shall seek from St. Paul as complete an exposition as possible of the nature of the whole Christ, of the prerogatives of the divine Head, and the attributions of the members. To this end, Part I will make a careful and detailed study of the principal epistles in which the Apostle describes so meticulously and with so much devotion, the constitution and the essential organs of the divine Body of Christ.

In Part II we shall follow the teachings of the Thomistic School in dealing theologically and by way of synthesis with the constitutive principles of this supernatural organism. We shall strive with the help of the clarifications of sacred science to bring out the great dogmatic riches contained in St. Paul's terse formulas. This will enable us to solve, to the extent that our limitations and our ignorance of the divine mysteries allow, the problem posed in our Introduction on the real nature of the unity, whether physical or moral, that exists between the Head and the members of the Mystical Body. This will be the most important part of our study, for it will provide a firm foundation for everything we shall afterwards say concerning our life in Christ.

Let us begin with a study of the doctrine of St. Paul.

---

[1] The author is referring here to Volume II of his work *Le Corps Mystique du Christ*, entitled *Vie du Corps Mystique*.

PART I

The Doctrine of St. Paul on the Mystical Body

Introduction

The development of the doctrine of the Mystical Body must be sought in Holy Scripture, and notably in the epistles of the great Apostle of the Gentiles.

It is true that the doctrine of our supernatural unity in Christ is to be found in other portions of the inspired Books. We find it mentioned here and there in the Old Testament, although in a veiled and discreet manner. It is the New Testament, however, that gives us the clues to the presence of this doctrine in the Old. Thus St. Paul shows Christ to us as the end and consummation of the Mosaic Law (cf. Rom. 10:4). He makes us see in the life of the Church the fulfillment of the figures of the synagogue (cf. 1 Cor. 10:11). He brings out forcefully the merit of the Patriarchs' faith in the Messias to come; and he attributes their salvation and the value of their meritorious actions to their union with Christ.[1]

Our vital and life-giving union with Christ the Redeemer has been revealed to us much more clearly in the Gospels. St. John, in particular, has preserved for us long fragments of the teachings of Jesus that set forth with utmost precision the doctrine of our incorporation into him. In Chapter I we shall cull the most important of these passages.

The other inspired writings of the Beloved Disciple are also replete with sublime thoughts and admirable revelations on the mystery of the supernatural unity of all the faithful in God and in Christ. We shall have occasion to refer to them throughout our study, and in the final chapter we shall borrow from the Apocalypse the description of what the whole Christ will be in heaven, in "the mature measure of [his] fullness" (Eph. 4:13).

However, we shall concentrate our attention primarily on St. Paul. In his writings the doctrine of the Mystical Body receives its full development and definitive expression. Divine Wisdom, which proceeds gradually in the manifestation of truth, has ordained that the Apostle of the Gentiles

---

[1] Cf. Hebrews, Chapter II, especially verses 13, 26, 39–40.

should be the Doctor *par excellence* of "the fullness of Christ." Jesus himself prepared his disciples for the developments that were to come after his ascension. Before leaving, he confided to them: "Many things yet I have to say to you, but you cannot bear them now. But when he, the Spirit of truth has come, he will teach you all the truth. . . he will receive of what is mine and declare it to you" (John 16:12–14).

In St. Paul, therefore, we shall find the teaching of Jesus himself, the teaching of "the Spirit of Jesus" (Acts 16:7) in its ultimate perfection. Thus we shall be in a position to make of it the principal and unshakable foundation of our theology of the Mystical Body. We shall study closely and at length the apostolic letters in which St. Paul makes us see, the eyes of our mind being enlightened, the sublime destiny to which God has called us and "the riches of the glory of his inheritance in the saints" (Eph. 1:18; cf. 1:17).

Nothing can take the place of this immediate contact with the thought of the great Doctor of the Gentiles. His ideas are so rich, so vibrant with love, so full of the breath of life. No analysis, no presentation at second hand can give a complete or exact idea of this complex and lofty doctrine.

Besides, there is a special grace attached to these inspired pages of St. Paul, a grace of faith and of charity that wins and penetrates the soul, enlightens the mind, stimulates the will, and kindles the heart. Did not St. John Chrysostom say in his fervent admiration for the great Apostle. "I exult with joy when I hear this spiritual trumpet. I am inspired and filled with fiery desires when I recognize this friendly voice, and I seem almost to see him and hear him."[2] And if we were to dispense with the direct study of St. Paul's epistles, we would be depriving ourselves of valuable spiritual benefits.

A cold, abstract concept is not what takes shape in St. Paul's style; rather, it is a living and lived thought, it is the entire soul of the great Apostle shining forth, with its powerful originality, with the vehemence and fire of his holy and impassioned love for Christ and for his Church. As Father Léonce de Grandmaison expresses it:

> Elevation, supplication, apostrophe, irony, imprecation, all the rhetoric of passion is there, but a rhetoric which scorns conventional rhetorics. In these writings are the cries, the appeals, the tears, the enthusiasms or the groanings of a man who loves, who suffers, who compassionates, who waxes indignant, who melts with tender pity, who is raised to a pitch of excitement. And it all goes to make up a unique style; all these metals are

---

[2] *In Epist. S. Pauli,* Introduction.

cast into a homogeneous alloy; for the love of Christ, whose Spouse and whose Mystical Body the Church unifies all in Paul's heart.[3]

Here indeed is the dominant idea of the Apostle, the idea that engrossed his whole life. This is the central truth of St. Paul's entire doctrine, around which all the others are grouped or into which they are integrated as parts of a whole. For this reason his doctrine has an indefinable depth and mystery that is beyond and above us. Even when we have understood it, we are still under the impression that we have missed something of its meaning.

St. Paul is visibly filled with the sense of the inexhaustible plenitude of the mystery he is preaching. He feels powerless to express it as completely as he would like. He is impelled to communicate his extremely rich and profound conception in its totality, and to this end he forges a new vocabulary, new and daring expressions, and overcharged sentences which are grammatically incorrect but filled with sublime ideas.[4]

Actually it is impossible to fully grasp the thought of St. Paul if we do not juxtapose the various passages of his epistles to make a synthesis of his doctrine. This fact, which holds true for the entire teaching of the Apostle, applies especially to his doctrine of the Mystical Body. The formula "*in Christo Jesu*" that sums it up and that St. Paul repeats at every opportunity, can be understood in all its complexity and its dogmatic depth only when considered in its doctrinal context. And that is what we shall strive to accomplish in the following chapters.

First we shall analyze the principal passages of our Lord's teaching concerning our subject, to make sure that the disciple is really giving us the Master's doctrine. We shall then see the various symbols, the diverse analogies that the Apostle uses to translate into human language the transcendent reality of our unity in Christ. Once these preliminaries have been established as succinctly as possible, we shall turn to a direct study of the epistles of St. Paul, at least of those in which the doctrine of the Mystical Body holds a superior place. We shall see the successive developments that the Apostle gives to this central dogma of his theology in his First Epistle to the Corinthians, in his Epistle to the Ephesians, and in the letter addressed to the faithful of Colossae.

---

[3] Léonce de Grandmaison, S.J., *Jesus Christ* (New York: Sheed & Ward, 1934), I, 26–27.

[4] On this subject, cf. Fernand Prat, S.J., *The Theology of Saint Paul*, (Westminster, Md.: The Newman Press, 1952), I, 68 ff.

CHAPTER I

The Origins of the Doctrine of the Mystical Body in Our Lord's Teaching

The origin of the dogma of our incorporation into Christ Jesus must be sought from a source higher than St. Paul, namely, in the Gospel teachings of our divine Savior himself. For Christ is the supreme Doctor, the Prophet predestined by God to reveal to us the truth that saves and the conditions under which we must recover the life we lost in Adam.

In the Old Testament, God had been content to make known to men in an obscure and veiled way the mystery of our unity in the Christ who was to come. Already in the Garden of Eden, the Lord had outlined the general plan in his solemn promise to our first parents. In the new order of things, that God was then inaugurating to make salvation possible to sinful humanity, he pointed out a twofold solidarity: the serpent and his cursed race on the one hand; and at the other extreme the Savior and all the redeemed: "I will put enmities between thee and the woman, and thy seed and her seed" (Gen. 3:15). The entire dogma of the Mystical Body is implicitly contained in this passage.

The seed of the Woman is Jesus Christ, but not Jesus Christ alone. It is everything that will ever be opposed to the devil's brood, everything that will nurture irreconcilable hatreds against Satan. The race of the Woman is Christ together with all those he was to redeem; Jesus with all his faithful; the Head with all its members; in a word, the whole Christ.[1]

Thus, from the earliest origins of the Christian economy, in the oracle of Genesis, we find revealed the ineffable mystery of our incorporation in the Savior. Many times afterwards, God confirmed and, in a certain measure,

---

[1] This generally accepted exegesis would find its confirmation in St. Paul's interpretation of the promise made to Abraham. Cf. Gal. 3:16; Gen. 22:18

7

clarified this initial revelation. But the clear and explicit knowledge of this dogma of salvation was to be given us by Jesus himself. Under many circumstances, our Lord explained "the mystery of the kingdom of God" to the crowds that followed him, and especially to the disciples whom he was initiating more intimately into the secrets of the faith. And he often spoke to them of the close union he had deigned to contract with mankind.

The most beautiful and powerful expression that Jesus has left us of our supernatural union with him is to be found in the parable of the vine. He said: "I am the true vine, and my Father is the vine-dresser. Every branch *in me* that bears no fruit he will take away; and every branch that bears fruit he will cleanse, that it may bear more fruit. . . . *Abide in me, and I in you.* . . . I am

the vine, you are the branches. He who abides in me, and I in him, he bears much fruit; for without me you can do nothing" (John 15:1–5).

In these words of our Lord, we have the whole doctrine of the Mystical Body. Even the analogy that Jesus uses differs scarcely at all from the one St. Paul prefers. The sacred vine is a living organism, all of whose parts, bound to one another, are quickened by the same divine life.

The same sap flows from the vine stalk into the branches, and the branches possess life only if they cleave to the vine. It is by virtue of the vinestock that the branch bears fruit. If it is separated from the stock, it loses all fruitfulness, all life, all beauty. It becomes a dried-up shoot, useless wood, good only to be cast into the fire.

The same holds true for us in our relationship with our Lord. Our spiritual life is of the same nature as his. We receive it from him through the sanctifying influences that his most holy soul continually exerts on our souls. His divine heart, beating constantly with love for us, communicates to us its most pure affections and its generous desires for goodness. Our good works, the salutary fruit that we must bear in every season, are produced only by the vital force of his grace. "As the branch cannot bear fruit of itself unless it remain on the vine, so neither can you unless you abide *in me*" (John 15:4).

Separated from Jesus, deprived of his grace, we are deadwood, doomed to the fires of hell. For us there is no middle ground between the excess of happiness that union with Jesus assures us and the utter misfortune of separation from him. "If anyone does not abide in me, he shall be cast outside as the branch and wither; and they shall gather them up and cast them into the fire, and they shall burn" (John 15:6). Our own happiness and the glory of the heavenly Father both demand that we be engrafted on the sacred humanity of our Savior, and manifest by the abundance of our good works the fruitfulness of the divine vine that bears us. "In this is my Father glorified, that you may bear very much fruit, and become my disciples" (John 15:8).

Jesus concludes his beautiful allegorical exposition with these words: "Abide in my love . . . as I abide in his love" John 15:9–10). Our union with Jesus is modeled on the union of Jesus with his Father. This idea is expressed still more forcefully by our Lord in his priestly prayer, the sublime prayer that Jesus addressed to his Father after the Last Supper, recommending to him his disciples and the Church that he was founding upon them: "That all may be one, even as thou, Father, in me and I in thee; that they also may be one in us" (John 17:21). It is in God himself that this perfect unity is consummated, and our Savior is the divine connecting link between us and his Father, as he himself makes clear: "I in them and thou in me; that they may be perfected in unity" (John 17:23).

Perfect unity—not a substantial unity, and yet a oneness that is above all other unions here on earth. It is a unity modeled on that of God himself: a union through the love that we bear to God the Father, to Jesus and to our brothers; a union through the continual action of Jesus on our souls; a union through the manifold bonds that unite us to our Savior; a union that finds expression particularly through the Holy Eucharist, whose great unitive power Jesus teaches us in his sermon at Capharaum.

Our Lord has said: "I am the bread of life." Yes, he is the bread of the life that he possesses in himself, that he has received from the Father, and that he has come to bring to us from heaven so that we might be quickened by his own life. For "as the living Father has sent me, and as I live because of the Father, so he who eats me, he also shall live because of me" (John 6:58). Jesus, as he himself has told us, receives the fullness of divine life from his Father by virtue of his eternal generation. And he wants to give us an eminent participation in this life through the eating of his sacred flesh. We do not receive the divine life in its essence, that is, the life that makes Jesus the only-begotten Son of God by nature. But we have a created participation in it that makes us children of God by adoption, heirs of heaven and coheirs with Christ.

Our Lord has told us: "He who eats my flesh and drinks my blood has life everlasting" (John 6:55)—the divine life of sanctifying grace that tends of its nature to remain within us forever and to attain its fullness in the life of heaven. This life, however, remains in us only in the measure that we remain united to Jesus who is its source. For "he who eats my flesh and drinks my blood abides in me and I in him" (John 6:57).

The fact is that Jesus does *abide* in us through Holy Communion. How is that possible? Sacramentally, he dwells within us only for a half-hour, more or less, after the reception of his sacred Body. Through his divinity, however, he remains the guest of our soul together with the Father and the Holy Spirit, according to his promise (cf. John 14:23). He dwells in us through the sanctifying grace that he preserves and increases in our souls at every moment, by the life-giving influences of actual graces, by the union of love that his divine Sacrament strengthens continually.

Jesus abides in us when we receive him in the Blessed Sacrament. But we also abide in him: "*In me manet et ego in illo.*" We abide in Jesus through the lively faith that keeps its gaze fixed on him throughout the day. We abide in him through the continual surging of an ardent love, through the frequent aspirations of our soul and heart. In a more perfect way still, we remain united to him through the gift of infused contemplation, through the mystical union of passive love that can continue even during the performance of our daily tasks, as St. Teresa of Avila teaches.[2] This is a mysterious prayer, the secret inclination of the heart toward the object of its affection, the union of a soul already advanced in the path of perfection and accomplishing ever more fully the words of our Savior: "*In me manet et ego in illo.*" These words of Jesus attain their perfect fulfillment here on earth only in the transforming union of spiritual marriage, and in heaven in the beatific union.

Our Lord showed us in a compelling way the divine union that he deigns to establish with us when he announced the Last Judgment. The divine Judge is seated on his throne, surrounded by his angels. Before him appear all the sons of Adam, the just on his right, sinners on his left. Addressing those on his right, Jesus pronounces this reassuring sentence: "Come, blessed of my Father, take possession of the kingdom prepared for you from the foundation of the world" (Matt. 25:34). Here are the grounds for the divine verdict: "I was hungry and you gave me to eat; I was thirsty and you gave me to drink; I was a stranger and you took me in; naked and you covered me; sick and you visited me; I was in prison and you came to me" (Matt. 25:35–36).

---

[2] Cf. St. Teresa of Avila, *Autobiography*, Chapter 17; *The Way of Perfection*, Chapter 32.

But the just express their astonishment. For they have never had the honor of serving their Master in person in this unusual way. And Jesus answers: "Amen I say to you, as long as you did it for one of these, the least of my brethren, you did it for me" (Matt. 25:40).

An analogous answer is given to the condemned, who are also surprised by the tenor of the divine judgment: "Depart from me, accursed ones, into the everlasting fire. . . . For I was hungry, and you did not give me to eat; I was thirsty and you gave me no drink; I was a stranger and you did not take me in; naked, and you did not clothe me; sick, and in prison, and you did not visit me" (Matt. 25:42–43). You have refused me the care I expected of your charity for my suffering members who are the poor. That is the criterion of the Savior's judgments. He holds as done to himself whatever we do to our neighbor. Are not all men *his brothers*, saved by him, filled to overflowing with his graces, called to share the heritage of heaven in union with him?

Such is the doctrine that Jesus himself has deigned to give us on the mystery of our union with him, a mystery that was to become the central teaching of St. Paul's preaching. While Jesus' doctrine has been preserved for us most completely by St. John, it is not absent from the writings of the other evangelists. And if we search carefully through the other Gospels, we shall see that this doctrine is, as it were, the foundation of all of our Lord's teaching.

Indeed, the idea most often emphasized in the first three Gospels, the idea that represents the essence of the redemptive mission of Jesus, is the establishment of the *kingdom* of God. Now the notion of a kingdom implies the solidarity, coordination, and the organic hierarchy of all who make up this social unity. The Church is the kingdom of God on earth, and by this fact the faithful are to be united in loving submission to the divine rule of our beloved King, Jesus Christ.

This analogy admittedly still does not express the whole supernatural reality of our union with our Lord. Less complete and less comprehensive when taken by itself than the symbol of the vine or of the Mystical Body, it expresses only one aspect of the bonds that unite us to Jesus and to his other members: namely, bonds of the juridical and moral order. But insofar as the question here is one of a heavenly and divine kingdom, we can at least glimpse the possibility of closer bonds than those existing in earthly societies whose vistas are purely temporal.

Among the specific functions of the Head of the Mystical Body is the exercise of kingship.[3] This is the point of view stressed above all in the Gospels of Sts. Matthew, Mark, and Luke, in their accounts of Jesus' doctrine on the kingdom of heaven.[4] It is the same doctrine, therefore, although less complete and less explicit than that of St. John, on the organism of the Mystical Body and its members.

From whom did St. Paul learn the doctrine of the Mystical Body of Christ? Beyond doubt he received the basic principles from the apostles and disciples of Christ, whom he made it a point to consult so that his preaching might conform fully with that of the Apostolic College (cf. Gal. 2:2). However, the Lord reserved for St. Paul a more complete revelation of this admirable mystery. We have it from the Apostle himself that God deigned to manifest to him the secrets of his ineffable life. The Acts of the Apostles also present him many times as being in immediate contact with the Lord.

It is truly remarkable that, from the very first moment of his apparition to Saul the persecutor on the road to Damascus, Jesus made known to him the unity of the Mystical Body, the union of Christ with his faithful: "Saul, Saul why dost thou persecute me?" (Acts 9:4). Saul was thrown to the ground, overcome, converted. From then on, according to God's merciful designs, he brought before kings and nations the name of this Jesus who had spoken to him on the road, of this Jesus who dwells in heaven but who likewise abides on earth, hidden within the person of those who love him, the Jesus who holds as done to himself the good or evil done to any of his followers, and who will some day judge the elect and the damned according to this rule.

Let us now listen to Saul, after he has become Paul, as he speaks to us of the mystery whose herald he was appointed by God.

---

[3] Cf. the author's *Le Corps Mystique du Christ*, Volume II.
[4] For the doctrine of the Mystical Body in the Synoptic Gospels, consult Emile Mersch, S.J., *Le Corps Mystique du Christ, Étude de théologie historique* (Louvain, 2d ed., 1936), Part I, Chapter 2.

CHAPTER II

The Various Expressions of the Doctrine of the Mystical Body in St. Paul

It belongs to the nature of supernatural mysteries to be beyond the scope of our limited intellects. Even when divine Mercy deigns to reveal something of their interior nature, human language possesses no expression that can adequately convey the divine reality. Man is then forced to multiply figures and analogies in an effort to translate by various forms of language what a single form cannot completely express.

This is the case for example with regard to the notion of sanctifying grace. We speak of it as a participation in the divine nature, as the supernatural or divine life of the sanctified soul, and as an adopted sonship. All these designations, and many others as well that might be found in Scripture or in theology, are exact, and reveal to us an aspect of this ineffable reality that the good God creates in our souls at the moment of baptism and that he afterwards perfects in many ways.

The same thing holds for the mystery of our union with our divine Redeemer, for the dogma of our incorporation into Christ Jesus. Our Lord has revealed it to us in various ways, as we have seen in the preceding chapter. St. Paul, following in his Master's footsteps, likewise uses diverse figures to express and to render intelligible to our faith the very profound and mysterious truth of our vital and life-giving union to the Word Incarnate, our Savior.

Chief among these figures, the one that he develops most assiduously and to which he continually returns, is the analogy of the body, of the human organism. We shall concentrate our attention, therefore, on this particular analogy. We should not, however, neglect the other analogies; by their very diversity they help us to understand the reality expressed by the words "Mystical Body," emphasizing the essentially analogical character of this term.

We shall examine briefly the most important analogies used by St. Paul. First there is the analogy of the building or the temple of God, whose stones are made up of the faithful. Then there is the plant or the seeded field. Then there is the symbolism of conjugal union, in which Jesus is the divine Bridegroom, and the Church has the role of the Spouse. Lastly comes St. Paul's favorite analogy, the one of the Head and members forming a single Mystical Body.

First of all, the faithful constitute, in union with Christ, a *mystical structure*. Writing to the Ephesians, the Apostle says: "Therefore, you are now no longer strangers and foreigners, but you are citizens with the saints and members of God's household: you are built upon the foundation of the apostles and prophets with Christ Jesus himself as the chief cornerstone. In him the whole structure is closely fitted together and grows into a temple holy in the Lord; in him you too are being built together into a dwelling place for God in the Spirit" (Eph. 2:19–20).

The unity of the divine plan shines through this passage, a universal unity joining the two Testaments in the fulfillment of a single plan of God, the divine architect of the supernatural world. This sacred structure rests upon a twofold foundation: the Prophets in the Old Testament; the Apostles in the New Law. On them all the faithful must rely who want to become stones of the mystical temple. Christ, too, is a stone in this divine building, but a stone of capital importance: he is the cornerstone.

The Prophets had already attributed the function of cornerstone to the Messias. And Jesus in one of his discourses addressed to the leaders of the synagogue a few days before his Passion, applied to himself the words of the Psalm: "The stone which the builders rejected, has become the cornerstone" (Matt. 21:42, quoting Ps. 117:22).

The role of the cornerstone is to unite and bind closely two walls of a building and to give them, by their union, the necessary strength that neither possesses alone. This role is all the more important when these walls terminate in a vault and receive their cohesion entirely from the top. According to the analogy, our Lord would be the *keystone* that gives unity and solidity to the whole structure *from above*.

The principle of unity that emerges most clearly from St. Paul's analogy is that of the juridical and social bond that brings together, unites, and hierarchizes within the supernatural society of the Church all of its different members, according to their mutual relationships of submission and superiority, and according to the rights and obligations established among them by the power of jurisdiction or of spiritual government. To this must be added the bond of moral union that supernatural charity welds among the members of this divine society. It is such a powerful and efficacious union of hearts that it gives strong cohesion to the diverse parts of the mystical edifice where the Lord deigns to dwell, and where he manifests his presence by the manifold effects of his grace.

The analogy of the plant or of the cultivated field lays greater stress upon this activity of grace, and brings out more cogently the unity of the Mystical Body through the active cause that operates within and communicates life. The mark of the plant which characterizes it, giving it its specific unity, is the fact that the same sap nourishes all its parts. The plant, therefore, symbolizes very well this intimate and penetrating action of God in the mystical organism of his Church. Our Lord used the image several times to symbolize the kingdom of God. In addition to the parable of the vine, which we analyzed above, he offered to his disciples the comparison of the mustard seed that grows and attains the size of a tree. He also used the figure of the sower, part of whose seed was lost on thin or rocky soil or among thorns, whereas another part, having fallen into good ground, brought in thirty-, sixty-, and even a hundredfold. Finally there is the parable of the good seed into which the enemy comes and sows weeds.

St. Paul in his turn makes use of the analogy of the vegetable kingdom, although he does so only in passing and without insisting too much on it. He uses it in the First Epistle to the Corinthians to show the unity of the Church in the diversity of evangelical ministries. For, in the Lord's field there are many different tasks, but only one life-giving principle.

Referring to the rivalries that had arisen among the faithful of Corinth on the occasion of the prestige that Apollos had acquired as an eloquent preacher among the Christian community, the Apostle said to them:

> For whenever one says, "I am of Paul," but another, "I am of Apollos," are you not mere men? What then is Apollos? What indeed is Paul? They are the servants of him whom you have believed—servants according as God has given to each to serve. I have planted, Apollos watered, but God has given the growth. So then neither he who plants is anything, nor he who waters, but God who gives the growth. Now he who plants and he who waters are one, yet each will receive his own reward according to his labor. For we are God's helpers, you are God's tillage, God's building (1 Cor. 3:4–9).

In this work of spiritual husbandry, everything cooperates toward the common end willed by God: the action of the preacher who sows the seed;

the care of the minister of God who watches over its springing up and its growth; Christ's influence from above, whose instruments and helpers these men are; the vital action of the sap flowing within; and finally above all of these, the supreme action of God who gives life and growth to the seed entrusted to the field of the Church.

And yet the mystical unity of Christ, of his ministers, and of his faithful is not as clear in this comparison used by the Apostle as in those our Lord borrowed from the vegetable kingdom.

Another and more expressive image of this divine reality is that of the *mystical marriage* between Christ and his Church. Already in the Old Testament conjugal union was the type of the union of God with the chosen people. The Canticle of Canticles makes of it the admirably apt symbol of the Convenant contracted between the Lord and the holy nation, as well as of the mystical wedding of the Word Incarnate with redeemed humanity.

In his Epistle to the Ephesians, St. Paul takes up this symbolism of the inspired Canticle and applies it more explicitly to Christ and to the Church. According to the doctrine of the Apostle, the divine Bridegroom has not only been joined to the Spouse. He first redeemed her and brought her out of the state of abjection, of servitude into which she had fallen: "*Christ . . . loved the Church, and delivered himself up for her*" (Eph. 5:25). He purified her of her stains in the bath of his blood, thus preparing himself a most beautiful Bride, "*in order that he might present to himself the Church in all her glory, not having spot or wrinkle or any such thing, but that she might be holy and without blemish*" (Eph. 5:27).

The analogy of the conjugal union brings out, as we can readily see, the moral bond of charity, for charity realizes in the mystical order a more perfect and no less fruitful union than the natural union of husband and wife.

Yet, in this same passage St. Paul indicates another principle of union between Christ and his members: "*No one ever hated his own flesh; on the contrary he nourishes and cherishes it, as Christ also does the Church*" (Eph. 5:29). The Savior nourishes his Spouse through the sacrament of the Eucharist, giving her his own Body, the principle and sign of his union with her. He warms her and increases her vital energies through his action on our souls in the production of grace.

The comparison of the conjugal union serves St. Paul as a natural transition, leading to the analogy of the Mystical Body. In fact, after the words: "No one ever hated his own flesh; on the contrary he nourishes and cherishes it, as Christ also does the Church," he adds without pause, "*because we are members of his body*" (Eph. 5:29).

This transition is based on the fact that husband and wife, in the language of Scripture, are not considered as two persons but rather as a single moral person, as constituting a single body and one flesh, according to the oracle of Genesis cited by our Lord and by St. Paul in the following passage: "For this cause a man shall leave his father and mother, and cleave to his wife; and the two shall become one flesh" (Eph. 5:31; cf. Gen. 2:24; Matt. 19:5).

The analogy of the Mystical Body is the most perfect of those used by the Apostle of the Gentiles, and it contains all the preceding ones in an eminent way. It is also the most complete expression of the many supernatural realities that constitute our union with Jesus. Thus, the term "*incorporation into Christ*" possesses a wealth of significance that nothing can equal. It contains everything that the other analogies express individually. This will become very clear in the following chapters, in which we shall follow St. Paul in his development of the doctrine of the Mystical Body.

This major doctrine of the great Apostle does not appear in all its scope from the start. Nevertheless we can easily follow its progress and maturation through his epistles.

Like the mustard seed of which our Lord speaks, the seed gathered by Saul on the road to Damascus strikes its roots into the faithful soul of the generous convert. Under the influence of new lights, his thought develops and soon makes itself manifest in his preaching. The doctrine of the Mystical Body is first discreetly intimated in the earlier epistles. It then takes on greater scope and precision in the apostolic letters to the faithful of Corinth and Rome, reaching its maturity in the epistles of the captivity.

Chronologically speaking, the first epistles of St. Paul are the two addressed to the Christians of Thessalonica. The dogma of our incorporation into Christ is already breaking through, but is scarcely above ground. This is quite noticeable by comparison with the teachings of his later writings. The doctrine of the *parousia*, of the second coming of Jesus in glory, revives in the Apostle's heart the yearning to be united to Christ forever (cf. 1 Thess. 4:16), and to live with him (cf. 1 Thess. 5:10). When Christ Jesus appears on the last day, he will manifest his glory *in his saints*, and he will show himself worthy of admiration in all those who have believed in him (cf. 2 Thess. 1:10). These latter will then be, as it were, the radiance of his own splendor.

With the Epistle to the Corinthians, the doctrine of the total Christ already takes on more substance. The analogy of the living organism, of the Mystical Body, as the expression of our spiritual unity through Jesus and in Jesus, appears for the first time. Pressed by circumstances and wanting to nip in the bud the ferments of discord that had begun to belabor his beloved Christians of Corinth, the Apostle held up to his faithful the imposing reality of the living Christ, whose members they were: "*Now you are the body of Christ*" (1 Cor. 12:7). Should not the reminder of this splendid dogma put an end to all disagreements and bring Christians back to their vocation to sanctity?

The description of the Mystical Body presented in the First Epistle to the Corinthians, however, is not complete. The role of Head, the function of Christ as Head of the mystical organism is not yet revealed in its full light. The Epistle to the Romans and the Epistle to the Galatians take up several aspects of the doctrine proposed to the Corinthians, without any further stress on the place and function of the head in the Mystical Body. Yet, several new ideas of the greatest spiritual interest concerning this doctrine are put forth. For instance, in the Epistle to the Romans we are shown the magnificent meaning of baptism, which buries as with Christ in death to sin so that we may rise again with Christ to a life of grace and of virtue (cf. Rom. 6:3 ff.). And, in the Letter to the Galatians we find the keen sense of our life in Christ, which the Apostle expresses in words that have long since become axiomatic: "*It is now no longer I that live, but Christ lives in me*" (Gal. 2:20).

In the epistles of the captivity, especially the Epistles to the Ephesians and to the Colossians, St. Paul shows us in noble terms the role of Christ the Leader, the principle and consummation of our life in God, the Head and plenitude of the Church (cf. Eph. 1:22–23; Col. 1:18), the firstborn of all creatures (cf. Col. 1:15), the Head of the heavenly hierarchies (cf. Eph. 1:21; Col. 1:16), and the Savior of the human race (cf. Eph. 1:7; Col. 1:13–14). Now that we are dead to sin through the mystery of the cross, we live henceforth in Christ, and we find in him inexhaustible riches (cf. Eph. 2:6–7; 3:8), for in him all fullness dwells (cf. Col. 1:19). Quickened by the Spirit of Christ (cf. Eph. 2:18–22), the whole Church grows and develops from day to day until it reaches the perfect age of Christ in the consummation of the saints (cf. Eph. 4:12–13).

We shall now study these sublime teachings in greater detail, allowing ourselves to be penetrated by them and meditating upon them in leisurely fashion.

CHAPTER III

The First Epistle to the Corinthians

The first great epistle of St. Paul, the first also in which he frankly approached and dealt at length with the doctrine of the Mystical Body is the one he wrote to the Church of Corinth about the year 57 A.D. The Apostles had been preaching the Gospel less than twenty-five years. Only five years before, St. Paul had founded a Christian community in the capital of Achaia, in the ancient and populous city of Corinth where the Lord had promised him many conquests (cf. Acts 18:10).

Actually, St. Paul's sojourn of a year and a half in this important center had brought many conversions and given him the opportunity to organize a flourishing Church, distinguished by the fervor of its faith and the abundance of graces lavished upon it by the Lord. But disorders soon arose as the result of the easy life in the opulent city, and the absence of a regularly constituted hierarchy to take over after Paul's departure. Jealousy led some to attack the Apostle's authority and to set up in opposition to him the prestige of the eloquent Apollos or the apostolic primacy of Cephas, the leader of the Twelve. In short, quarrels and divisions arose within the Corinthian cenacle.

Many other troubles soon made their appearance, as the result of disunion and discord. Among them were relaxation of morals, participation in the meals of idolatrous sacrifices, disorders in the celebration of the agapes and of the Eucharist, contention concerning the use and relative worth of various miraculous graces, such as the gifts of tongues, prophecy, and so forth, with which certain of the faithful were endowed, as well as other abuses that made the great Apostle's heart bleed. To remedy these ills, St. Paul took up his inspired pen and addressed his First Epistle to the Christians of Corinth, the first at least that has come down to us addressed directly to them.

We do not need to analyze it in its entirety. We shall pause only at those portions dealing with the doctrine of the Mystical Body, and in particular, the remarkable Chapter 12 in which this doctrine is developed with such clarity and precision. Actually, we may well consider this teaching of the Apostle on the Mystical Body as the central doctrine of the whole epistle. The purpose of the letter, as we have already pointed out, was chiefly to put an end to the divisions that were decimating the Church of Corinth. To attain this goal, St. Paul brings out the unity that characterizes the mystical Christ. At the very beginning of his letter, he asks: "Has Christ been divided up?" (1 Cor. 1:13) This thought dominates the entire epistle, and finds its full expression in Chapter 12.

Let us consider the substance of Chapter 12. From the very beginning the apostolic writer brings out the essential principle of the unity of the Mystical Body—in other words the "soul" of the total Christ. This soul is the Holy Spirit.

Thus: "No one speaking in the Spirit of God says 'Anathema' to Jesus. And no one can say 'Jesus is Lord,' except in the Holy Spirit. Now there are varieties of gifts, but the same Spirit; and there are varieties of ministries, but the same Lord; and there are varieties of workings, but the same God, who works all things in all. Now the manifestation of the Spirit is given to everyone for profit" (1 Cor. 12:3–7).

This is the general principle that assures the unity and harmony of the various manifestations of the Christian life. All of them proceed from the same divine source and tend toward the same end, the good of the whole community. And the Apostle details the charismatic gifts [1] lavished on the Primitive Church, showing that each and every one of them proceeds from the life-giving Spirit:

> To one through the Spirit is given the utterance of wisdom; and to another the utterance of knowledge, according to the same Spirit; to another faith, in the same Spirit; to another the gift of healing, in the one Spirit; to another the working of miracles; to another prophecy; to another the distinguishing of spirits; to another various kinds of tongues; to another interpretation of tongues. But all these things are the work of one and the same Spirit, who allots to everyone according as he will (1 Cor. 12:8–11).

---

[1] This is a generic term covering all the extraordinary and miraculous graces that the Lord gives to certain souls especially for the good of others, and that theology also calls *gratis datae*.

Thus God's good pleasure is the supreme arbiter in the distribution of his many gifts to the faithful. St. Paul, however, is not content to give a general reason for the difference in the way the Holy Spirit works in various individuals. He foresees an objection and anticipates a question. Why does a diversity of gifts exist? Why does not the Holy Spirit, who is given to all, communicate himself to all in the same way and in the same measure? The reason, says the Apostle, lies in the diversity of the members who compose the one Body: "For as the body is one and has many members, and all the members of the body, many as they are, form one body, so also is it with Christ" (1 Cor. 12:12).

St. Paul does not say, as we may have expected, "So also is it with the Church." He says: "So also is it with Christ"— "*ita et Christus.*" The Christ of whom the Apostle speaks in this verse is not our Lord Jesus Christ alone. Paul includes all of us with him; he includes all the faithful united to Jesus in one Spirit and through the common grace of baptism. He is speaking of the Mystical Christ. Thus, he continues: "For in one Spirit we were all baptized into one body, whether Jews or Gentiles, whether slaves or free; and we were all given to drink of one Spirit (1 Cor. 12:13).

If we make up one Mystical Body with Jesus, it is because we have one Spirit with him. This divine Spirit, however, this soul of our common supernatural life, is communicated to us by baptism, which is both our spiritual birth and our incorporation into the whole Christ. We shall see later on the consequences that the Apostle himself draws from this conception of baptism.

After having established the unity of the Mystical Body, the Apostle brings out the diversity of its members, the variety of their functions, their solidarity, their mutual interdependence in the exercise of their respective activities, and their tendency to the common good of the whole divine organism. In two symmetrical pictures that complement one another like two panels of a diptych, he describes first the natural body and then the Mystical Body, giving more details on the former and speaking of the latter more soberly. He leaves to the faithful the task of completing the comparison and of applying to the Mystical Body the characteristics he stresses in his analysis of the human organism.

Let us examine each of these pictures carefully. In studying the first, a description of the human body, we must not lose sight of the second. For the idea of the Mystical Body dominates St. Paul's thinking from the start, and commands the choice of all the characteristics he stresses in his model.

After saying in 1 Corinthians 12:13, that we have all been baptized in one Spirit, to form one Body, he continues:

> For the body is not one member, but many. If the foot says, "Because I am not a hand, I am not of the body," is it therefore not of the body? And if the ear says, "Because I am not an eye, I am not of the body," is it therefore not of the body? If the whole body were an eye, where would be the hearing? If the whole body were hearing, where would be the smelling? But as it is, God has set the members, each of them, in the body as he willed. Now if they were all one member, where would the body be? But as it is, there are indeed many members, yet but one body (1 Cor. 12:14–20).

After showing the diversity of the members and of the organs that the integrity of the body requires, and thus answering indirectly the unreasonable claims of the faithful of Corinth who envied their brothers their more excellent charisms, St. Paul passes on to another order of ideas, stressing the union and solidarity of the various members of the organism:

> And the eye cannot say to the hand, "I do not need thy help"; nor again the head to the feet, "I have no need of you." Nay, much rather, those that seem the more feeble members of the body are more necessary; and those that we think the less honorable members of the body, we surround with more abundant honor, and our uncomely parts receive a more abundant comeliness, whereas our comely parts have no need of it. God has so tempered the body together in due portion as to give more abundant honor where it was lacking; that there may be no disunion in the body, but that the members may have care for one another. And if one member suffers anything, all the members suffer with it, or if one member glories, all the members rejoice with it (1 Cor. 12:21–26).

Such is the first picture presented to us by St. Paul, showing the unity of the body amid the diversity of its members. Now what is true on the level of the natural and sensible order is equally true in the supernatural and spiritual order. For this reason the Apostle immediately juxtaposes his second picture, rapidly outlining the similarities between the Mystical Body and the human body. In fact he goes right on to say:

> You are the body of Christ! You are THE BODY OF CHRIST, member for member. (1 Cor. 12:27)

> God indeed has placed some in the Church, first apostles, secondly prophets, thirdly teachers; after that miracles, then gifts of healing, services

of help, power of administration, and the speaking of various tongues. Are all apostles? Are all prophets? Are all teachers? Are all workers of miracles? Do all have the gift of healing? Do all speak with tongues? Do all interpret? Yet strive after the greater gift. (1 Cor. 12:28–31)

"Now you are the body of Christ, member for member." This is the central assertion of the entire chapter, indeed of the entire epistle. The other dogmatic ideas and practical recommendations set forth in the epistle flow from this one statement as conclusions of a general principle. Thus: the pressing appeals to concord and charity (cf. 1 Cor., Chapters 1 and 6); the urgent appeals to the chastity that befits members of Christ and temples of the Holy Spirit (cf. 1 Cor., Chapters 5 and 6); the prohibition to eat of the food sacrificed to idols (cf. 1 Cor., Chapters 8 and 10); the requirements for worthy participation in the Eucharistic mysteries (cf. 1 Cor., Chapter 11); finally, the necessity of our future resurrection, which the Apostle demonstrates at the end of this epistle to be the rigorous consequence of the resurrection of Christ Jesus, by reason of the fact of our incorporation in him (cf. 1 Cor., Chapter 15).

Several of these points of doctrine have been developed in our study of the life of the Mystical Body (*Corps Mystique*, Vol. II). Let us note for the present the role attributed by St. Paul to the Holy Eucharist in the formation of the Mystical Body: "The cup of blessing that we bless, is it not the sharing of the blood of Christ? And the bread that we break, is it not the partaking of the body of the Lord? *Because the bread is one, we though many, are one body, all of us who partake of the one bread*" (I Cor. 10:16–17).

The last verse, which is filled with more meaning in the Greek text than in the Vulgate, makes of the Eucharistic bread not merely the symbol but the active principle of our union in the Mystical Body. Jesus our divine Head, by giving us his sacred Body as food, communicates his life and his Spirit to us, and intensifies the supreme principle of union, namely, divine charity.

Charity! Nowhere does St. Paul speak of it in more magnificent terms than in the admirable Chapter 13 of the First Epistle to the Corinthians. Chapter 13 follows directly after the one we have just analyzed, and the sequence is not purely accidental.

St. Paul sets up charity in opposition to the dissensions that destroy the essential and indispensable unity of the Mystical Body, or at least lessen its power of assimilation and expansion. He opposes charity to cliques, to party interests, and to the jealous rivalries of egoism and ambition. For he sees charity as the power of attraction and of coordination that cleaves first of all to the infinite Good, and thereby unites all souls in the pursuit of this divine object and incomparable treasure. He affirms from the start the supreme necessity of this divine charity. He then enumerates all its qualities and closes his panegyric by showing the permanence of this virtue even in the life of the blessed in eternity.

The Apostle has just spoken of the various gifts that the Lord makes to his Church for the common good, and declares by way of conclusion: "Yet strive after the greatest gifts" (I Cor. 12:31). But he adds at once: "And I point out to you a yet more excellent way" (I Cor. 13:1), the way of divine charity. This way is more excellent than the way of the charismatic gifts, because even without infused knowledge, without the gift of prophecy, without the power of the miracle worker and the gift of tongues, man can save his soul and attain to perfection. He cannot do so without charity, however, because to attain to salvation it is necessary to be united to Christ and to be a part of his Mystical Body. Furthermore, without charity there is no vital union with Christ nor living incorporation in his Mystical Body.

St. Paul cries out passionately:

> If I should speak with the tongues of men and of angels, but do not have charity, I have become as sounding brass or as a tinkling cymbal. And if I have prophecy and know all mysteries and all knowledge, and if I have all faith so as to remove mountains, yet do not have charity, I am nothing. And if I distribute all my goods to feed the poor, and if I deliver my body to be burned, yet do not have charity, it profits me nothing (1 Cor. 13:1–3).

The qualities attributed by St. Paul to this most necessary virtue make it even more appealing. The Apostle delights in stressing the diverse properties of true love of God and of neighbor, whose absence has been noted among the lax Christians of Corinth (cf. 1 Cor. 1:11).

> Charity is patient, is kind; charity does not envy, is not pretentious, is not puffed up, is not ambitious, is not self-seeking, is not provoked; thinks no evil, does not rejoice over wickedness, but rejoices with the truth; bears with all things, believes all things, hopes all things, endures all things. (1 Cor. 13:4–7)

What more is needed to cement an enduring union among souls that possess the treasure of indulgent, patient charity, ready to forgive anything, ready for every renunciation and immolation? The lives of the saints, the examples of such men as St. Francis de Sales and St. Vincent de Paul show us distinctly the unitive power of this virtue when generously practiced. But they also show us that here on earth charity is nourished by sacrifice because it demands stern warfare against the self-love which constricts hearts and divides souls. And a smile like the one on the lips of a St. Thérèse of Lisieux, a simple and efficacious means of spiritual conquest, is often the fruit of an interior immolation whose price is known to God alone. This has been the condition of charity on earth since the day our divine Master declared that the supreme proof of love was to lay down one's life for one's friends. In heaven, charity will remain, but it will no longer need to sacrifice, for it will have reached its perfection. It will no longer meet any obstacle or barrier in its movement toward God. It will be the indissoluble embrace of the Creator and his creatures in the consummate unity of the whole Christ. This is what St. Paul teaches in the third part of the chapter: "Charity never fails, whereas prophecies will disappear, and tongues will cease, and knowledge will be destroyed. For we know in part and we prophesy in part; but when that which is perfect has come, that which is imperfect will be done away with" (1 Cor. 13:8–10).

He continues: "When I was a child, I spoke as a child, I felt as a child, I thought as a child. Now that I have become a man, I have put away the things of a child. We see now through a mirror in an obscure manner, but then face to face. Now I know in part, but then I shall know even as I have been known. So there abide faith, hope and charity, these three; but the greatest of these is charity" (1 Cor. 13:11–13).

On this note the sublime meditation on charity closes. Next, in Chapter 14, the Apostle examines the charisms of the Holy Spirit, to regulate their use in the Christian assemblies and to indicate those to which preference should be given. Without going into every detail of the chapter, let us note that again the criterion the Apostle uses is borrowed from the doctrine of the Mystical Body: "Since you strive after spiritual gifts, seek to have them abundantly *for the edification of the church*" (1 Cor. 14:12).

In consequence, St. Paul prefers the gift of prophecy (which tends to the common good) to the gift of tongues (which often proves beneficial only to the one endowed with it). Let us remember the general lesson that emerges from these directives of St. Paul, namely, the necessity of orientating the action and the piety of the faithful in a Catholic direction, of making them tend toward the common good of the Church, of making Christians aware of the divine solidarity that binds them in Christ. Then Christian fraternity, apostolic charity, and Catholic piety will regulate the heartbeats of each of the faithful by the beats of the divine heart of Jesus, setting every heart on fire for the overriding interests of the Church, for the holy cause of God and of his Christ. This disinterested piety and conquering charity must strive to spread the kingdom of Jesus in the souls of many Christians who have forgotten their vocation. This compassionate and helpful charity must be poured out as a balm of consolation and salvation upon the souls of the poor and the sick, the suffering members of Christ Jesus. Finally, this unitive charity must seek perfect union with Christ our divine Head, including daily Eucharistic union and constant mystical union insofar as possible. Then our souls will seek at their very source the vital influences that they will be able to transmit to the souls of our brothers.

This is the first important outline of the doctrine of the Mystical Body bequeathed to us by St. Paul. It is not yet presented with the perfection to be found in his Epistle to the Ephesians or in his Epistle to the Colossians. True, it affirms the role of Christ as Head of the Mystical Body, especially in the last chapter regarding our glorious resurrection through Christ (cf. 1 Cor. 15:21–22; 47–49). But the prerogative of Headship is merely indicated in passing, in reference to other truths, rather than treated *ex professo*.

In writing to the Corinthians, the Apostle considers the Mystical Body more directly in the totality of its members, abstracting in a certain measure from the Head of the divine Whole. No doubt the reason for this is that he is preoccupied primarily with difficulties of the practical order that face the Christian community of Corinth. He seeks to remedy the divisions that have arisen within it. Consequently he insists on the urgent need of maintaining the strong spiritual cohesion that must unite all members of the same supernatural organism.

The principles of this mystical union brought out in the First Epistle to the Corinthians are essentially three. The first principle is, as we have said, the influence of a single Spirit of supernatural life and action. From him proceed all the vital manifestations of the Church. The second principle is the very powerful action of the sacrament of union, the Holy Eucharist. Finally, the third principle is the bond of supernatural love that charity establishes among the members of the same Body.

To these fundamental elements constituting the unity of the Mystical Body, others will be added in the epistles we shall study, notably in the Epistle to the Ephesians which we turn to next.

CHAPTER IV

The Epistle to the Ephesians

In the epistle to the Romans, the doctrine of original sin and its consequences, the dogma of our predestination and our justification, take on proportions that we would seek in vain elsewhere, and the Epistle to the Hebrews presents in an incomparable way the divine Sonship of Christ and his eternal priesthood. In spite of this, however, the Epistle to the Ephesians[1] is perhaps the most beautiful, the most sublime, and, although relatively brief, the richest in doctrine that St. Paul ever wrote.

We find in the Epistle to the Ephesians an overall view of the designs of divine providence in the world, a general presentation of the economy of grace in the work of our salvation, and especially a doctrinal synthesis of the "mystery" par excellence of the total Christ to be found nowhere else.

The very circumstances in which this epistle was composed must have contributed to its more transcendent and universal character. Written in prison, at the beginning of his Roman captivity during the year 67 A.D., the letter is the fruit of long meditations. Taking advantage of the leisure provided by his solitude, he was able to contemplate in the light of the Holy Spirit the harmony of the great work in which he more than anyone else had collaborated for twenty years. Besides, since he was not addressing himself to one Church in particular but rather to the various Christian communities he had established in Asia Minor, the great Doctor of the Gentiles was freed to some extent from the concerns of individual places and persons. He was not concerned with current and pressing practical needs, as in the majority of the other letters, and notably in his First Epistle to the Corinthians. He was able, therefore, to write at greater length and

---

[1] While this was probably an encyclical letter intended for several Churches, we shall accede to general custom and call it the Epistle to the Ephesians.

more objectively of the great mystery by which he lived and which was the burden of his apostolate.

Thus, in the Epistle to the Ephesians, the Apostle, from the very start, rises above consideration of created things and seeks his conception of the sublime destiny of regenerated humanity in God himself, in the counsel and preordination of eternal Wisdom (Cf. Eph. 1:3 ff.).

Before viewing the unity of the Mystical Body in its temporal fulfillment, he discovers and contemplates it in the eternal decree of predestination that has ordered all things to the glory of Christ, the divine Exemplar and universal end of all creation. In a magnificent flight of thought filled to overflowing with doctrine, he develops the great and merciful plan of divine Goodness, which predestines us to become, through Christ, the adopted sons of the Father, to the glory of the three divine Persons: "*Ad laudem gloriae ejus*—"unto the praise of the glory of his grace" (Eph. 1:6; cf. 1:12; 1:14). This formula, repeated three times, reveals to us in succession the relation of our supernatural life to the Father who predestined us, to the Son who redeemed us at the price of his Blood, and to the Holy Spirit who sanctified us and signed us with his seal. But let us allow St. Paul to speak for himself:

> Blessed be the God and Father of our Lord Jesus Christ, who has blessed us with every spiritual blessing on high *in Christ*. Even as he chose us in him before the foundation of the world, that we should be holy and without blemish in his sight in love. He predestined us to be adopted through Jesus Christ as his sons, according to the purpose of his will, unto the praise of the glory of his grace, with which he has favored us in his beloved Son (Eph. 1:3–6).

Here is the origin of our supernatural vocation. It comes to us from the Father. For the Father, from all eternity, has borne us in his mind and heart. He has lavished upon us "every spiritual blessing on high," a thousand times more precious than the temporal and earthly blessings granted to the people of the promise.

What are these blessings? They are not mere words, but real and operative. They tend to make us "holy and without blemish in [God's] sight." They make us *holy*, sharers of the holiness of God himself through sanctifying grace, which unites us to him. They tend to make us *without blemish*, without reproach before the Lord, because we have been purified of the stain of sin and the defects of the old man. They place us *in God's sight*, by the faith that shows him to us as dwelling in our hearts, and by the love that roots us in him and him in us. And our Father in heaven has prepared these blessings for us "before the foundation of the world."

One pious commentator says: "Even though we have come into being. God's love and his gratuitous choice had no beginning. We have been carried in an eternal cradle in the mind and heart of our God, and the blessings of time have come only as the fulfillment of this first election."[2]

Our infinitely tender Father in heaven, however, intended to endow us with this heavenly benediction, the gift of his grace, the state of holiness, only in his beloved Son. St. Paul repeats over and over this formula of our spiritual inclusion in Christ, of our mystical incorporation in Christ. The Father has blessed us "in Christ." He has chosen us from all eternity "in him." He has predestined us "through Jesus Christ." And when he enriches us with his grace, it is still "in the Beloved."

Cornelius à Lapide observes concerning these last words that, "according to the original text, St. Paul does not say: *'in dilecto Filio suo'*— in his Beloved Son,' but only: *'in dilecto'*—in the Beloved'— that is to say, in the one who is loved absolutely, in all and before all, without whom none other is loved, and who is the reason why all the others are loved."[3]

Of ourselves we merit no love, since by nature we are nothingness and by our demerits we are sin. What consoles and reassures us is that God loves his own divine Son in us, whose grace has placed the divine image within us. In his name we can always come into his divine presence, certain of being welcomed with love and benevolence; whereas we would have every reason to fear if we relied on our own excellence and if we placed our trust in our own merits. The reason is that Jesus was constituted by his Father our one universal Mediator and our sacred Head, and the blessings of our heavenly Father are communicated to us only through Christ and on condition that we be in living communion with Christ.

The Apostle, however, clarifies the nature of this spiritual benediction that the heavenly Father grants us through his Son, and indicates the profound reason for the mediation of Jesus and the nature of our incorporation in Christ. God the Father, says Paul, "predestined us to be *adopted through Jesus Christ as his sons*" (Eph. 1:5). He wanted to make of all of us not servants but beloved sons and thus admit us into his divine company, indeed into his very family. Only through Christ could we receive the benefit of divine

---

[2] Dom Delatte, *Les Epitres de saint Paul replacées dans le milieu historique*, Volume III.
[3] *In Epist. S. Pauli*, Eph. I.

adoption, for he is the only-begotten Son, the Beloved of the Father, the Son of God by nature. It was only by communing in his divine Sonship, by becoming his brothers through grace that we could attain the incomparable nobility of being the adopted sons of God the Father.

As Dom Delatte says: "We cannot improvise our ancestors. We belong to a lineage only if we have a rightful claim to it. I hold my claim from our Lord Jesus Christ and from my union with him. For he is not only the Mediator of this filiation, for only through him can we become sons, he is also the treasure of this filiation, since we can be sons of God only in him."[4]

Therefore quite justifiably Jesus is called our elder Brother: "*that he should be the firstborn among many brethren*" (Rom. 8:29). Yes, he is our elder brother, and not in any accidental way as happens among us because of the fact of a simple precession in the order of time. Jesus is our older brother in a necessary and essential way, by the very exigency of the divine sonship that he possesses by right from all eternity and that we receive from him by participation, in time.

Here we touch the very depths of the ineffable mystery of our incorporation in Christ; for the whole purpose of this mystery is to communicate to us the riches of Christ. Now Christ's own and strictly divine possession, the thing that is most *personal* to him, is the fact that he is the only-begotten Son of the Father. And if, in addition, he assumed our human nature, it was in order to fling it like a bridge of mercy above the abyss that separated us from his Godhead, and thus allow us to be united to him, to become his brothers.

St. Paul tells us from the start how the Son brought about this reconciliation between sinful humanity and God its Father. After describing, in the first part of the prologue, the work of the Father who predestined us and adorned us with his grace in his beloved, he goes on to reveal the redemptive work of the Son in the following terms:

> In him we have redemption through his blood, the remission of sins, according to the riches of his grace. This grace has abounded beyond measure in us in all wisdom and prudence, so that he may make known to us the mystery of his will according to his good pleasure. And this his good pleasure he purposed in him to be dispensed in the fullness of the times: to re-establish all things in Christ, both those in the heavens and those on the earth. In him, I say, in whom we also have been called by a special choice, having been predestined in the purpose of him who works

---

[4] *Op. cit.*

all things according to the counsel of his will, to contribute to the praise
of his glory—we who before hoped in Christ (Eph. 1:7–12)

The role of Christ the Savior, itself subordinate to the eternal design
of the Father of mercies, is defined by the Apostle in two complementary
formulas. The first presents him to us as our Redeemer immolated for our
salvation, the second reveals him as the new Head of redeemed humanity.

"In him," says St. Paul, "we have redemption"—deliverance. We were
indeed captives, but Jesus has broken our chains. We were slaves, but Jesus
has restored us to the holy liberty of the children of God. Captives of hell,
slaves of the devil through the sin of the first man, we have found in the
New Man the price of our redemption, the payment of our debt for sin.
And what is this emancipating ransom? We know what it is. Perhaps we
have grown too accustomed to hear it repeated, but it is no less admirable
and worthy of our eternal gratitude. The Blood of Christ ransomed us.
He is our Redeemer because he is the voluntary victim sacrificed for our
salvation, to such a point that we identify the idea of the Redeemer in our
minds with the sacrifice of the shedding of blood. And yet, strictly speaking,
Jesus could have offered something else as the price of our redemption. We
know that a single tear and a single sigh of our divine Savior, through the
infinite merit of each of his actions. would have sufficed to save us from
death. But such was not the will of the Father who wanted to lavish upon
us with *superabundant* liberality, to use the Apostle's words, "the riches of
his grace" by the virtue of the Blood of our Lamb.

Still more beautiful and more fruitful is the second formula in which
St. Paul shows God re-establishing the universal order under a *new* Head,
Christ the Savior. The first head of the human race, spiritual as well as
natural, was our common father Adam. If he had remained faithful, grace
would have flowed through him into all his descendants. But he went astray,
transfusing into his entire posterity the consequences of his disobedience,
the stain of sin.

God restored the harmony of the supernatural world by constituting
Christ not only as our Redeemer, a term that expresses only a part of the
truth, but also as our universal Head with all the prerogatives befitting a
Head. Christ is the Head not only of men but also of the choirs of angels.
"To re-establish all things in Christ, both those in the heavens and those on
the earth": such is the whole plan of divine Wisdom. The entire doctrine
of the Mystical Body is contained in these few words.

To the work of the Father and the redemptive action of the Son, however, the activity of the Holy Spirit is added, consummating the great work of our salvation in Christ. The Apostle continues, following the verses just cited above: "And in him [Christ Jesus] you too, when you had heard the word of truth, the good news of your salvation, and believed in it, were sealed with the Holy Spirit of the promise, who is the pledge of our inheritance, for a redemption of possession, for the praise of his glory" (Eph. 1:13–14).

The Holy Spirit is the Spirit of Christ himself. He is in us, Bossuet remarks, as coming to us from the outside, as received on loan. He is not our own Spirit, but the Spirit of Jesus Christ.[5] For he proceeds from Christ, and he abides in his sacred humanity as in his most inviolable temple. Moreover, it is through Christ our Savior that this Spirit of holiness is poured into us, to bring about a twofold effect: the marking of Christians with a divine *seal*, an indelible character of their belonging to Christ the Savior, constituting them his members and quickening them with his own life; the giving to Christians the *pledge* of their admission to the *heavenly heritage*, and still more to be himself this infinitely precious pledge. For how could a member of Christ, quickened by the Spirit of his Head, fail to share some day in the glory and heavenly consummation of the divine Head? Only in the fulfillment of the mystical Christ in heaven will the Blessed Trinity receive in plenitude the "*praise of glory*" that all the works of creation and sanctification are intended to render to him.

———·———

After revealing to us in this sublime introduction the whole plan of the *Hidden Mystery,* St. Paul makes known to us in greater detail the various aspects of the Mystical Body, considered in its totality and in its diverse members. We must not seek, in this development of the apostolic doctrine, a rigorous order or a perfectly logical unity. Let us allow ourselves to be dominated and possessed, after the example of Paul, by the sublime idea of *Christ the fullness of the works of God.* Let us allow ourselves to be penetrated and carried away as he was by immense love and a consuming zeal for the growth and perfection of the Church. Then we shall discover in the succession of St. Paul's ideas a powerful and closely-knit unity, the unity that belongs by nature to the Mystical Body of Christ.

Since the constitution of this mystical organism, its increase in beauty, its completion, imply the constant and generous cooperation of the faithful,

---

[5] Cf. *Elévations sur les mystères,* Thirteenth Week, Second Elevation.

the first thing the Apostle demands of them is that they become aware of what it means for them to be Christians, and what is the meaning of the total Christ in whom they are incorporated. They must have a lofty understanding of the great mystery, an understanding that is not merely abstract, but living and practical, rooted in conviction and love.

The Apostle continues:

> Wherefore I on my part, hearing of your faith in the Lord Jesus, and of your love for all the saints, do not cease to give thanks for you, making mention of you in my prayers, that the God of our Lord Jesus Christ, the Father of glory, may grant you the spirit of wisdom and revelation in deep knowledge of him: the eyes of your mind being enlightened, so that you may know what is the hope of his calling, what the riches of the glory of his inheritance in the saints, and what the exceeding greatness of his power towards us who believe. Its measure is the working of his mighty power, which he has wrought in Christ in raising him from the dead, and setting him at his right hand in heaven above every Principality and Power and Virtue and Domination—in short, above every name that is named, not only in this world, but also in that which is to come (Eph. 1:15–21).

The complexity and doctrinal richness of this passage tend to obscure the clarity of the thought. But the essence of it can be summed up in the following terms: the Apostle wishes the faithful to understand the grandeur of the *hope* to which God has deigned to call them, the excellence of the *heritage* that God has prepared for them in glory.

He is speaking of benefits to come, however, of spiritual benefits so far above human weakness that Christians might easily doubt they could ever obtain them from divine liberality, or ever see the effect of such magnificent promises. St. Paul reassures them, saying, in effect: Have no fear. Depend on the exceeding greatness of God's power. And if you do not know what divine power is capable of accomplishing in your favor, look at Christ, see what it has realized in him, your Head. It raised him up from the dead, and seated him in heaven at the right hand of the Father, above all the choirs of angels. In him you have the Exemplar and pledge of what God will do for you. For if Christ has been glorified, you who are his members and his fullness will share in his glory.

St. Paul then goes on to stress the place of the Savior in the plan of God's works. He says that God has made "all things . . . subject under his feet, and him he gave as head over all the Church, which indeed is his body, the completion of him who fills all with all" (Eph. 1:22–23).

This formula synthesizes with truly Pauline terseness and power the entire doctrine of the Mystical Body. The Church is the fullness of Christ; it is the mystery of our incorporation in Jesus. And Christ, "who fills all with all" is a Doctor among the doctors of the Church, an Apostle among the apostles, the divine Sanctifier in the various ministries. This sums up his functions as the divine Head of the Church.

It would be quite a task to comment in detail on the rest of the epistle. In order to stay within the scope of our proposed study, we shall limit ourselves to stressing the Apostle's key ideas relating to our subject, and, when necessary, indicate their place in any doctrinal *summa* of the Mystical Body.

Chapter 2 of Ephesians can be said to follow two principal lines of thought: first, the notion of the life-giving action of Christ who snatches us from the death of sin and communicates his divine life to us through grace and glory; secondly, the notion of the union of the two peoples, Jews and Gentiles, in a single supernatural Body.

To bring out more clearly the wonderful efficacy of the life-giving influence of Christ the Savior on our souls, St. Paul reminds us of the abyss of misery in which we were plunged before.

Divine Mercy came to rescue us from the darkness of sin, to lead us through his Word Incarnate to the light of his truth and grace. God has called us from the state of spiritual death to the supernatural life, raising us from the dead with Jesus:

> You also . . . were dead by reason of your offenses and sins, wherein once you walked according to the fashion of this world, according to the prince of the power of the air about us, the prince of the spirit which now works on the unbelievers—indeed, in the company of these even we, all of us, once led our lives in the desires of our flesh, doing the promptings of our flesh and of our thoughts, and were by nature children of wrath even as the rest. But God, who is rich in mercy, by reason of his very great love wherewith he has loved us, even when we were dead by reason of our sins, brought us to life together with Christ (by grace you have been saved), and raised us up together, and seated us together in heaven in Christ Jesus, that he might show in the ages to come the overflowing riches of his grace in kindness towards us in Christ Jesus (Eph. 2:1–7).

These are the incomparable gifts of divine mercy, gifts that are purely gratuitous and in which no one can glory. St. Paul repeats: "For by grace you have been saved through faith; and that not from yourselves, for it is the gift of God, not as the outcome of works, lest anyone may boast. For by his workmanship we are created in Christ Jesus in good works which God has made ready beforehand that we may walk in them" (Eph. 2:8–10).

To keep the Gentile Christians more firmly in this spirit of humility, which makes them realize the gratuitous favors of infinite Goodness, St. Paul reminds them that they were long excluded from the Covenant God had made with his people. He reminds them that through grace they have been joined to the holy nation in order to be one people in Christ; indeed, far more than this, to become a single man, the new man whose Head is Jesus.

"Wherefore, bear in mind that once you, the Gentiles in flesh, who are called 'uncircumcision' by the so-called 'circumcision' in flesh made by human hand—bear in mind that you were at that time without Christ, excluded as aliens from the community of Israel, and strangers to the covenants of the promise, having no hope, and without God in the world" (Eph. 2:11–12).

The Apostle continues:

> But now in Christ Jesus you, who were once afar off, have been brought near through the blood of Christ. For he himself is our peace, he it is who has made both one, and has broken down the intervening wall of the enclosure, the enmity, in his flesh. The Law of the commandments expressed in decrees he has made void, that of the two he might create in himself *one new man*, and make peace and reconcile both in one body to God by the cross, having slain the enmity in himself. And coming, he announced the good tidings of peace to you who were afar off, and of peace to those who were near; because through him we both have access in one Spirit to the Father (Eph. 2:13–18).

St. Paul completes this doctrinal statement on the union of the two peoples with the passage cited earlier,[6] in which he tells those Christians converted from paganism that they are built upon the foundation of the Apostles and Prophets to form one Temple whose supreme cornerstone is Jesus.

The Apostle describes in general terms the conditions of the human race before the coming of the Redeemer, in order to bring out afterwards in bold relief the work of the restoration by our Savior. The whole human race was divided into two factions: one, the Jewish nation, serving Yahveh and enjoying his Convenant; the other, the Gentiles, separated from God and without hope of a return to the truth. Between the two a deep severance, a

---

6   Cf. Chapter II above, referring to Eph. 2:19–22.

profound enmity, rising like an impassable wall between the chosen people and the masses of the pagan nations. Furthermore, the wall of separation of which the Apostle speaks was not a simple grammatical figure, since the inner enclosure of the Temple, to which only the circumcised were admitted, was a tangible sign of the exclusion of all others from the society of Israel.

This enmity seemed all the more insurmountable in that it was legitimate as far as the Hebrews were concerned, even holy and willed by God. It was based both on the fidelity of the chosen people to the true worship, and on the separation from the true God in which the idolaters lived. The means of spiritually reuniting the two fragments of humanity was the return of the Gentiles to the worship and love of their Creator and Lord. In the divine plan, however, this return was not destined to be a conversion of the pagans to the religion of Israel, but rather a simultaneous conversion of the Jews and of the Gentiles to the worship "in spirit and in truth" inaugurated by Jesus. The union of the two peoples was to be not an absorption of the one by the other, but their fusion in Christ Jesus, the true cornerstone joining the two walls of a single structure.

No doubt the Jews were in a more advantageous position. God had made use of them to lay the deepest foundations of the mystical building. The Prophets belonged to their nation, as did the Apostles, and, by his humanity, Christ himself (cf. Rom. 9:4–5). But by reason of his Messianic role, Jesus belongs to the whole human race, which finds its lost unity in him. It is he who "made peace through the blood of his cross" (Col. 1:20). "The arms of the cross, stretching out to the left and to the right, call to God's embrace the nations of the whole world reconciled among themselves because reconciled with God. Thus, the divine idea finds completion in the eradication of all divisions, in the unity of all peoples in Christ."[7]

Chapter 3 of the Epistle to the Ephesians begins with a long parenthesis that continues until verse 13. Here St. Paul tells us the role that has devolved upon him in the carrying out of God's plans for the nations. The parenthesis is not a digression, however, since it simply develops the Apostle's favorite idea in a new form:

> For this reason, I, Paul, the prisoner of Christ Jesus for the sake of you, the Gentiles—[the thought remains unfinished, and is taken up again at verse 14][8] for I suppose you have heard of the dispensation of the grace of God that was given to me in your regard; how that by revelation was made known

---

[7] Dom Delatte, *op. cit.*

[8] Cf. Eph. 3:14. "For this reason I bend my knees to the Father . . . ."

to me the mystery as I have written above in brief; and so by reading you can perceive how well versed I am in the mystery of Christ, that mystery which in other ages was not known to the sons of men, as now it has been revealed to his holy apostles and prophets in the Spirit: namely, that the Gentiles are joint heirs, and fellow-members of the same body, and joint partakers of the promise in Christ Jesus through the gospel.

Of that gospel I was made a minister by the gift of God's grace, which was given to me in accordance with the working of his power. Yes, to me, the very least of all saints, there was given this grace, to announce among the Gentiles the good tidings of the unfathomable riches of Christ, and to enlighten all men as to what is the dispensation of the mystery which has been hidden from eternity in God, who created all things in order that through the Church there be made known to the Principalities and the Powers in the heavens the manifold wisdom of God according to the eternal purpose which he accomplished in Christ Jesus our Lord. (Eph. 3:1–12).

The Church, the fullness of Christ, *is the Mystery* par excellence, the center of the wonders of God, the subsistent revelation of the secrets of divine Wisdom.

And now, taking up the sentence he began in verse 1, St. Paul makes a fervent supplication, bending his knees to ask God to strengthen the inner man of his faithful through the grace of his Holy Spirit, and *to make Christ dwell in their hearts* through faith and charity (cf. Eph. 3:16–17). These two expressions have long been appropriated by Christian spirituality to characterize the essence of the interior life.

Union with Christ through faith: through faith we enter the supernatural order; through faith we contemplate the infinite riches of Christ our Savior, through faith we are transformed to the likeness of our divine Exemplar and Model (cf. 2 Cor. 3:18); through faith we measure, with astonished eyes, the unspeakable extent of the great mystery, or, to use the Apostle's words, its "breadth and length and height and depth" (Eph. 3:18), which encompass all times and places in the unity of a single divine plan.

Union with Christ through charity: through charity we are established, *rooted* in him, yielding habitually to his life-giving action. Charity communicates his divine benefits to us, and finally, according to the Apostle, fills us "unto all the fullness of God" (Eph. 3:19).

In Chapter 4 of Ephesians, St. Paul exhorts Christians to "walk in a manner worthy" (Eph. 4:1) of their vocation. Here begins the moral portion of his epistle, which we have dealt with in our study of the life of the Mystical Body (cf. *Corps Mystique*, Volume II). And yet, starting with verse 4 of the chapter, the Apostle returns to dogmatic considerations and continues in this vein until verse 17, thus completing and condensing the entire doctrine presented up to this point.

From the point of view of the Mystical Body, there are three different parts of this passage. First, the sacred writer enumerates all the principles that intervene in the constitution of the whole Christ. Then he calls to mind the diverse ministries instituted by God to cooperate in the completion of the Mystical Body. Finally he describes in an overcharged and complex sentence the varied articulations of this divine organism.

The generating principles of the supernatural unity of the Mystical Body are indicated by the Apostle with reference to the precept of fraternal charity, in the following manner:

> I therefore, the prisoner in the Lord, exhort you to walk in a manner worthy of the calling with which you were called, with all humility and meekness, with patience, bearing with one another in love, careful to preserve the unity of the Spirit in the bond of peace: one body and one Spirit, even as you were called in one hope of your calling; one Lord, one faith, one baptism; one God and Father of all, who is above all, and throughout all, and in us all (Eph. 4:1–6).

These then are the diverse elements that constitute our union in Christ, summed up in a few concise words. We shall analyze each of them at length in the chapters to follow. The unity of the Mystical Body is assured by the unity of the life-giving Spirit, the soul of the total Christ; by the unity of a single supernatural end; by the unity of a single sacrament that incorporates us in Christ; and finally by the unity of our common God and Father, the supreme author and ultimate principle of the divine life communicated to us by his beloved Son.

This essential unity of the Mystical Body coexists with a diversity of functions and of ministries, as St. Paul points out in the following passage. Christ, says the Apostle, "gave some men as apostles, and some as prophets, others again as evangelists, and others as pastors and teachers, in order to perfect the saints for a work of ministry, for building up the body of Christ, until we all attain to the unity of the faith and of the deep knowledge of the Son of God, to perfect manhood, to the mature measure of the fullness of Christ" (Eph. 4:11–13),

The Mystical Christ, just like our natural organism, must progress through successive stages of growth to attain the ultimate term of development which is perfect manhood.

Finally, before resuming his moral exhortations and practical counsels, St. Paul delineates the total Christ with vigorous strokes: "Rather are we to practice the truth in love, and so grow up in all things in him who is the head, Christ. For from him the whole body (being closely joined and knit together through every joint of the system according to the functioning in due measure of each single part) derives its increase to the building up of itself in love" (Eph. 4:15–16).

This terminates the dogmatic exposition of the doctrine of the Mystical Body which the Apostle of the Gentiles has left us in his Epistle to the Ephesians. True, he does refer to it again in Chapter 5 in the context of the reciprocal duties of Christian spouses, showing the relationship between Christ and the Church as the ideal type of the sacrament of matrimony. But we have already discussed this passage in speaking of the various analogies by which St. Paul expresses the mystery of the total Christ.[9]

As of now we possess a substantial, complete doctrine of this great mystery. It is a living and life-giving doctrine, the most fruitful doctrine of all, offering inexhaustible resources for our life of union with God, as well as powerful inspiration to stimulate and to sustain our apostolic ardor, our priestly and lay activities, and favoring the growth of the new man to "the mature measure of the fullness of Christ" (Eph. 4:13).

The Epistle to the Colossians will now provide interesting complements to this body of doctrine.

---

[9]   Cf., 17–18 above, referring to Eph. 5:21.

CHAPTER V

The Epistle to the Colossians

Colossae, a city in Phrygia, had not had the advantage of hearing St. Paul's preaching (cf. Col. 2:1), It owed its faith to St, Epaphras, one of the Apostle's disciples. The Doctor of the Gentiles felt obliged, nonetheless, to watch carefully over the preservation and the progress of the faith in this Christian community that he had founded only indirectly.

In the year 62 A.D. or 63 A.D., when Paul was a prisoner of Caesar in Rome, he learned through St. Epaphras that serious unrest had arisen among the faithful of Colossae. False prophets were beginning to corrupt the truth of the Christian dogmas. The role of Christ Jesus as universal Mediator was being contested and denied. This brought into question the very essence of Christianity.

Aflame with zeal and impelled by the Holy Spirit, St. Paul took up his inspired pen to prevent the spiritual ruin that threatened his beloved Christians of Colossae, whom he remembered constantly in his prayers (cf. Col. 1:3; 1:9). He had just written his Letter to the Ephesians,[1] which treats in a general way, and without pointing to any particular error, the point of doctrine attacked by the innovators. He counseled the Colossians to read this epistle which answered all their difficulties (cf. Col. 4:16). In the Letter to the Colossians he dealt with the same subject, to offer them further recommendations relating to the necessities of the moment.

Precisely what was the heresy, for heresy it was, by which the false teachers were corrupting Christian truth? It was already the nucleus, the embryo of Gnosticism, a mixture of Eastern philosophy and Christianity. It contained fantastic conceptions without any objective foundation, related to

---

[1] According to several authors, notably Father Prat in *The Theology of Saint Paul*, (Westminster, Md.: The Newman Press, 1952) I, 280 ff., this epistle was written simultaneously with or even a bit earlier than Ephesians.

the seductive ideology of Neo-Platonism and born of an intellectual pride that would not submit to the simplicity of faith. The Apostle warned: "Let no one deceive you by persuasive words" (cf. Col. 2:4). And a little further on: "See to it that no one deceives you by philosophy and vain deceit, according to human traditions, according to the elements of the world, and not according to Christ" (Col. 2:8).

The basis of the system worked out by the Colossian innovators consisted, as is made clear throughout the epistle, in replacing the mediation of Christ by that of the angels: "Let no one cheat you who takes pleasure in self-abasement and worship of the angels, and enters vainly into what he has not seen, puffed up by his mere human mind. Such a one is not united to the head, from whom the whole body... attains a growth that is of God" (Col. 2:18–19).

Through a false humility that was a cloak for their pride, these precursors of Cerinthus, Marcion, and Valentinius deemed God to be too far above matter to deign to bend down to the visible world and to extend his providence to corporeal beings. Creatures and the governance of this world, they said, are too unworthy of God and must be attributed to inferior powers intermediary between the Supreme Being and corporeal nature—in a word, to the angels.

Moreover, they held that the work of the Redemption was no more fitting to the divine Majesty than that of creation. What, then, was the Redemption in the eyes of the Colossian doctrinaires? Conceived in a purely rationalistic and gnostic way, it was to be a liberation of the spirit from the shackles and defilement of matter, by means of a superior knowledge or *gnosis*, which was the privilege of an elite. This supposed redemption was accomplished only by the mediation of the heavenly spirits. In such a system there could no longer be any question of Christ, the Son of God-made-man, as the Mediator between God and humanity. Thus the whole doctrine of the Mystical Body and of Christianity itself were abolished.

To the vain speculations of these proud doctors were added restrictive practices borrowed from Judaism. Since matter was reputed to be impure, it was deemed fitting to abstain from contact with it insofar as this was possible. Certain foods and beverages were, therefore, forbidden to the adherents of the new sect. St. Paul stormed against these superstitious prohibitions. While he did not stress their relationship to doctrinal errors, this relationship was to become clearly evident in the full-blown Gnosticism of the following epoch. Here is what the Apostle warned:

Let no one, then, call you to account for what you eat or drink or in regard to a festival or a new moon or a Sabbath. . . . If you have died with Christ to the elements of the world, why, as if still living in the world, do you lay down the rules: "Do not touch; nor taste; nor handle!"—things that must all perish in their very use? In this you follow "the precepts and doctrines of men," which, to be sure, have a show of wisdom in superstition and self-abasement and hard treatment of the body, but are not held in esteem, and lead to the full gratification of the flesh. (Col. 2:16, 20–23)

Instead of being ordered to Christ as shadows to substance (cf. Col. 2:17) to signify interior detachment, the circumcision of the heart (cf. Col. 2:11–13), and death to sin, these practices of a bygone age were becoming ends in themselves, impediments, and fomenters of pride.

In short, both of the deviations that the Apostle stigmatizes in his epistle, the dogmatic error and the Judaizing practices, turned the mind away from Christ. The mediation of the angels took the place of the mediation of the Son of God-made-man and Redeemer of the human race. The clinging to precepts of abstinence borrowed from the Mosaic Law discounted the benefits of the spiritual order that Christ brought by liberating us from sin and enriching us with his grace. It was against these two errors that the Doctor of the Gentiles strove to forewarn the faithful of Colossae. But fittingly he placed much greater stress on the former. In order to completely demolish this error he placed a great deal of emphasis on the doctrine of Christ the Head.

The Epistle to the Ephesians gave us an overall view of the Mystical Body considered in its Head and in its members. The First Epistle to the Corinthians dealt more exclusively with the members of the total Christ. The Letter to the Colossians, on the contrary, makes known to us more particularly the sacred Head of the Mystical Body in the fullness of his perfection, and shows us his mediatory mission in relation to the members united to him. Thus these two last epistles taken together contain the message of the Epistle to the Ephesians.

Let us now delve into the Epistle to the Colossians. After the salutation and prologue, the Apostle enters the very heart of his subject and frankly approaches the doctrine of Christ as Head and universal Mediator. Beginning with Colossians 1:12, the doctrine fills the second half of Chapter 1 and all of Chapter 2, and is followed in Chapter 3 with practical applications, including the well-known text: "*Igitur, si consurrexistis cum Christo . . .*"—"therefore, if you have risen with Christ . . ."

The false doctors claimed that God does not concern himself with our earthly world, and does not intervene directly in human matters nor in the regulation of our destinies. As they saw it, he left these tasks to the pure spirits that he created and set up between himself and corporeal nature. To refute these negations, St. Paul first shows us the heavenly Father predestining us to the heavenly heritage and snatching us from the power of darkness. These benefits of his fatherly mercy come to us not through the angels but through his beloved Son.

The Apostle counsels us to render thanks "to the Father, who has made us worthy to share the lot of the saints in light. . . [and] rescued us from the power of darkness and transferred us into the kingdom of his beloved Son, in whom we have our redemption, the remission of our sins" (Col. 1:12–14).

From the start Jesus is revealed to us as our true Mediator: he is both God and man, placed between the supreme Creator and his wretched creatures as the bridge between them. He is God, for he is the beloved Son of the Father. He is man likewise, for he has shed every drop of his sacred Blood for our salvation. The angels could not by themselves lead us to God, for they are far removed from us. Christ our divine Redeemer, on the contrary, inspires full confidence, for he is our brother through his human nature. But he is also very close to God; indeed, he rests on the bosom of the Father, being eternally begotten of him.

The Colossian heretics disputed the dominion of God and of Christ the Son of God over the works of nature and the works of grace, attributing both to the heavenly spirits. Taking the opposite stand to this bold error, St. Paul proclaims the Son as the Creator of the universe and even of the angels, as well as his role as Mediator in the universal Redemption and restoration:

"[The beloved Son] is the image of the invisible God, the firstborn of every creature. For in him were created all things in the heavens and on the earth, things visible and things invisible, whether Thrones, or Dominations, or Principalities, or Powers. All things have been created through and unto him, and he is before all creatures, and in him all things hold together" (Col. 1:15–17).

So much for the world of created beings. Through him, the Wisdom of the Father and the subsistent image of his infinite perfection, creatures come into existence. Through him they attain the perfection of their being, and toward him they all converge, as toward the one who is the substantial glory of the Father and by whom all things are brought back to their first principle.

The same order has been observed by God in the economy of sanctification. All the works of grace are accomplished in the Church. The Head of this Church, however, the synthesis of the wonders of God, is Christ. St. Paul continues: "He is the head of his body, the Church; he, who is the beginning, the first born from the dead, that in all things he may have the first place. For it has pleased God the Father that in him all his fullness should dwell, and that through him he should reconcile to himself all things, whether on the earth or in the heavens, making peace through the blood of his cross" (Col. 1:18–20).

Here we find the notion of the restoration of all things under a single Head, an idea already presented by St. Paul in his Epistle to the Ephesians (cf. Eph. 1:10). However, the Apostle adds two new elements. First, he shows us that the consummation of Christ and of his supernatural mediation is his *Resurrection*. Twice he speaks of Jesus as the firstborn from the dead. And a little farther on he proposes the risen Christ to the faithful as the Exemplar of their new life.

The fact is that the Redemption attains its ultimate term and its most glorious triumph in the resurrection of our divine Savior. The resurrection manifests the full efficacy of the redemptive Blood, and is the certain pledge of our total liberation from the yoke of sin and of death.

Secondly, Christ is shown to us in this passage not only as the sacred Head who communicates life and movement to all its members, but as the one who possesses in himself the fullness of all grace and perfection. Returning to this idea, St. Paul clarifies it still further in these words: "For in him dwells all the fullness of the Godhead bodily, and in him who is the head of every Principality and Power you have received of that fullness" (Col. 2:9–10).

Not only the created perfections of Christ make of him our Head and the source of our holiness. His divine nature and the grace of the hypostatic union, which the Apostle calls "the fullness of the Godhead" dwelling in Christ, also and primarily cause this. From his divine nature all heavenly gifts flow into the Church. Through the grace of the hypostatic union we are filled in Christ with every supernatural treasure: "*And in him who is the head. . . you have received of that fullness.*" We must cleave to Christ our Head, to Christ our God, to Christ our brother through his humanity, to Christ our divine Mediator.

Let us not stop at creatures, holy as they may be, nor even at angelic spirits. Let us go to them, yes, let us call upon their help. But let us go beyond them, let us go through them to Christ. For Christ is "the throne of grace" (Heb. 4:16), the source of all holiness, the fullness of all perfection. He is the infinite Good who, through his union with our finite nature, dispenses every grace to us. The saints understand this doctrine of salvation and find in it the divine supplement to all their insufficiencies. That is what gave St. Thérèse of Lisieux her "daring confidence" of becoming "a great saint."

"I am not trusting in my own merits, for I have none; but I trust in him who *is* Virtue and Holiness itself. It is he alone who, pleased with my poor efforts, will raise me to himself, and by clothing me with his merits make me a saint."[2]

The same faith in the infinite riches of our heavenly Mediator also dictated the following verses:

> Too well I know that all our just acts
> > Are valueless in your eyes.
> To give my sacrifices value
> > I want to cast them into your divine heart.[3]

This truly apostolic doctrine cannot be esteemed too highly, and it should be preached boldly and untiringly to souls eager for perfection. It can lead them to the summits of sanctity and fill up the void of their human deficiencies with the infinite treasures of our divine Redeemer. Let us borrow from Dom Marmion the following thoughts which make an excellent commentary on St. Paul's "in him . . . you have received of that fullness":

> The thought of our riches in Jesus Christ should give us a holy boldness to draw near to the Father. When we are filled with this spirit of St. Paul, the sight of our miseries does not discourage us, we lean on Jesus Christ alone. When a soul tells me: "All that is useless for me . . . I am too full of miseries . . ." I see that it is a soul who has never understood the greatness of our riches in Jesus Christ, who has never understood these words: 'God so loved the world, as to give his only-begotten Son.'"[4]

Indeed our deficiencies should not make us lose our trust in our sweet Savior, since our weaknesses are the reason and condition for his redemptive

---

[2] *St. Thérèse of Lisieux, the Little Flower of Jesus*, "The Autobiography" (New York: P. J. Kenedy & Sons, 1927), 70.

[3] *Loc. cit.*

[4] Don Raymund Thibaut, *Abbot Columba Marmion*, (St. Louis: B. Herder Book Co., 1932), 141.

mission, for his divine mediation. St. Paul reminds us of this in the following passage of his Epistle to the Colossians: "You yourselves were at one time estranged and enemies [of God] in mind through your evil works. But now he has reconciled you in his body of flesh through his death, to present you holy and undefiled and irreproachable before him" (Col. 1:21–22).

Our spiritual resurrection, our quickening, our sanctification come to us from our divine Fullness, Christ. This does not mean that we do not need to cooperate. We must remain steadfast in the faith, St. Paul tells us; we must defend our treasure against those who would snatch it from us (cf. Col. 1:23). We must follow the Apostle's example and fill up in our flesh "what is lacking of the sufferings of Christ . . . for his body, which is the Church" (Col. 1:24). But our cooperation can never match the merits of Jesus. And our sufferings perfect us and contribute to the welfare of the Church only when they rest on the passion of the Savior, whose prolongation and re-edition they are in each of his members.

After stressing the role of Christ as universal Head and Mediator, St. Paul returns to general considerations on the Mystical Body, as seen in the plan of divine Providence. After speaking of the Church, the Body of Christ, for whose sake he shares in the Savior's passion, the Apostle adds: "[I have become the Church's minister] in virtue of the office that God has given me in your regard. For I am to preach the word of God fully—the mystery which has been hidden for ages and generations, but now is clearly shown to his saints. To them God willed to make known how rich in glory is this mystery among the Gentiles—Christ in you, your hope of glory!" (Col. 1:25–27).

Here again St. Paul brings out the universality of the economy of grace that belongs no longer to the Jews alone, but to all nations, to the whole human race. With this thought in mind he goes on to say: "Him [Christ] we preach, admonishing every man and teaching every man in all wisdom, that we may present every man perfect in Christ Jesus. At this, too, I work and strive, according to the power which he mightily exerts in me" (Col. 1:28–29).

He carries the thought over into Chapter 2: "For I wish you to know what great concern I have for you and for the Laodiceans and for all who have not seen me in the flesh; that . . . they . . . [may] know the mystery of God the Father of Christ Jesus, in whom are hidden all the treasures of wisdom and knowledge (Col. 2:1–3).

With these words St. Paul closes his direct and objective explanation of his doctrine on the Mystical Body and on the prerogatives of its sacred Head.

Although he has not yet so much as mentioned the false teachers who are disturbing the Church of Colossae, nor revealed their errors, he opposes the divine truth to the sacrilegious modifications that the heretics introduced.

From this point on and throughout Chapter 2, the Apostle makes a frontal attack on error, and places the faithful on their guard against the pernicious teachings of the innovators. "See to it that no one deceives you by philosophy and vain deceit . . . (Col. 2:8),[5] and so on. We have already anticipated this polemical portion of the epistle in order to place the teaching of St. Paul in its historical and doctrinal context. We need not lay too much stress on it here.

We shall merely cite the magnificent passage in which Paul refutes the twofold error of the Colossian doctrinaires, at the same time depicting in sublime language the victory Christ won by his cross. The false teachers commended physical circumcision. St. Paul answers that Christ abolished this rite and replaced it by a spiritual circumcision. They stressed the mediation of the angels, through whom God gave the Law to Moses (cf. Gal. 3:19). Christ, retorts the Apostle, has dispossessed them of their mediatory function, by substituting his own universal mediation on Calvary (cf. Col. 2:15).[6]

> In him . . . you have been circumcised with a circumcision not wrought by hand, but through putting off the body of the flesh, a circumcision which is of Christ. For you were buried together with him in baptism, and in him also rose again through faith in the working of God who raised him from the dead. And you, when you were dead by reason of your sins and the uncircumcision of your flesh, he brought to life along with him, forgiving you all your sins, cancelling the decree against us, which was hostile to us. Indeed, he has taken it completely away, nailing it to the cross. Disarming the Principalities and Powers, he displayed them openly, leading them away in triumph by force of it (Col. 2:10–15).

Here we are back to the central dogma of Christianity. For, as Bossuet has remarked, if Christ is the center of religion, the cross and the passion are the center of the life of Christ.

---

[5] Cf. also p. 51 above.

[6] Another interpretation of this passage is also possible. The Principalities and Powers here mentioned might be the infernal spirits whom Christ despoils of their domination. The sense of this verse is not obvious. Cf. Prat, *op. cit.*, 201, and *Recherches des Sc. relig.*, 1912, 201–29, in which the same author proves that in this verse, whose meaning is very controversial, the reference is indeed to the angels, stripped by Jesus of their temporary mediation.

The remainder of the Epistle to the Colossians is discussed elsewhere in our study of the activity of the Mystical Body,[7] the supernatural and renewed activity of the Christian risen with Christ, whose "life is hidden with Christ in God" (Col. 3:3).[8]

We shall not make a detailed study of the interesting passages in the other epistles of St. Paul that might relate to the constitution of the Mystical Body of Jesus Christ. The Epistles to the Romans, to the Galatians, and to the Hebrews would all provide beautiful texts on the dogma of our incorporation into Christ. In the Epistle to the Hebrews especially, the Apostle presents Christ to us as our divine Exemplar, become like to us in all things by reason of the infirmities and sufferings of his sacred humanity, so that he might be a merciful High Priest, capable of compassionating the weaknesses of those whose Mediator and Head he has been appointed by God.

These passages, however, will find their proper place in other portions of this work. We know enough now about the doctrine of St. Paul on the Mystical Body, and the pre-eminent place he assigns to it in the totality of Christian truths. On this solid foundation of apostolic doctrine we can establish and develop the theology of the Mystical Body. And this we shall strive to do in Part II which follows.

---

[7] Author is referring to Volume II of his work *Le Corps Mystique du Christ* (English translation forthcoming from Arouca Press).

[8] Cf. also Col. 3:1–2.

PART II

·

Theological Notions on
the Nature of the Mystical Body

Introduction

The mystery of the whole Christ, Jesus the Son of God made man, the Head of redeemed and sanctified humanity; all men called to become members of Christ the Redeemer and to form a single supernatural organism in union with him; the Church considered as the Mystical Body of Jesus, its extension and plenitude: this is the substance of the doctrine we have received from St. Paul concerning our salvation through Jesus Christ, our union with Jesus Christ.

But the question arises once again which we formulated earlier: "How are we to define this union according to St. Paul? Is it an essential union . . . like the substantial union of soul and body? Is it a personal union like the hypostatic union . . . ? Is it a moral or a physical union?"[1] This is the question which, with God's help, we shall strive to answer now, thus determining, in accordance with the principles of theology, the nature and constitution of the Mystical Body.

The Mystical Body of Christ, which forms an organic whole, can be known in its constitutive elements only if we clarify the residing place of the essence of the organism: the *unity* of the whole and the *diversity* of its parts. Every organism evokes an idea of unity, but this unity necessarily implies, in the case of a living body, the multiplicity of its members and the diversity of its organs, adapted to the many functions that the life of the body requires.

In our study of the constitution of the Mystical Body, therefore, we shall first consider the nature of the unity of this divine organism. We shall then indicate the various parts that make it up and whose harmoniously ordered diversity gives to the Body of Christ its supernatural beauty.

Part II which follows will be divided as follows:

Article I: The Constitutive Principles of the Unity of the Mystical Body.

Article II: The Diverse Parts of the Mystical Body: The Head and the Members.

---

[1] Duperray, *Le Christ dans la vie chrétienne*, Chapter 1, par. 2.

ARTICLE I

THE CONSTITUTIVE PRINCIPLES OF
THE UNITY OF THE MYSTICAL BODY

CHAPTER VI

On the Unity of the Mystical Body in General

The Mystical Body! This expression, so simple and so brief, contains a world of supernatural realities that we must strive to discern by the light of faith and by the help of theology.

What do we mean by the term "Mystical Body"? What is its general signification? This is what we shall determine in the present chapter, analyzing each of the words that compose it and indicating the principles of unity of this *Body*, as well as its mystical character.

The word BODY implies an *organic whole*, composed of dissimilar parts that are called *members*, all of which are subordinate to the principal and governing part—the *head*. Both head and members are united and informed by a single principle of life—the soul— and tend under the impulsion of the soul, through diverse and harmoniously coordinated operations, to a *common end*, which is the preservation of the organism and its ultimate perfection.

All the elements of this definition are to be found in the supernatural organism called the *Mystical Body*. The various members that make it up are the faithful and their pastors, each with distinctive functions. The Head who rules them is Christ the Redeemer. The soul of the Mystical Body, as we shall see, is the Holy Spirit, the Spirit of Jesus and the vital principle who gives life to his members. The common end to which all the parts of the Mystical Christ tend is, according to the Apostle's words, the perfection of the saints and "the fullness of Christ" (cf. Eph. 4:12–13).

The diverse elements of the definition formulated above apply literally only to the natural organism, and must be applied to the Mystical Body of Christ in an analogical manner, according to an analogy of proportion.

In a natural body, or to be more precise, in the human body, the members exist only within the whole, and form a single physical being none of whose parts can subsist alone or live apart from the whole. In the Mystical Body, on the other hand, the members that constitute it are living beings complete in themselves, numerically distinct, and existing prior to their incorporation into Christ.[1]

In the natural order likewise, the soul is an essentially incomplete principle of being, ordered to the body as to its necessary complement to form a single substance with it; whereas in the supernatural order of the soul of the Mystical Body is a subsistent divine Person who does not contract a substantial union with the divine organism to which he communicates his life.

Is the unity of the Mystical Body, then, merely a moral union of its various parts, as is true of all human societies? Certainly not. There is more, much more in the constitution of the Mystical Christ than a simple moral union. Jesus exerts a physical influence in the very depths of souls, and he is the efficient principle of their supernatural life. There is nothing like this in any moral body, in any social unity. No one would dare maintain that the subjects of a kingdom are the members of the head who governs them; for the bonds of dependence and social solidarity that unite the subjects to their ruler are far from being as excellent, as numerous, and as close as those that bind the faithful to Christ their Head.

Moreover, the Body of Christ is qualified as MYSTICAL, an epithet that expresses something hidden, mysterious, and supernatural, something surpassing human understanding. The Mystical Body, like everything that relates to the economy of grace and to the work of the sanctification of souls, belongs to an order of things that does not fall within the domain of the senses, nor can it be perceived by unaided reason. It can be known only through divine revelation and the interior illumination of the Holy Spirit. Even this supernatural light allows us only a glimpse of the surface, if we may say so, of the divine realities. For we cannot penetrate their inner nature here on earth. It is, therefore, with the greatest respect and in a spirit of sober truthfulness (cf. Acts 16:25) in all that concerns divine matters that we approach the study of these admirable mysteries accomplished by eternal Wisdom in the constitution of the Mystical Body of Christ.

We have said that the union of the faithful with our Lord is not a *substantial union* like the one uniting the various parts of a natural being, inasmuch as Christ's "to be" is distinct from that of each of the faithful who are his

---

[1] Cf. the Encyclical *Mystici Corporis*, par. 61: "In a natural body the principle of unity unites the parts in such a manner that each lacks its own individual subsistence; on the contrary, in the Mystical Body the mutual union, though intrinsic, links the members by a bond which leaves to each the complete enjoyment of his own personality."

mystical members. For a similar reason there can be no question here of a hypostatic union such as the one that unites the human nature of Christ to the Divine Word in the unity of a single Person. For even though we have been incorporated into Christ and even though our dependence upon Christ our Head may be very close, we still retain not only our own nature but our personal and independent being, with full and entire responsibility for our acts and for our life.

On the other hand, the union we contract with our divine Savior in the Mystical Body is not a simple union of the moral order, even though this mode of union is not to be excluded.

Indeed, many bonds of obedience, social dependence, and love unite us to Christ. But there is more than that.

What, then, is the nature of this union of the Mystical Body, and what make up the supernatural bonds uniting the faithful to our Lord, bonds so close and so strong that through them we become his members, and he our sacred Head?

The bonds are many, and we shall enumerate them briefly now, explaining them in detail later in the following chapters. There are seven ways in which we are united to Jesus, each of them a distinct mode of union from which results the unity of the Mystical Body:

1. Union of the juridical order. Christ has sacred rights over us by the fact of his Incarnation, and because he redeemed and reconquered us through his redemptive passion. Thus we are his inalienable property even before our sanctification by baptismal grace. The rights of Jesus over us and our duties toward him as our Redeemer form the first bond of cohesion and solidarity joining us to Christ our Head.

2. Union of the moral order. The juridical bond, in itself glorious and holy, is closely related to the bond of reciprocal charity that unites us to our Savior and unites him to us through love. This mutual love ratifies spontaneously and voluntarily our obligatory submission to Christ by reason of our creation and redemption.

3. Union through efficient causality. Not content to possess us as his property and to love us with a divine love, our Savior sanctifies us in the very substance of our being through sanctifying grace, and in all our faculties through the infusion of the virtues and gifts. In addition, his sacred humanity is constantly projecting into our souls many life-giving influences that make us act supernaturally and live divinely, in accordance with our condition as adopted sons of the heavenly Father.

4. Sacramental union. In an inexpressible embrace of love the divine Savior deigns to visit his creatures in the ineffable sacrament that not only brings his grace and the influence of his sacred humanity into our innermost being, but gives us his very humanity as our divine food to transform us into himself.

5. Union in the Holy Spirit. In making us his members, Christ our Head has deigned to quicken us with his own Spirit, and he has given this sanctifying Spirit to his Church as its permanent principle of life, as the *soul of the Mystical Body* which we form in union with him.

6. Union through exemplary causality. In the development of our spiritual life and in the exercise of the manifold virtues adorning the mystical organism that God has willed to establish, we tend to reproduce in ourselves the Model offered us by our divine Head. For our heavenly Father "has predestined [us] to become conformed to the image of his son" (Rom. 8:29), so that the Head and the members might be homogeneous and be harmoniously united in the same supernatural Body.

7. Union through final causality. All who are incorporated in Christ must join with him in glorifying God the heavenly Father for all eternity in the splendor of glory, through the full development of the Mystical Body and the full deployment of its supernatural activity.

These are the constitutive principles of this unique organic unity, which will permit us to penetrate the specific essence and the ineffable perfections of what we call, together with St. Paul, the Body of Christ. They are enumerated and analyzed in the Encyclical *Mystici Corporis*. They can be ordered under the four modes of causality that embrace the universality of things and, when applied to a given object even in the field of theology, enable us to envisage all its aspects and contents. It will be useful to the order and clarity of the ideas we are going to develop to apply this mode of adequate division to the subject before us:

I. *Material Cause* (Principle of multiplicity): The Head and members.
Cf. Article II, following.

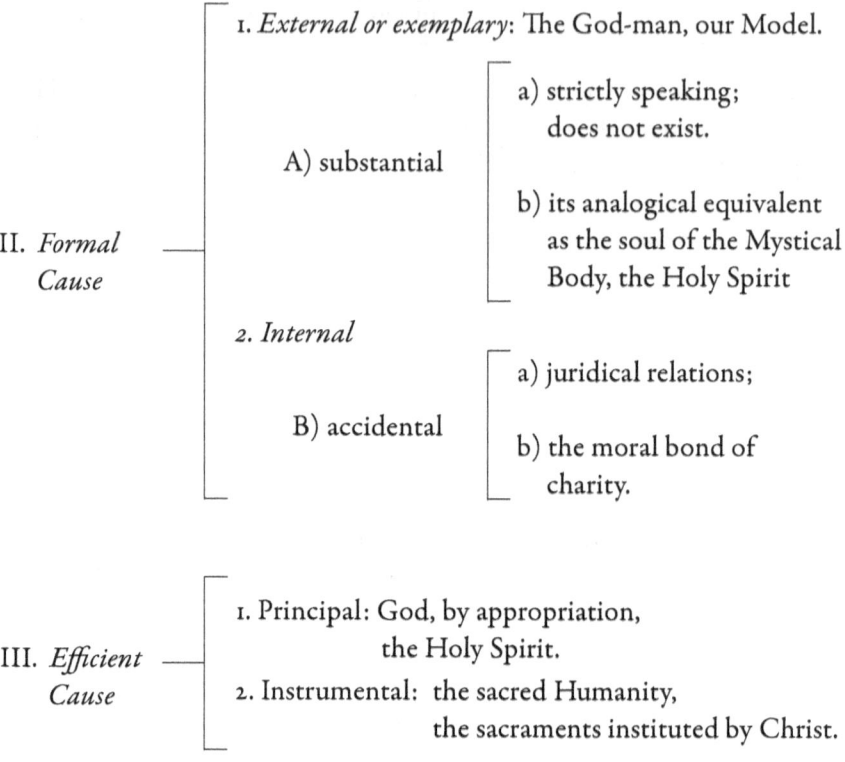

I. *External or exemplary*: The God-man, our Model.

A) substantial

  a) strictly speaking;
    does not exist.

  b) its analogical equivalent
    as the soul of the Mystical
    Body, the Holy Spirit

II. *Formal Cause*

2. *Internal*

B) accidental

  a) juridical relations;

  b) the moral bond of
    charity.

III. *Efficient Cause*

1. Principal: God, by appropriation,
    the Holy Spirit.
2. Instrumental: the sacred Humanity,
    the sacraments instituted by Christ.

IV. *Final Cause*: The fullness of Christ for the glory of God.

Before undertaking a deeper study of these constitutive elements of the Mystical Body of Jesus, we feel it necessary to satisfy a need for order and synthesis. A question arises in the minds of some of our readers.[2] Are the theological notions concerning the Mystical Body all of equal importance, and must we treat them on an equal par? Is there not a hierarchy among these various supernatural realities? What is the most important among the principles of unity? Which of the principles is the one around which a true theological synthesis of the total Christ may be realized, the principle that is as it were the prime constitutive of the unity of the members of the Mystical Christ?

---

[2] Cf. for example, *Vita cristiana* (November, 1938), 645–46.

In answer to these questions, we shall establish the two following points:

1. Of all the principles of unity of the Mystical Body, the most important one, the one that more than any other accounts for the mysterious reality of the total Christ, is the principle of efficient causality.

2. Around the principle of supernatural efficient causality, of the life-giving action of Christ the Savior on his members, can be grouped all the other principles of unity, whether because they are the presupposed conditions, or the means of applying this vital influx of Christ, or because they are its necessary consequence and complement.

In the first place, it is efficient causality above all which, in the total Christ, accomplishes the close cohesion of the many parts, the vital dependence of the members with regard to their Head, thanks to which Jesus and we form a single supernatural organism.

In the natural order, the unity of the members of a living being is of the substantial order and depends on the *one substantial form* which actuates and unifies the diverse parts of the body. In the supernatural order, on the contrary, there can be a question only of an *accidental unity*, even though it may be close and profound. And this unity cannot stem from a single substantial form, but depends on the *action* that Christ exerts on us, on the life-giving influx that the Head exercises on his members, on the continual communication of life that the Word Incarnate pours into our souls through the canal of his sacred humanity: "*It is now no longer I that live, but Christ lives in me*" (Gal. 2:20).

We have explained elsewhere the nature of this influx of our divine Head into us and the many manifestations of this *Christian life*, of this *life of Christ* in us. We can guess already the inestimable value of this life of grace through which Jesus wills to continue in each of us in particular and in his Church as a whole his own divine and human life, his *theandric* life. This life begins for us at the time of our baptism, in the very act of our incorporation into Christ, and will attain its consummation in glory.

It is principally in terms of the vital influx of Christ into his members that the Angelic Doctor explains the unity of the Mystical Body. Speaking of Christ the Head in his *Commentary on the Epistle to the Ephesians*, St. Thomas Aquinas enumerates three elements that concur in the constitution of the total Christ, by similitude with the natural body:

> The natural body consists of three things: the union of several members, their being joined together by means of nerves, and their mutual interrelations. Spiritually also, everything that the head gives to the body flows from

Christ, our Head, into the body of the Church. And first of all, the union [of the faithful] . . . through faith . . . Then from Christ the Head there flows into his Mystical Body the power that connects and joins together [the members] through faith and charity. . . In the third place, from Christ the Head there proceeds into his members the spiritual virtue that makes them act with a view to their growth.[3]

Here as well as elsewhere St. Thomas distinguishes other elements of unity, but he sees them as deriving from the *vital influx* of Christ, whose Body we are and upon whom we depend at every instant.

In his commentary on Chapter 12 of the Epistle to the Romans,[4] St. Thomas says with even greater clarity:

In the second place the Apostle speaks of the unity of the Mystical Body, saying: "We are one body" (Rom. 12:5). Now this spiritual unity of the Mystical Body consists in our being united to one another and to God through faith and charity, according to these words spoken to the Ephesians: "one body and one spirit" (Eph. 4:4). And because it is from Christ that the spirit of unity flows into us, according to these words: "If anyone does not have the Spirit of Christ, he does not belong to Christ" (Rom. 8:9). And for this reason St. Paul adds: "*in Christo unum corpus sumus*" (cf. Rom. 8:9). In Christ we are one, in him who unites us to one another and to God through his Spirit whom he gives to us, according to St. John: "that they also may be one in us . . . even as we are one" (John 17:21–22).

This enlightening text orientates our faith in our analysis of the unity of the total Christ. Many principles intervene in the constitution of the Mystical Body, and St. Thomas enumerates quite a number of them at various points in his writings.[5] But in the last analysis these elements tend to mold all the mystical members into the Body of Christ. And we are united in Christ only by our vital dependence upon our divine Head by reason of the causality of grace he exercises over us.

But the life-giving influx of Jesus presupposes various conditions, is accomplished by diverse means, and produces various kinds of grace in us. Hence, it follows that all the other principles of unity enumerated above will be grouped around this principle of efficient causality.

---

[3] *In Eph. IV*, lect. 5.
[4] *In Rom. XII*, lect. 2.
[5] Cf. De *Veritate*, q. 19, aa. 4–5; *In Col. 1*, lect. 6; *In 1 Cor. XII*, lect. 3.

First there are the conditions. Before any fulfillment in the natural or supernatural order, there exists in God a conception of the end to be realized: this is the principle of *final causality*.

The end that comes last in the order of execution appears first in the order of intention, according to the axiom *"ultimum in ordine executionis, primum in ordine intentionis."* Now God has willed us in Christ and for the glory of Christ, the Word Incarnate.

Passing to the order of execution, we are placed at once in the presence of the admirable mystery (cf. Eph. 3:4; Col. 1:26), the mystery of godliness (cf. 1 Tim. 3:16) that God inaugurated upon earth through the Incarnation of his Son, that he perfected through the work of the Redemption, and that he consummated with the establishment of the Church, the beloved Bride and mystical prolongation of his incarnate Son.

The Incarnation places at the summit of the spiritual and corporeal world the "first born of every creature" (Col. 1:15), the Son of God-made-man. And by that very fact it gives all creation a Head, and makes all men subjects of this divine King, members of the organic unity that he came to establish upon earth. Then by redeeming us in his precious Blood, Jesus added to his right over us by reason of birth, the right of conquest. And here we have the principle of *juridical causality*.

But everything that is acquired in principle must afterwards be progressively won in fact. Even though we belong to Christ by right (St. Thomas would say "in potency")[6] from the moment we come into the world, we still do not begin to live in Christ, to be in fact living members of our Head until the day of our engrafting upon the Mystical Vine (cf. John 15:1 ff.).

Baptism initiates this divine incorporation, the Eucharist completes it, and the other sacraments extend its benefits to the various phases of our activity and the diverse situations of our individual and social life: this is the *principle of sacramental unity*.

Once incorporation into our sweet Savior has been accomplished, we are habitually under his life-giving influence, under the influx of the efficient causality that is at the summit, or better at the center of all these mysteries of life and grace within the Mystical Body. By the same token, however, we are also placed under the influence of the Spirit of Jesus, the Spirit of the Son (cf. Gal. 14:6), the Soul of the Mystical Body, the common Spirit of the Head and of its members.

---

[6] Cf. *Summa*, IIIa, q. 8, a. 3.

Jesus and his Spirit of love devote all their divine power to uniting all the members of the Mystical Body among themselves by inspiring absolute oneness in their aspirations, views, intentions, and operations, as well as submission to the authority of the ecclesiastical magisterium. This is another aspect of *juridical unity*.[7] The resemblance of all the members to Christ the Head through the sacramental character, through the grace of adopted sonship, and through the supernatural virtues is *the principle of exemplary or formal causality*. The union of all through the common views of a single faith, through the hope of the same beatitude, and through bonds of the same supernatural charity is *the principle of moral union*, of the unanimity, of the "one soul and one mind" (Phil. 2:2) that St. Paul urged so strongly upon the Philippians.

This is the order, as far as we are able to establish it, the hierarchy of the many supernatural realities, of the "joints and ligaments" (Col. 2:19) that constitute the cohesion and unity of the structure of the Mystical Body of Jesus Christ. In the following chapters we shall adopt this order of presentation insofar as possible, but without any exaggerated slavishness, in our effort to analyze more thoroughly "the unfathomable riches of Christ" (Eph. 3:8), and to increase our love for the beautiful mystery of the mystical Christ.

---

[7] While the use of a strictly logical order is useful on the whole, it is not always opportune in specific instances. To avoid a separate treatment of related subjects, we have grouped everything concerning *juridical causality* in a single chapter.

CHAPTER VII

Union in Christ,
the Universal Final Cause

At the beginning as well as at the end of every undertaking is the consideration of its purpose. At the beginning, the end in view is the motive that induces to action, the reason that justifies the work begun. And when the work is completed, the end is its final realization, its consummation, and its reward.

The end is a principle of being, and therefore a principle of unity. For the unity of a thing, according to the philosophical axiom, follows from its being and is an inseparable property of its being. If, therefore, we want to know the nature of this mysterious unity that is the total Christ, if we want to live it in a fully conscious way, we must first know what is its final end pre-established by God for "building up the body of Christ" (Eph. 4:12).

In the plan of divine Wisdom, everything has been conceived and willed in order to manifest the glory of the only-begotten Son, because he is the substantial glory of the Father (cf. Heb. 1:3). Every creature must glorify the Son, as the Son glorifies the Father, whose living image he is (cf. Heb. 1:3). Did not Christ say so in his sublime prayer before his passion: "I have glorified thee . . . and I am glorified in them" (John 17:4, 10)? I have glorified thee, O Father, and I am glorified by my disciples.

The glory of the Father through the Word Incarnate, the glory of the Son through those who are his complement and his fullness as members of his Mystical Body: this is the end God has foreseen from all eternity in the creation of all things outside of himself.

Whatever God, infinite Wisdom, does is for this end that is worthy of himself. This is the end that presides over the realization of all his works, that illumines all the paths which his creatures follow, which determines in advance the efficacious means and necessary helps to attain the end in view: a universal and supremely efficacious ordering that theology designates by the name of *Providence*.[1]

When this order of divine Providence concerns not merely an indifferent end, whether proximate or remote, but the supereminent and final end which is the beatific vision, then the Providence of God takes on a special name and is called *Predestination*. The formal reason of Predestination resides in the merciful design of divine Goodness that ordains certain creatures to attain the end of eternal beatitude.[2]

Now a principle of order exists in this plan of divine Wisdom and Goodness. Among all the predestined there is one whom the Father of mercies has in mind before all others, and to whom all the elect are ordered as to their end:[3] his Incarnate Son, Jesus Christ. He has been predestined to receive the fullness of grace in his human nature, to be the source of all other grace. Through the hypostatic union the Son of God is a real man by nature,[4] and the only-begotten Son of God has become the term and Exemplar to whom all the adopted children are conformed.

In his Epistle to the Ephesians, in the magnificent prologue that we analyzed above,[5] St. Paul showed us our vocation to the supernatural order, our predestination *ante mundi constitutionem*, conceived by God the Father in his Christ. The Apostle tells us that the Father *"predestined us to be adopted through Jesus Christ as his sons"* (Eph. 1:5); that "he chose us in him before the foundation of the world, that we should be holy and without blemish in his sight" (Eph. 1:4).

---

[1] Providence is the ordering of all things toward their end, an ordering that pre-exists from all eternity in the mind of God. "It is necessary that the type of the order of things towards their end should pre-exist in the divine mind: and the type of things ordered towards an end is, properly speaking, providence" (*Summa*, Ia, q. 22, a. I).

[2] Cf. *Summa*, Ia, q. 23, a. I.

[3] And at the same time he is the Exemplar and the efficient cause of their predestination. Cf. *Summa*, IIIa, q. 24, aa. 3–4.

[4] St. Paul's famous words to the Romans (Rom. 1:3–4) must be applied to this predestination of Christ according to his human nature: "... concerning his Son who was born to him according to the flesh of the offspring of David, who was foreordained Son of God by an act of power in keeping with the holiness of his spirit ..." This lesson, which is quite difficult to interpret, is very well explained in theological terms by St. Thomas in his *Commentary* on this Epistle, Chapter 1, lect. 3: "Whereas the Person of Christ has always been the Son of God (and as such could not be predestined to *become*), nevertheless he has not always had a supposit of human nature that was the Son of God: that was the effect of an ineffable grace." This then is the proper object of the predestination of Christ, the exemplar and term of ours. Cf. *Summa*, IIIa, q. 24. In Greek the word *praedestinatus* does not occur in our text. The word *destinatus*, ὁρισθέντος, is used, which makes the exegesis easier.

[5] Cf. Chapter IV.

Therefore, in the mind of God himself, in the original design of divine preordination directing all creation to its end, we must seek the first principle of this unity and of this divine and ineffable solidarity that binds us to and incorporates us in Christ Jesus. That is the source of all grace, of all love; by an eternal act of inconceivable love our heavenly Father has included us with his Beloved in the same decree of filial predestination.

Filial predestination means that the entire ordering of God's mercies concerns this divine sonship which, belonging by nature to the only-begotten Son, is communicated in its entirety through the hypostatic union to the human nature of Christ, and then poured out through grace and participation upon us, poor mortal creatures.

In the strictest sense, it is due to the grace of filial adoption that our incorporation into Jesus Christ is realized. And it is as adopted sons that we are willed by God, predestined by God to become the members of his Christ.

To quote Abbé Anger:

> We are, therefore, loved by God only in the measure that in us he sees his son. And we have already seen that we do not resemble Jesus Christ, we are not true images of him or exact photographs, except by grace conferred within the Mystical Body. It is not outside of himself that our Savior molds us to be his image and his likeness; it is in uniting us to himself, in incorporating us into himself; in making us participants of that life divine of which he is the Source. By an act which bespeaks an ineffable dispensation, he elevates us to himself, he makes us one with himself. Now we see how in Jesus we are the beloved of God and how in Jesus we are the object of God's tenderness evinced before time by predestination, witnessed to in this world by our sharing in the blessings of Redemption, while we await the supreme beatitude of heaven.[6]

In heaven the grace of divine adoption will attain its blessed term in the beatific vision, for glory, as we have shown elsewhere,[7] is nothing but a consummate participation in the Sonship of the one who is the Son of God. Thus the term and the principle are brought together. The order of predestination is adequately realized in the order of execution, in the consummation of God's eternal plan.[8]

Christ the Son of God, however, is not merely the end and the archetype of rational creatures, of men and angels, who are called to a *formal*

---

[6] *The Doctrine of the Mystical Body* (New York: Benziger Brothers, 1931), 345.

[7] Cf. the author's *Le Corps Mystique du Christ*, Volume II, Chapter 27.

[8] According to the axiom: "The end, being first in intention, is last in the order of execution."

participation in his divine Sonship. Every creature is ordered to him as to its end; every created being tends to glorify him, reflecting a ray of the substantial glory that he himself is to the praise of the Father (cf. Heb. 1:3). He is the center of all the works of God. He is their principle and their term. In the work of creation, "all things were made through him, and without him was made nothing that has been made" (John 1:3). All things are ordered to him and through him to the Father, for the work proclaims the excellence of the artisan. The Divine Word, by the fact that he is "the image of the invisible God" (Col. 1:15) and "the image of his substance" (Heb. 1:3) is the prototype of all creatures. All beings, from the highest angel radiant with light at the summit of the heavenly hierarchies down to the puniest insect and to the atom on the very threshold of nothingness, all these many productions of creative power imitate the infinite perfections of the Word of God in various ways and celebrate his praises.

This symphony of creation singing the glory of its Author was marred by a discordant note that destroyed its harmony. Sin contested God's supremacy and usurped the honor due to the Lord, claiming it for his creatures. Lucifer revolted, wanting to become like to the Most High. But he was at once thrown into the abyss, and divine justice re-established the equilibrium broken to the detriment of love, admitting the faithful angels to the face-to-face vision of the infinite beauty of God in his Word.

Man in his turn fell by refusing obedience to his sovereign Lord. This time the whole human race in the person of Adam its head fell from its lofty condition and betrayed its vocation by robbing God of his glory. By this fact the entire material universe was turned away from its end. Beings without reason, the splendors of the heavens and the beauties of earth had been created for man and were meant to exalt the Author of all these wonders. Man lent his voice to creatures devoid of intelligence to sing the glory of the Creator. Through Adam's sin the ordering and concurrence of creatures to the glory of the Creator were abolished.

It was then that God resolved to send his divine Son, his Word, to earth to restore the broken harmony. The Son of God assumed our mortal nature, he became the new Head of the human race, the new Adam who would give back to us the grace lost by the first Adam. Through him we became new children of God. Through him the whole of creation found its voice again to offer the Lord its sacrifice of praise. Jesus, the Son of God made man, recapitulating the corporeal and spiritual world in his human nature (matter and spirit) (cf. Eph. 1:10), became the perfect praise of the Father and the necessary voice by which the glory of the universe would henceforth rise toward its Creator. Such was the plan of restoration determined by divine Mercy.

Immediately after the fall of man in the Garden of Eden, God promised forgiveness and revealed the divine Redeemer to our first parents in a prophetic vision. From that moment Christ became the hope of humanity, the expectation of the nations, and the one way of salvation for all men of good will. The entire Old Testament is filled with the thought of the promised Liberator. The sacrifices prefigured him; the Patriarchs lived in hope of him and already gloried in preparing his lineage; the Prophets announced him and described beforehand his life, his sufferings, and his glorious triumph. Christ is the center of history. He fills the centuries; he is the term toward which all events, great and small, converge upon this earth: "Jesus Christ, yesterday and today, yes, and forever" (Heb. 13:8).

It was the mission of an entire people to prepare his coming. The life and history of the Chosen Nation were the figure of what Christ the Savior would realize among us. The crossing of the Red Sea, the manna in the desert, the water that Moses caused to gush out of the rock, the conquest of the promised land, were images and anticipations of the Messias' gifts, of our spiritual liberation, of the manna of heaven, of our entrance into the kingdom of heaven. The ark of the covenant, the temple, the holy city of Jerusalem, the paschal lamb, and the immolation of victims symbolize the sacrifice of Christ and the establishment of his Church for the salvation of the whole human race.

When Jesus finally appeared, after the long expectation of the centuries, the figures ceased, the veil of the temple was torn, the ancient priesthood was abolished, and Christ became the eternal Priest through whom a purified and sanctified humanity glorifies the Lord.

If the Old Testament was already filled with the glory of Jesus, this is even truer of the New. He is the head of the new people, the life of the nations, the perennial source of all the spiritual riches of the human race. Everything in the Church relates to Christ, everything glorifies Christ. He is the principle and the term of our religion and our worship, and through him alone we return to the Father, to whom we offer up "all honor and glory"[9] through his beloved Son.

We are called by a divine vocation to be part of Christ, to be his plenitude and his completion. The whole life of the Church tends by a prolonged

---

[9] From the Canon of the Mass.

effort from century to century to form the members of the total Christ, some occupying pre-eminent places because of the sanctity of their lives, whereas others fill up the ranks in this society of saints. When this great work is completed, the fullness of time will come. Then the history of the world will end, and the Lord will come on the clouds to pass all things in review and to judge each man according to his works. Then will begin the eternal reign of Christ in his saints and the reign of God in his Christ (cf. I Cor. 15:28). Then will the Mystical Body have attained its full stature and the blessed term of its spiritual growth that St. Paul calls "the mature measure of the fullness of Christ" (Eph. 4:13).

The mature measure of the fullness of Christ: this is the end to which all the members of Christ tend here on earth. This is the ultimate term of all the operations of God *ad extra*, the reason for the Incarnation, the end of all the graces granted to the angels and to men. Then the glory of God will fill the whole Body of Christ. Like a ray from the countenance of the Most High, it will shine on our divine Head and through him be communicated to all his members, irradiating souls with the heavenly splendors of the beatific vision and transforming even their corporeal, earthly substance, restored to life by the resurrection so that it may participate in its own way in the qualities of the glorious soul.

Let us see by what means God accomplishes this admirable plan in time, this blessed unity of all the predestined in Christ that his divine Wisdom has conceived and decreed for his glory and our happiness from all eternity.

CHAPTER VIII

Union of the Juridical Order

The juridical order embraces the totality of the rights (*jus, juris*) and correlative duties that establish a hierarchy of relationships of superiority and subordination among men living in society. The family, the smallest society founded by God, sets up the husband as the head of the family and establishes reciprocal rights and duties between husband and wife and between parents and children. It is a tiny society when compared with the great groupings of the political order, and especially with the supernatural unity of the whole Christ. And yet, even in the family, small as it may be, God himself, the author of nature, creates the close cohesion that molds several beings into one entity and makes one life out of several. Now this cohesion, this social unity is built in great part[1] on the delicate relationships of superiority and submission that bind the members of a family to one another. This is unity of the juridical order.

These same social relations exist on a broader scale in civil society. The bonds born of hierarchical subordination are the more numerous in the measure that the attributions of the governing authority or the functions of the executive power are more varied and shared by a greater number of titulars. These rights and duties, stemming from the social hierarchy, constitute the order of *legal justice*. To these are added others that exist among equals and that stem from *commutative justice*. They are the rights or obligations resulting from the various facets of life in society: contracts of purchase or sale; loans or gifts; the acquisition or transfer of property; social aids of various sorts.

This whole aggregation of relationships and bonds tends to create and to maintain the unity proper to the social body, and is called *juridical unity*.

---

[1] For the moment we are abstracting from the other elements that cement the union among the members of the family, namely bonds of blood, love, and so forth.

This same unity exists on an immeasurably superior level in the Mystical Body of Christ.

In the supernatural order, in the order of the superior realities in which God invites us through a purely gratuitous love to be participants of his own divine Life and of his happiness, there is also a society, a great family, the society of those whom St. Paul calls very clearly "citizens with the saints and members of God's household" (Eph. 2:19). It is a vast family comprising all who in one way or another belong to Christ, either on earth, in heaven, or in purgatory. We shall enumerate these various members later on.

In this supernatural society, the Head, the principle of unity and cohesion, the summit where everything converges and to which all the parts are linked, is Christ. For God has made him "head over all the Church, which indeed is his body, the completion of him who fills all with all" (Eph. 1:22–23). *Juridically* all the baptized belong to Christ and are by right members of the supernatural society which is the Church.[2] Far more important, in a broader sense all men are subjects of the divine Redeemer, who by his Incarnation and passion acquired imprescriptible rights over all creatures.

Bound to Christ the Head by bonds of subjection and of dependence, the members of the Mystical Body are also joined to one another by a certain community of supernatural goods, by reciprocal influences which in their totality make up the mystery of the *Communion of Saints*.

Thus, the element of oneness that we call the principle of juridical unity involves the relationships of dependence of all redeemed men to Christ their Head, and the relationships of supernatural solidarity among the members of Christ. Let us now consider this principle in greater detail.

The Dependence of the Members upon Christ their Head

St. Paul tells us that God made all things subject under the feet of Christ, and gave him "as head over all the Church" (Eph. 1:22). These words permit us to envisage the primacy of Christ in a twofold aspect, and to distinguish as it were two categories of subjects under his supreme jurisdiction, one group being more extensive and the other more limited in scope. The first

---

[2]   It should be noted that the bonds of the juridical order, this social subordination, while they do not formally imply a physical or ontological reality, do in fact, in the supernatural order, imply a physical supernatural entity, the principle of all ecclesiastical hierarchy. God has founded the social order of his Church on the diversity of sacramental characters. And character is a spiritual reality, a divine mark that impresses upon the soul the seal of Christ. The same observation will be applied in the next chapter to the union based on love, which is intrinsically a moral bond but which flows from the divine reality that is the infused virtue of charity.

includes all creatures, whose Head he became by right of birth and redemption. The second includes only those who are members of his Church,[3] who belong more completely to him by the fact of their baptism, and who are governed by the pleasant kingship that he exercises over them in the divine society that is the Church.

We must carefully explain the nature of this twofold juridical belonging to Christ: that is, the belonging of all men to the Word Incarnate, the Redeemer of the human race; and the belonging and subjection of all the baptized to Christ the Head of the Church. We are concerned with both, especially as the second does not suppress the first but rather confirms and reinforces it.

In the first place, *Jesus, as the Son of God and Redeemer of the world*, is the obligatory Head not only of all men but of the whole universe. By his Incarnation and redemptive Passion he acquired sovereign rights over our souls and bodies, and over all created beings.

First, the Incarnation makes of Jesus the Head of all creation by right of birth. It makes of him the masterpiece and synthesis of all creatures, both spiritual and temporal. It confers upon him, through the grace of the hypostatic union, a unique excellence that is in a certain sense infinite. The Word Incarnate is truly *"the first born of every creature"* (Col. 1:15), the necessary Mediator between God and man—indeed, between God and all creatures. For God, says the Apostle, willed to "re-establish all things in Christ,[4] both those in the heavens and those on the earth" (Eph. 1:10). Because of this fact, he can freely dispose of all the creatures under his power, bringing them to God and making them contribute to the glory of his Father. That is his *right* as a Sovereign. He is the Master and the Head.

And yet this all-powerful Master, whose greatness and power are presented in such magnificent terms by St. Paul, this Head of the universe appeared among us in such a lovable manner that some were scandalized and refused to receive him. *Sion, ecce Rex tuus venit tibi mansuetus.* He comes toward his subjects a meek and peaceful King (cf. Zach. 9:9; John 12:15), not so much to break and dominate them with arrogance as to win them and rule them with love.

---

[3] However, we are giving the word "Church" its greatest extension, including within it not only the faithful here on earth, but also the saints in heaven and the souls in purgatory.

[4] The Latin word *instaurare* (re-establish) is the one used to translate the much richer Greek word ἀνακεφαλαιώσασθαι, which means to recapitulate. And this can signify either the recapitulation of all created things in the masterpiece that is Christ, or the headship of Christ over the whole created universe.

Or rather he comes to deliver himself up so that he may conquer them and incorporate them into his kingdom by the shedding of his Blood (cf. Col. 1:13–14).

Through the Redemption Jesus Christ possesses another claim to headship. Through it we become his conquest, his thing, his property. Even before receiving the baptismal character every man belongs to him and is obligated to him for having redeemed him at such a heavy cost to himself. The Redemption cannot be disregarded with impunity. Those who disregard the rights of Christ the Redeemer now will one day face him as their Judge, and those who have not lovingly accepted their subjection to him will be forced to acknowledge the rights of his justice.

In order to understand to what extent the Redemption of Christ binds us to him, we must distinguish in the work of our salvation a threefold benefit and hence a threefold claim of Jesus to be the Head of the human race:

First, Jesus satisfied the rights of divine justice over us.

Secondly, Jesus delivered us from our slavery to the devil.

Finally, Jesus merited for all men all the graces of salvation and of life with God.

SATISFACTION

The first benefit we received from Christ the Savior, his first claim to us, is that of the *vicarious*[5] satisfaction he offered *in our place* to the majesty of God his Father.

Sin had gravely attacked the honor of the sovereign Lord. We could redeem our guilt only by offering God a suitable reparation. But the offense to God, because of the nature of the Person wronged, was infinite in its gravity and thus made us insolvent debtors. It was then that Jesus, the Son of God-made-man, with infinite condescension, took *our debt* upon himself. "For our sakes he made himself to be sin" (2 Cor. 5:21).[6] For our sakes he paid the debt with usury. By his expiatory sufferings, by his bloody immolation, he, the true Lamb offered in sacrifice, presented to divine justice a satisfaction, a reparation equal to the offense.

Jesus was able to do what all the men in the universe could never do: make reparation equal to the gravity of the debt. His dignity as the Son of God gave infinite merit to the least of his acts. In the words of St. Thomas: "By suffering... Christ gave more to God than was required to compensate

---

[5]   *Vicarious* signifies done in the place of another, by substitution.

[6]   2 Cor. 5:21. When we say that he who knew nothing of sin was made sin for us, we are referring not to the act, but to the debt to be paid, and this Jesus took upon himself for *his brothers.*

for the offense of the whole human race . . . on account of the dignity of his life which he laid down in atonement, for it was the life of One who was God and man."[7]

In addition to the personal value of Christ's reparation inasmuch as he is the Son of God, his satisfaction also possessed in itself, by the nature of the work, an unparalleled *objective* value,[8] by reason of the severity and the number of the sufferings he endured.[9] Our divine Redeemer did not want to take advantage, if we dare say so, of his condition as Son of God to acquit himself of the debt at the smallest cost. He chose to make the intensity of the pain endured equal as nearly as possible to the gravity of the offense.[10]

Through this voluntary expiation offered up for all of us, Jesus freed us from the formidable weight of the *offense* against God and of the *punishments* incurred by our sins. Holy baptism, by configuring us to the Passion of Christ by a sort of mystical burial, applies to us in its fullness the redemptive satisfaction of our Lord. The sacrament of reconciliation, together with the penance attached to it, also makes us commune in the expiation of Jesus and applies its fruits to us. Even if, as the result of less perfect dispositions, this sacrament often allows a portion of the punishment to remain, it is still the Passion of Jesus, our divine Substitute, that gives our satisfactions their value and efficacy.[11]

This is the first bond of supernatural solidarity that Jesus as Savior has contracted with us. It is the juridical relationship of the *accredited Respondent* for indebted humanity, through the substitution, ratified by God of the innocent for the guilty. It is a juridical relationship, but one completely imbued with love and mercy, that obligates us and binds us irrevocably to the Savior of our souls. For if he has delivered himself up for us, how can we be anything but completely his as a just return?

---

[7] *Summa*, IIIa, q. 48, a. 2.

[8] Cf. Edward Hugon, *De Verbo Inc.*, q. 15, a. 1, n. 10.

[9] Cf. *Summa*, IIIa, q. 46, a. 6.

[10] Cf. ibid., q. 48, a. 2.

[11] Regarding the punishments due to sin that the Passion wiped out, St. Thomas raises an objection whose solution deserves attention. He asks: How can we say that the Passion of Christ has freed us from the punishment due to sin, when we still must undergo death, as a consequence of sin? And here is his answer: "Christ's satisfaction works its effect in us inasmuch as we are incorporated with him, as the members with their head. Now the members must be conformed to their head. Consequently, as Christ first had grace in his soul with bodily passibility, and through the Passion attained to the glory of immortality, so we likewise, who are his members, are freed by his Passion from all debt of punishment, yet so that we first receive in our souls the spirit of adoption of sons, whereby our names are written down for the inheritance of immortal glory, while we yet have a passible and mortal body: but afterwards, being made conformable to the sufferings and death of Christ, we are brought into immortal glory" (*Summa*, IIIa, q. 49, a. 3 ad 3).

However, in addition to this first title of Christ the Redeemer to be our Head, there are two others. The deliverance or redemption that he has promised; the merit by which he has won supernatural life for us.

REDEMPTION OR DELIVERANCE

St. Thomas, together with the whole body of theologians, usually distinguishes in the redemptive Passion of Jesus, its character of *satisfaction* and its formal nature of redemption or *repurchase*.[12] By repurchase, the Angelic Doctor means the onerous liberation by which Christ delivered us from slavery to the devil at the price of his Blood, at the same time freeing us from punishment due to sin.[13]

Sin made all of us debtors of God and the forced subjects of Satan, his slaves, captives of hell. In our servitude to the devil, to sin, to our passions, we could no longer aspire to the liberty of the children of God. Jesus snatched us from this shameful bondage: he broke our chains; he vanquished the powers of evil that dominated us by paying the ransom of our freedom with his Blood. This is how he won his glorious title of *Redeemer*.

A redeemer is one who buys back a valuable object that has fallen into other hands. Jesus our Redeemer paid the price of our liberty not to the devil whose captives we were, but to his Father who had punished us by justly delivering us up to the slavery of hell (cf. 2 Peter 2:19).[14] Being a generous Redeemer, he shed the very last drop of his precious Blood for our deliverance: "*In him we have redemption through his blood*" (Eph. 1:7).

But if Christ has bought us back, it was so that he might possess us, might become the absolute Master of our souls and of our lives. For, as St. Paul says explicitly: "Christ died for all, in order that they who are alive may live no longer for themselves, *but for him who died for them and rose again*" (2 Cor. 5:15).

CHRIST'S MERIT FOR US

Jesus made satisfaction for us. Jesus redeemed us. He did more than that, however. We must add a third benefaction, still another right by which he is our Head, one that is the *most important* of the three. Jesus merited a new life for us, life in God through grace. It was not enough for us to be discharged of our debt to God, it was not enough that we be liberated from the servitude of hell. We also had to be restored to our original condition,

---

[12] Cf. ibid., q. 48, aa. 2, 4.
[13] Cf. *Summa*, IIIa, a. 4 c. and ad 2.
[14] Cf. also *Summa*, IIIa, q. 48, a. 4 ad 3.

to the state of grace, to our dignity as children of God. Now the Passion of Christ and his entire life have assured us of this return to life, of this re-entry into the state of grace. And how did he do it? He did it by way of merit.

Each of our Savior's sufferings, each of the actions of his life, has a meritorious value to obtain for us an influx of divine life, a grace of salvation, of virtue, of holiness. Far more, the actions of Christ have an *efficient power* to produce in us this grace that they merited in the first place. This final point will be treated later on, in the chapter on efficient causality.

But how was Christ able to merit for us? Is not merit the price of a personal work? Merit, St. Thomas tells us, is the reward or the price of work.[15] It is a *right* founded on *justice*, according to which all work must receive suitable wages. Where God is concerned, the notion of justice and therefore of merit is verified only in a reduced and analogical way. For justice in the strict sense implies equality between what is given and what is received, equality also between the one who gives and the one who receives. Now there exists no such equality between man and God, for everything that man possesses and everything that he accomplishes already belongs to God and proceeds from him. Nevertheless, God deigns to order our acts to a reward, and thereby render them capable of merit.[16]

But if merit is a right in justice, can merit be gained for others? And could Christ merit for us? Does not justice render to each one what is due *him* personally? And can anything be due to Paul for a good work accomplished by Peter?

In order to explain Christ's merit on our behalf, St. Thomas calls upon the notion of the Mystical Body and the capital grace of Jesus: "Grace was bestowed upon Christ, not only as an individual, but inasmuch as he is the Head of the Church, so that it might overflow into his members; and therefore Christ's works are referred to himself and to his members in the same way as the works of any other man in a state of grace are referred to himself."[17]

St. Thomas is really speaking of a twofold bond between the Head and the members of the Mystical Body. First, the bond based on the efficient causality of his capital grace, which produces an analogous grace within us. We shall come back to this point later. Secondly, the *juridical* solidarity by reason of which the works of Christ, the source of all merit, are juridically attributable

---

[15] Cf. *Summa*, Ia-IIae, q. 114, a. 1.
[16] Cf. ibid., *Sed contra* and ad 3.
[17] Ibid., IIIa, q. 48, a. 1.

to me as a right to grace, as a right to God's benefactions. From the point of view of acquired merit, Christ is, in a certain sense, identical with us.

From this splendid truth flow magnificent consequences for Christian life. It is the basis for unlimited trust. Jesus belongs to us. His sufferings, the merits of his death, the treasures of his grace are at our service. He is our Savior, and he is totally dedicated to our welfare in his role as our Redeemer. When we sense our indigence, we are permitted to appropriate his infinite riches.

When we experience shame for our sins in God's presence, we can present ourselves confidently to him, clothed in the merits of our elder brother, Christ Jesus. If we dare not hope for the forgiveness of our sins, or if we fear we cannot pay the debt we owe because of our countless sins, Jesus is the divine *Respondent* whose satisfactions we can always count on, for they far exceed all our debts.

The saints and interior souls have a very clear understanding of this truth, and they know how to make it the fulcrum of their boundless trust. Let us cite, in this connection the very expressive and theological words of Sister Elizabeth of the Trinity, the Carmelite nun of Dijon: "I am convinced that all the treasures within the soul of Christ are mine. Hence I am infinitely rich."

And before her, St. Thérèse of the Child Jesus had written these luminous words in her act of offering to Merciful Love: "Since you have loved me, O my God, to the point of giving me your only-begotten Son to be my Savior and my Spouse, *the infinite treasures of his merits are mine.* I offer them to you joyfully, beseeching you to look at me only through the face of Jesus and in his heart burning with love." This thought of the little Saint of Lisieux recurs many times in her counsels and in her poems. Her life was totally imbued with this profound faith in *"the unfathomable riches of Christ"* (Eph. 3:8).

> Your riches are mine,
> My Beloved, my King,
> Remember this!

So sings the wise virgin, whose faith is always aware of the great mystery of Christ, and whose doctrinal message is so consoling for everyone: for weak souls and for sinful souls, even and especially for the latter. Jesus came to save sinners, and during his earthly life, he lived among them. Even though the Pharisees were scandalized, he ate with the publicans, and allowed repentant women to approach him. Is not his name Jesus, that is, Savior? And how would he be a Savior if only the just had access to him? He said: "I have come to call sinners, not the just" (Matt. 9:13). It is for sinners that he became man and that he died on the cross. Jesus, therefore, belongs to them; indeed he belongs to all of us, since we are all sinners.

If Christ is ours, with his merits and his grace, the converse is equally true. We are Christ's; our whole life is pledged to the service of Christ Jesus. Our life belongs to him, it must be worthy of him.

Our life belongs to Jesus. It is upon him that the glory of our holy works reflects. To him in the first place goes the honor of our meritorious acts, of our virtues. But the reverse is true as well. The dishonor of a sinful life strikes directly at our divine Head and mars the beauty of his Mystical Body. The sins of the Church's children fall back upon her, to the great detriment of her sanctifying mission. The Church is the Spouse of Christ, entrusted with the function of making the sanctity of her heavenly Spouse shine forth to the eyes of the world. She is the Sulamitess whose supernatural charms win souls for the divine Solomon. Many are the Christians, however, who sully her immaculate garment, who cast a shadow upon the beauty of her face, and thereby rob Christ of his glory and of the honor of more numerous victories!

Christ belongs to us, therefore, and we belong to Christ. This mutual communication of actions, sufferings, and prayer between the Head and his members has been translated by St. Augustine with amazing boldness in the following passage from his *Commentary* on the Psalms:

> Christ, by a sort of transfiguration, assumed our likeness when he willed to be tempted by Satan. We were just reading in the Gospel that our Lord Jesus Christ allowed himself to be tempted by the devil in the desert. In Christ, it was you who were being tempted. For Christ has taken on from you an infirm flesh, so that salvation might come to you from Christ. From you to Christ, an exchange of humiliations, from Christ to you, an exchange of honors. From you to Christ, a communion of temptations, from Christ to you a communion of victories. If we suffered temptation in him, in him also we shall triumph over the devil. You notice that Christ was tempted, and you pay no attention to his victory? Recognize in him, therefore, your own temptations, so that in him also you may recognize your own victories! Jesus could keep the devil at a distance, but if he had not been tempted he would not have taught you to conquer.[18]

---

[18] *Enarr. in psalmos*, Ps. 60, n. 3, *PL* 36:724.

The lives of the saints could furnish ample confirmation of St. Augustine's teaching. Remarkable among them is the account reported in the acts of Sts. Felicitas and Perpetua and their companion-martyrs. All of these confessors of Christ were awaiting in prison the day of their blessed death. Only Felicitas, who was eight months pregnant, regretfully saw the hour of her martyrdom deferred because of a certain humaneness in Roman law that forbade the execution of women about to become mothers. Her companions in captivity shared her regret. As they did not want to be separated in combat, they obtained through their prayers that the Lord hasten the delivery of Felicitas. Now when the servant of God was in labor, she groaned. The prison guard insulted her suffering, saying: "If you complain today, how will you be able to endure the tortures of death tomorrow?"

"Today," answered the noble Christian lady, "it is I who suffer and pay tribute to nature. But tomorrow another than I will suffer in my place, in the combat that I shall wage for him."

In the first case, Felicitas was suffering in a sense on her own personal score, according to the common condition of her sex. In her martyrdom, on the contrary, she suffered for Christ. Her tortures turned to the glory of her Redeemer and became, juridically speaking, the sufferings of her Jesus, who owed it to himself in the moment of trial to strengthen his faithful servant.

More than all the rest, the sufferings of Christ's faithful belong to him who chose to be called the "Man of Sorrows" (cf. Is. 53:3). He who came to suffer and to enter into his glory willed that his Mystical Body should complete what was still lacking to his passion. That is what made St. Augustine say in his beautiful explanation of the Psalms:

> The sufferings of Christ are not to be found only in Christ, and on the other hand, the sufferings of Christ exist only in Christ. If by Christ you understand the Head and the Body, the sufferings are all in Christ. But if you refer only to the Head in Christ, then the sufferings of Christ are those of Christ only. For in that case, how could one of his members, the Apostle Paul, have said: "What is lacking of the sufferings of Christ I fill up in my flesh for his body, which is the Church"[19]

St. Augustine continues:

> If therefore you are among the members of Christ, O man . . . everything you suffer through those who are not members was lacking of the sufferings of

---

[19] *Enarr. in psalmos*, Ps. 61, n.4, *PL* 36:730–31.

Christ. These are added because they were lacking. You fill up the measure, you do not make it overflow. The measure of what you suffer is that of the sufferings you need to add to the universality of the Passion of Christ, who suffered in our Head and suffers in his members, that is to say, in us.

This is a magnificent truth that shows us the divine reality of this reciprocal belonging of Christ to his members, and of the members to Christ their Head.

Thus far we have considered this supernatural solidarity of the Head and members only as a function of the Incarnation and Redemption of Christ. It remains for us to inquire briefly how the juridical relations between the Redeemer and those he has redeemed are realized and completed in this divine society which is the Church.

Jesus Christ as Head of the Church actualizes the *rights* he possesses over every creature through his condition as Word Incarnate, as well as the rights he has acquired through the work of his merciful Redemption. We are obligated to him because of this twofold benefaction, and he has an absolute right of dominion, of sanctifying power over us. But he chooses to exercise this right through the divine society that he founded and that he calls his *Church* (cf. Matt. 16:18).

Jesus was not content to save us and sanctify us, and afterwards leave us to our own devices, wandering "like sheep without a shepherd" (Mark 6:34). He has wanted to unite us all under a common Head, to form a supernatural and divine society. This society of the faithful he conceived not merely as an invisible and mystical communion of souls. He constituted it into a social, organic, visible body, and he endowed it with all the necessary powers to lead men to salvation and to the blessed society of heaven.

The invisible unity of souls through charity and the Holy Spirit does not exclude visible unity through the hierarchy and through social subordination. It presupposes it and is founded on it, just as the soul exists only in the body and because of it. He who said "Love one another!" (cf. John 15:17) also said: "If [anyone] refuse to hear . . . the Church, let him be to thee as the heathen and the publican" (Matt. 18:17). The Master who promised his disciples the Spirit of truth also commanded his apostles: "Go, therefore, and make disciples of all nations . . . teaching them to observe all that I have commanded you" (Matt. 28:18–19).

And if Jesus counseled the Twelve to consider themselves as servants of their brothers, it was without prejudice to their authority, which he opposed to that of the temporal sovereignties only to show the character of humility which must accompany it. "*The kings of the Gentiles*[20] lord it over them, and they who exercise authority over them are called Benefactors. But not so with you. On the contrary, let him who is greatest among you become as the youngest, and him who is the chief as the servant." (Luke 22:25–26)

Moreover, the apostles themselves and their successors the bishops must recognize a superior authority over them, a visible head, in whom the social unity of the Church is completed here on earth. Peter, however, the foundation of the City of God upon earth, is only the lieutenant, the *vicar* of the invisible Head who from his triumphal throne in heaven rules the kingdom founded by him and conquered at the price of his Blood.

If the Church governs her faithful, it is not at the expense of the kingship of Christ. It is Jesus who holds the scepter of supreme power in the Church. He is the King. His ascension was not an abdication, but an investiture, an entry into possession of the throne of David where he is to reign for all eternity (cf. Luke 1:32). From there he rules his Church through the visible Head whom he has appointed and through the subordinate heads whom he has associated with him.

Therefore all the sons of the Church are subject to Christ.

Together they form the social Body whose juridical Head is Jesus. The various degrees of the holy hierarchy are, as it were, the manifold joints spoken of by St. Paul (cf. Eph. 4:16), that unite all the members of this divine organism to one another and bind them to Christ their Head. Through them as through many vital ligaments and motor nerves, the head transmits life and movement to the humblest cells of the organism, and directs the activity of all the members toward the common good.

Thus is established among the members of the Church "the immanent [and unifying] orientation that the activity of the Church receives from the jurisdictional power."[21] Through it the faith of all the faithful is orientated toward the same First Truth, as it makes itself known to us in the documents of Revelation. Through it the hope and charity of all turn toward the same divine Good and seek from the same sources of grace the necessary help to attain to it. Through it the exterior worship of the Church is organized in a uniform way, together with the apostolic action of her ministers and the totality of the efforts of zeal and manifold works,

---

[20] We should note the comparison here and the use of the words: "the kings of the Gentiles."

[21] Charles Journet, "L'Eglise, issue de la hiérarchie," *La Vie Spirituelle*, Supplement (May, 1934), 70. It will be noted that Abbé Journet considers as the soul of the Church every "unifying form" of this same Church, whereas we give the name "soul of the Church" only to the Holy Spirit, the ultimate principle of unity and life in the Mystical Body. Cf. below, Chapter 11.

whose very diversity, corresponding to the various needs of the Church, brings out more clearly the unity of the goal pursued and the harmonious convergence of the means used.

But this visible cohesion of all the members of the Church, this subordination and hierarchical action, what are they in the last analysis if not the manifestation of these juridical relationships, of this totality of rights and obligations that is called authority, power of jurisdiction, in those who rule, and subjection, submission in those who are ruled. We are thus brought back to the notion of juridical relationships which we analyzed at the beginning of this chapter in reference to the constitution of natural societies. When the Church is in question, however, these juridical relations transcend by far those that we find in the family or in the state. For all relations are specified by their term, and the term here is Christ, the Son of God made man, Christ the Redeemer and Sanctifier, Christ whose divine authority is entirely dedicated to making us beneficiaries of his infinite merits and sharers of his divine life.

After considering the juridical relations between the members and their Head, we must now consider the analogous relations of the members among themselves, through the communication of supernatural riches that is called the Communion of Saints.

Relationship of the Members among Themselves Through the Communion of Saints[22]

Taken in its broad sense, the Communion of Saints is identical with the mystery of the total Christ, and designates our union with Christ and with his members through all the means God has established for this end. It implies our unity in the same faith and in a common love, our participation in the same worship and in the same sacraments, our configuration to the same Model, our vital adherence to the same Head, and finally our striving toward the same supernatural end. The problem we are analyzing in these chapters is the whole problem of the unity of the Mystical Body of Christ.

In a more restrained sense, however, the Communion of Saints is sometimes taken to mean the exchange of supernatural goods that takes place among the members of the Church, the pooling of their merits and

---

[22] We shall not discuss further the relationships among the members of the Mystical Body resulting from the power of jurisdiction. We feel we have spoken of these sufficiently *per modum unius*, with regard to the relationships that this same jurisdiction establishes between the Head and the members.

satisfactions which, united to the merits of Christ their Head, constitute the Treasure of the Church. Without excluding the first sense, which is more complete and comprehensive, we shall consider the Communion of Saints in the present section only in the second sense.

Within the Mystical Body exists a communication of spiritual goods, a transfer of rights and of juridical titles, thanks to which certain members of the Church benefit from a good work, a prayer, or an expiation accomplished by another. This type of communion in the supernatural goods of one's neighbor takes three forms: prayer of intercession, merit, and satisfaction.

PRAYER

This mode of acting on behalf of others is insistently inculcated in the Old and the New Testaments. Scripture shows us Abraham interceding in favor of the inhabitants of Sodom and Gomorrha (cf. Gen. 18), and obtaining life and health for King Abimelech (cf. Gen. 20:7, 17); Moses praying on the mountain for the victory of Israel (cf. Exod. 17), and fighting with God to save, by dint of supplications, the idolatrous people from punishment (cf. Exod. 32); and Job offering God prayers and sacrifices to obtain the forgiveness of his friends who had treated him shamefully (cf. Job 42:8–10).

In the New Law the efficacy of prayer to come to the aid of one's neighbor is often shown. St. James writes: "Pray for one another, that you may be saved. For the unceasing prayer of the just man is of great avail" (Jas. 5:16). St. Paul often requests prayers for himself, for his apostolate (cf. Rom. 15:30–32; Heb. 13:18; 2 Thess. 3:1–2), for the common good of Christianity and of all men (cf. 1 Tim. 2: 1–4). And preaching by his own example, he prays unceasingly for the Churches under his watchful care (cf. Phil. 1:4; Col. 1:9).

Moreover, the Church has always followed the practice of praying for all her children and of making them pray for one another. Her liturgy gives ample proof of this, and the faithful, following the example of their Mother, delight in bringing before God the special and general interests of their brothers in the faith. Commonplace as it may be, this affirmation of spiritual solidarity is a magnificent reality, a very beautiful and valuable expression of the dogma of the Communion of Saints.

MERIT

The communion of supernatural goods is also realized by way of merit. We already know that Christ, as Head, could merit for all of us. Is the same true of his members? To give an adequate answer to this question, we must first distinguish two kinds of merit: merit that is called *de condigno*; and merit that is less strict, called *de congruo*. In other words, there is a merit *of justice* and a merit *of fittingness*. By the first, we acquire a right in the strict sense, based on the intrinsic value of the work accomplished. By the second, without having a right in justice properly speaking, man still acquires a certain right based on a sort of exigency of friendship, to receive a certain favor.[23]

Now the faithful, the man in the state of grace, is capable of meriting in these two ways. He can merit by a merit of justice, *de condigno*, for himself, he can merit by a merit of fittingness, *de congruo*, on behalf of his neighbor.

The Christian in the state of grace can merit eternal life for himself through the least of his good works. In the words of St. Paul, he can merit "an eternal weight of glory" (II Cor. 4:17). He can also, by his holy works, that is to say those informed and quickened by charity,[24] merit an increase in sanctifying grace and a proportionate increase in beatifying grace. This progressive increase is in the order of providence and of grace. Deposited like a seed in the soul, it is destined to grow and to flourish. And it is through the soul's cooperation and sanctified activity that man obtains these successive increases.[25]

Finally, he can merit actual graces, those manifold helps, illuminations of the intellect, impulsions and strengthenings of the will that assure the soul's progress and facilitate its perseverance. With regard to effective final perseverance, it is the great gift of God that no one can merit *de condigno*, but that we can, however, obtain infallibly through prayer.[26] All the more true is it that we cannot merit for ourselves initial grace or the grace of conversion. For this would demand that we already possess the principle of merit—grace itself.[27]

But what possibility is there of our meriting on behalf of other members of the Mystical Body? Here, as we have said, the question is no longer one of merit in justice. Only Christ can merit in this way for others, inasmuch as his works belong juridically to all his members. His members, however, cannot extend the meritorious value of their acts for the benefit of others.

Nonetheless every faithful Christian, united to Jesus by charity, can obtain God's graces for others, through the merit of fittingness, *de congruo*: graces of fidelity and progress, and even first grace, the grace of baptism

---

[23] Cf. *Summa*, Ia-IIae, q. 114, a. 6.

[24] Cf. ibid., a. 4.

[25] Cf. ibid., a. 8; Council of Trent, Session VI, Chapter 10.

[26] Cf. ibid., a. 9 ad 1.

[27] Cf. ibid., aa. 5 and 7.

or conversion. And this merit, founded on the *right of friendship*, is all the more efficacious in the measure that the soul offering it up to God is holier, more united to God and to the members of Christ through the bond of charity. For charity is precisely a holy friendship, the principle of merit of fittingness, that exerts pressure on the merciful heart of our Lord. We can then understand how important it is for the Church to possess great saints, souls eminent in virtue, ablaze with love for God and their brothers; and we realize the great influence that a St. Francis of Assisi or a St. Catherine of Siena can have on Christendom.

To enable our neighbor to profit from the merit of our good works, it may be useful to formulate this intention and apply it specifically to a given soul whose spiritual welfare we desire. For we are the proprietors of our good works and can dispose of them as we please, in accordance with the order of providence.[28]

It is in virtue of this faculty that the custom has been introduced in many religious orders or institutes of granting to their outstanding benefactors the title of associate members, with a share in the merits accruing to all the good works of the institute. St. Thomas speaks of this communication of spiritual goods as a practice already accepted in his own day.[29]

An explicit intention is not necessary, however, to make others benefit from these merits. There is a certain form of merit that benefits all the members of Christ in proportion to their dispositions. Father Congar writes: "Every good work profits the perfection of the whole body, and hence all the other members. In the words of Elizabeth Leseur: 'Every soul that elevates itself elevates the world. On the contrary, every time a soul goes astray, the common treasure of life is in some way lessened."[30]

The reason is that all the faithful, united by charity and forming a single body with Christ, have a certain right to this mutual aid, to this beneficent influence of the other members of Christ. For it is a law governing the well-being of every living organism that the health or infirmity of any one member has repercussions within the entire organism. St. Thomas declares: "Through the union of charity that makes of all the faithful a single body, the act of one person turns to the advantage of the others, as we likewise see in the members of the human body."[31]

---

[28] Cf. St. Thomas, *Quodl.*, VIII, a. 9 *in fine*.

[29] Cf. *In Symb.*, a. 10 *in fine*.

[30] *La Vie Spirituelle* (January, 1934). Cf. also the article by Edouard Hugon, O.P., in *La Vie Spirituelle* (September, 1924).

[31] *Quodl.*, VIII, a. 9.

A member of the Mystical Body of Christ, however, can participate to the fullest extent in the good of the other members only if he is in the state of grace and of charity. The state of grace is necessary because it is the life of the soul and because, in order to benefit from the life-giving influences of the other members, one must be alive and not withered or dead through sin. Charity is likewise necessary because it constitutes one of the principal bonds among the members of Jesus Christ, and hence is a prerequisite for the reciprocity of vital influences among them. St. Thomas also writes: "The merit of the life of Christ and all the good that the saints have accomplished is communicated to those who abide in charity, because they are all one. Also, he who lives in charity participates in the good that is accomplished throughout the world."[32]

Furthermore, this participation is not equal for all. And since charity conditions the benefits to be received, those whose charity is more intense have a greater share of this treasure of the Church.

The Angelic Doctor tells us: "Each one profits from the acts of others inasmuch as every man living in charity benefits from every good work accomplished. And the greater his charity, the more he benefits, whether he be in purgatory, in heaven, or on this earth."[33] Many Christians, even in the state of grace, benefit only in a mediocre way from this communion of merits, because their fervor is dead, their charity is weak, and their life drags on in habitual routine and negligence. Great riches are within their reach, but they lack the necessary dispositions to receive them. The saints, on the contrary, as well as fervent and generous souls, find precious helps at every moment in this communion with all the members of Christ.

SATISFACTION

Satisfaction is the third means of sharing one's spiritual riches with other members of the Mystical Body.

To satisfy is to expiate punishment for sin. In this connection, our capabilities on behalf of our neighbor are greater than they are for merit. No one can merit for another in justice strictly so-called, *de condigno*. He can communicate his good works to another only by a merit of fittingness, on the basis of friendship. In the case of satisfaction, it is a different matter. Each

---

[32] *In Symb.*, a. 10. However, those who are in the state of sin, but not separated from the Church, still participate, even if in a limited way that cannot be precisely determined, from the sacrifices and good works of the Church in view of their conversion.

[33] *Quodl.*, VIII, a. 9.

one can in all justice expiate the sins of his brothers, for to expiate is to pay a debt. It matters little or not at all who pays the debt, provided it is paid.

The beneficiary of this expiation, however, must be in the state of grace and of charity: first, for the general reason that these exchanges of influences among the members of the Mystical Body presuppose life in the members; but primarily because the good God cannot remit the punishment, the *reatus poenae*, of someone who remains his enemy through habitual sin.

The state of grace is all the more necessary, therefore, in the one who makes satisfaction for his neighbor. For no work of satisfaction has any value in the eyes of God except through the grace from which it proceeds and through union with Jesus and his divine expiations.

St. Thomas makes an interesting remark on this point. He says that the punishment required to cover the debt of another is less than that which the guilty one would have to pay himself.[34] The reason for this is that God does not judge our works on the basis of how difficult or tedious they are, but according to the intensity of our love in performing them. The saints, a St. Thérèse of Lisieux for example, merited more and made greater satisfaction through commonplace actions quickened with great charity than have other souls by more painful exercises performed with less love. There is greater love in the one who generously offers himself to bear the sins of others than in the one who is forced to expiate his own sins. Does not the former, through this charitable substitution, resemble our divine Head who took our sufferings upon himself and accepted the punishment for our sins?

Just as we can apply merit to a particular person, so also with regard to satisfaction we can, by a special and explicit intention, apply the fruit of our good works to a particular person. We can also, without determining the beneficiary, place in God's hands or, as St. Louis de Montfort suggests, entrust to Mary the total disposition of all our works of satisfaction.[35] However, even without this formal intention the expiatory value of the good that is accomplished in the Church adds up, in a certain measure, to constitute a common treasure from which all can profit.

Cajetan, in one of his tracts on indulgences, gives us a profound reason for this pooling of works of satisfaction. The intention of the saints in accomplishing their expiations, he says in substance, tends not only to their

---

[34] Cf. *Summa*, Suppl., q. 13, a. 2.

[35] It is in this sense that St. Thérèse of Lisieux said: "Had I been rich, I could never have seen a poor person hungry without giving him to eat. This is my way also in the spiritual life. There are many souls on the brink of hell, and as soon as I earn anything, it is scattered among sinners. The time has never come when I could say: Now I am going to work for myself" (St. Thérèse of Lisieux, the Little Flower of Jesus, "Counsels and Reminiscences": New York: P.J. Kenedy & Sons, 1927, 323).

own benefit; it conforms to the very intention of Christ the Redeemer and encompasses his whole work, so as to cooperate in it and complete it. And Cajetan goes on to say: "The intention of Christ was to suffer for the whole Church. Likewise [therefore] the intention of the saints, after they have expiated for themselves, is to suffer for the Church in general. For the suffering of the saints is the consummation, the complement of the sufferings of Jesus Christ, as the Apostle Paul bears witness: What is lacking of the sufferings of Christ I fill up in my flesh for his body which is the Church.' "[36]

This passage brings out the fact that the treasury of the Church contains only the surplus of the expiations which a person has called down upon himself by his own sins. This is also the teaching of St. Thomas on the subject of indulgences:

> The reason [indulgences] avail is the oneness of the Mystical Body in which many have performed works of satisfaction exceeding the requirements of their debts; in which, too, many have patiently borne unjust tribulations whereby a multitude of punishments would have been paid, had they been incurred ... And the saints in whom this superabundance of satisfactions is found, did not perform their good works for this or that particular person, who needs the remissions of his punishment (else he would have received this remission without any indulgence at all), but they performed them for the whole Church in general, even as the Apostle declares that he fills up those things that are "lacking of the sufferings of Christ ... for his body, which is the Church" (Col. 1:24). These merits, then, are the common property of the whole Church.[37]

We see the significance of the doctrine of indulgences for the dogma of the Communion of Saints. The doctrine on indulgences is an illustration and a continual profitable use of the dogma of the Communion of Saints. Through indulgences the Church uses, for the benefit of all her indigent children, both living and dead, the inexhaustible treasure whose foundation is Christ and his mother, and which her more fortunate children—"the leaders of the people" (Ps. 44:13)—have accrued during the course of the centuries. Speaking of the satisfaction of the saints, St. Thomas says: "So great is the quantity of such merits that it exceeds the entire debt of punishment due to those who are living at this moment."[38]

---

[36] Cajetan, *Opuscula*, XV, Chapter 8
[37] *Summa*, Suppl., q. 25, a. 1.
[38] *Loc. cit.*

One of the logical consequences of Protestant individualism has been the denial of the value of indulgences. Only a complete repudiation of Christian solidarity and interdependence could bring into question the worship and intercession of the saints, and the possibility of participating in their merits that the indulgences assure us.

The Church, however, ever aware of her juridical and social unity and knowing the worth of the "spiritual treasure"[39] entrusted into her hands by Christ, is careful not to imitate the jealous servant who buried his master's talent in the ground, and she continues to exploit this spiritual treasure for the common profit of all the members of Christ.

We have analyzed at length a complex principle of unity and of our incorporation into Christ the Redeemer, namely, the principle of juridical unity: the supernatural solidarity by which we belong to Christ and by which Christ also belongs to us together with all the merits of his life and of his death. It is a unity and solidarity that binds us to one another, by the bonds of the social hierarchy, in this organic body which is the Church of Jesus Christ. It is a solidarity and mutual dependence that places in a common treasury the spiritual goods, the merits, and the satisfactions of both Christ and his members.

This juridical and social bond, however, far from exhausts the resources of the power and goodness of God to unite our souls to Christ and to one another. Bonds of the physical and ontological order incorporate us in a far more real and profound way to our divine Head, Jesus, and first among these bonds are those established by the sacraments.

---

[39] Canon 912.

CHAPTER IX

Sacramental Union

In order to exercise his function as our mystical Head through appropriate means, Jesus has established between himself and us ways of communication, channels through which his life-giving influence could fittingly reach us. These are the sacraments, whose reason for being and precise role in the constitution of the Mystical Body we shall now discuss.

Our Lord had no need whatever of these intermediaries to reach our souls. Through a virtual contact, his sanctifying action can extend to the men of all times and places. The order of divine Wisdom, however, which always adapts itself with admirable condescension to the weakness of its creatures, willed that these salutary influences of the Humanity of Christ should come to us through means proportioned to our nature.[1] Since man is a spirit imprisoned in a body, divine Providence willed that spiritual graces should likewise be communicated to him within a sensible wrapping, through the means of instruments and of material signs.

Especially since original sin, we are strongly inclined toward sensible goods, we are unduly impelled toward the things we see and touch. Jesus, who came to deliver us from our slavery to the elements of this world (cf. Gal. 4:3), and to cure us of our original infirmity, did not want to withdraw strong attachments from us too suddenly. Being a prudent physician, he limited the doses of the remedy. In order not to jar his patients, since he knew how much we loved the things of sense, he made of these very things the instruments of our sanctification. He made them sacraments of divine life. St. Thomas tells us:

> Man ... in sinning subjected himself by his affections to corporeal things.
> Now the healing remedy should be given to a man so as to reach the part

[1] Cf. *Summa*, IIIa, q. 61, a. 1 ad 1.

affected by disease. Consequently, it was fitting that God should provide man with a spiritual medicine by means of certain corporeal signs. For if man were offered spiritual things without a veil, his mind being taken up with the material world, would be unable to apply itself to them.[2]

Jesus therefore has condescended divinely toward our human weakness, and communicates the life of grace to us by way of the sacraments. But since we become members of Christ by participating in this divine life, the sacraments, vehicles of grace, become the proximate means by which is realized our union with Christ, our engrafting upon the sacred Vine whose life-giving Trunk he is, is realized.

Christ himself is the great sacrament, the living and subsistent SACRAMENT, the supremely efficacious Sign of God's munificence, the Word of life, the Word of God rendered sensible and palpable (cf. John 1:1). In all the manifestations of his temporal life he became the principle of grace and the universal cause of justification. Jesus is the living Sacrament, says Bishop Gay, "the plenary gift of God, his door to enter us, his organ to speak to us, his throne to rule us, his heart to love us, receive us, enlighten us, console us, and sanctify us."[3] The other sacraments are merely particular applications and, as it were, derivatives of this superior and unique Sacrament: Christ himself.

Jesus has established an order among the sacraments. Among all these sacred symbols, these efficacious signs of our life in Christ, he has established the Holy Eucharist as the principal sacrament, the one that contains in its fullness what the others give us only in part. Jesus has imprisoned himself in a wonderful way—a miracle of love and of power—in the mystery of the altar. He is both sacrifice and sacrament, the memorial of all God's work (cf. Ps. 110:4), pouring forth into our souls the torrents of supernatural life whose source lies within him.

At the same time our poor human nature does not suffer in being suddenly transported to such heights, or from the experience of receiving without other preparation the plenitude of incorporation in Christ through the sacrament of the Eucharist. Furthermore, Jesus, before giving us his own Body, chose to communicate to us the power of his sacred Humanity. Before mingling his flesh with our infirm flesh, before implanting his Body within us, as St. John Chrysostom says,[4] so that we might become a single thing

---

[2] Ibid., a. 1.

[3] *Elevations*, Second Elevation. Cf. also *Exposition des psaumes*, Ps. 1.

[4] *In Joan.*, homily 46, *PG* 59:260.

with him, he willed to purify us from sin and to infuse his divine life into us through the sacrament of regeneration, holy baptism.

Baptism is an anticipation of the Eucharist, according to the teaching of the Angelic Doctor. It incorporates us into Christ and makes us his members by orientating us toward the sacrament of the Body of Jesus Christ and by communicating its grace to us long beforehand.[5]

We shall, therefore, give special attention to these two sacraments, each of which is the principle of our incorporation in the Savior in an eminent way. We shall then deal briefly with the relationships of the other sacraments to the Eucharist, from which they also draw their sanctifying power.

Our Incorporation into Christ through Baptism

"For you are all the children of God through faith in Christ Jesus. For all you who have been baptized into Christ, have put on Christ" (Gal. 3:26–27). It seems to us that this twofold assertion of St. Paul's contains in substance the whole doctrine of our incorporation into Christ through baptism. First, the Apostle reminds the Galatians of the great dignity of Christians. They are sons of God. But is that possible? Is there not one and only one Son of God? Yes, answers St. Paul, but baptism extends this divine Sonship to you, by clothing you with Christ. This is incorporation and its admirable effect.

Commenting on this text from St. Paul, St. John Chrysostom asked: "Why does not St. Paul say: all you who have been baptized in Christ, are born of God? And yet that was what he should have said to show that they are sons of God. The reason is in order to affirm this truth in a much more compelling way. For if Christ is the Son of God, and if you have put him on, thus having the Son within yourself and being assimilated to him, you become a single race and a single thing with him."[6]

This is the great wonder realized by baptism. It makes a man a sort of God. The poor son of Adam, fallen, sullied by sin, excluded from the heavenly heritage and doomed to perdition, is seized by the sacrament and plunged into Christ. When he is immersed in the holy water the sacrament communicates to him the divine life of Christ, raising him up to the dignity of being a son of God. Thus he has become mystically an integral part of Christ, his member through the grace of incorporation. Thus by holy baptism is realized the eternal plan of the Father, who has predestined us

---

[5] Cf. *Summa*, IIIa, q. 73, a. 3.
[6] *In Gal. III, PG* 59:656.

to filial adoption in Christ Jesus. The ineffable gift that the Incarnation of the Word and the mystery of the Redemption have won for us by *right*, we obtain *in fact* through baptism, which is in all truth the sacrament of incorporation.

The primary end of baptism, incorporation in Christ, is precisely what the Angelic Doctor, with his keen sense of supernatural realities, stresses most when he speaks of the effects of baptism. From this fundamental effect all the fruits of this sacrament flow: "The effect of baptism is that the baptized are incorporated in Christ as his members, according to John 1:16: 'of his fullness we all have received.' Hence, it is clear that man receives grace and virtues in baptism."[7]

In the subsequent article, St. Thomas likewise proves, through the grace of incorporation received in baptism, the communication of the supernatural life and operations to the Christian:

> By baptism man is born again unto the spiritual life, which is proper to the faithful of Christ, as the Apostle says: "And the life that I now live in the flesh, I live in the faith of the Son of God" (Gal. 2:20). Now life is only in those members that are united to the head, from which they derive sense and movement. And therefore it follows of necessity that by baptism man is incorporated in Christ, as one of his members.[8]

But how is this incorporation into Christ through baptism realized? St. Paul gives us a more detailed explanation of his Epistle to the Romans. Here he presents baptism to us as a symbolic configuration to the death and resurrection of Christ. Now these symbols instituted by God realize spiritually what they express: "For he spoke and they were made" (Ps. 32:9). Thus the faithful, through the sacrament of Christian initiation, die with Christ and rise with him, and in so doing die to sin and rise to grace.

Paul asks the Christians of Rome: "Do you not know that all we who have been baptized into Christ Jesus have been baptized *into his death*?" (Rom. 6:3). Yes, says St. Paul, into his death. For when we were immersed in the waters of the sacrament, we were buried with Jesus, and thereby won a right to the spiritual fruits of his redemptive death. We were buried with him by baptism in death, so that after the example of his Resurrection from the dead for the glory of the Father, we might walk in a new life.

---

[7] *Summa*, IIIa, q. 69, a. 4.
[8] Ibid., a. 5.

A new life, the life of Christ in us, a supernatural and divine life, is the immediate consequence of the grace of incorporation into Christ's death and resurrection. St. Paul insists on this thought, as we have brought out elsewhere in dealing with the life of the Mystical Body.[9]

Because of this new life in Christ the Apostle designates baptism by a name that has long since passed into the current language of Christianity. He calls it the bath of regeneration, *lavacrum regenerationis* (cf. Tit. 3:5). A thought inculcated by Jesus himself to Nicodemus, and which so greatly surprised the "ruler of the Jews": "You must be born again of water and the Spirit" (cf. John 3:3–5).

To be born of water to the Christian life: this conception, when related to the symbol by which the first Christians designated our Lord, the Fish— Ιχθυς—inspired Tertullian to express a gracious thought: "Like little fish, we are born in water, in the likeness of our Ιχθυς, Jesus Christ, and it is only by staying in the water (faithful to the grace of our baptism) that we have the life of salvation."[10]

Incorporation into Christ dead and risen again is the meaning of baptism, the divine reality produced by baptism in the soul of the neophyte. The Church assimilated this doctrine of the Apostle from the beginning, and in order to better show to the faithful the mystical identity between the sacrament of regeneration and the mysteries of the death and Resurrection of the Savior she set Easter as the date for baptism. The entire liturgy of the Easter Vigil, and a great part of the seasonal liturgy as well, is orientated toward the administration of baptism. Easter is both the Resurrection of Christ and the resurrection of the neophytes. It is as if the Church wished to show that Jesus, in rising again from the dead, snatches from death these new members whom he unites through baptism to his Mystical Body.

We should read the Lessons of the Easter Vigil in the light of this dogma. And we should take inspiration, in order to better understand their meaning, from the prayers that the Church recites after each of them. Then, instead of finding these passages from Scripture tedious because of our indifference, our well-informed piety will find in them a rich savor, a precious instruction, and, as it were, the renewal of baptismal grace. During the long Paschal Vigil, as we hear the account of the wonders of God's goodness, we invoke with faith and love his supreme power that brings forth all creatures out

---

[9] Cf. the author's *Le Corps Mystique du Christ*, Volume II, Chapter 12.

[10] *De Bapt.*, Chapter I: "Sed nos pisciculi secundum Ιχθυς nostrum, Jesus Christum in aqua nascimur, nec aliter quam in aqua permanendo salvi sumus." We know that the symbol of the Fish is based on the Greek word Ιχθυς, whose letters form the initials of the words corresponding to Jesus Christ, Son of God, Savior.

of nothingness,[11] that saves the chosen people from death in their journey over the Red Sea,[12] and that purifies Israel and promises the ultimate victory of the Church.[13] These transparent symbols will help us to understand the even greater wonders accomplished at the baptismal fount.

In union with the whole Church, we can then say: "O God, we behold thine ancient wonders shining even to our own time; for that which the power of thy right hand did, for one People . . . thou accomplishest now for the salvation of all men by the waters of rebirth. Grant that the whole world may become children of Abraham and enter into the heritage of Israel . . ." (Prayer after the Second Lesson).

We can do no more than indicate in passing one aspect of the baptismal doctrine, so valuable in the development of a Christian and liturgical mentality among the faithful.[14]

If the faithful are configured to Christ through baptism, it is not in a purely transitory way. The sacramental sign marks his being with an indelible *character*, the physical expression of the divine transformation. Baptism imprints into the very substance of a soul the character of his Christianity. The character of baptism, according to St. Thomas, is, as it were, the form of our regeneration that makes us Christians.[15] While sanctifying grace is more excellent, speaking in absolute terms, inasmuch as it is a participation in the divine nature, it enters our souls only after the character and as though called by it. "When a man is baptized, he receives the character which is like a form; and he receives in consequence its proper effect, which is grace whereby all his sins are remitted."[16]

Character is a configuration to Christ the Priest, St. Thomas tells us elsewhere. It is properly the character of Christ, to whose priesthood the faithful are configured by the various sacramental characters.[17] Character makes us participate in an analogical way in the grace of the hypostatic union, which consecrates the Humanity of Christ as if by a priestly unction and makes of him our Mediator and our Priest before his Father.[18]

---

[11] Cf. First Lesson of the Easter Vigil Service, Gen. 1:1–2:2.

[12] Cf. Second Lesson of the Easter Vigil Service, Exod. 14:24–15:1.

[13] Cf. Third Lesson of the Easter Vigil Service, Is. 4:2–6.

[14] Cf. especially Dom Guéranger, *Liturgical Year*, Volumes V and VI; Cardinal Schuster, *The Sacramentary*, Volumes II and IV; Louis Bouyer, "The Paschal Mystery" *La Maison-Dieu*, (VI), on baptism, the Paschal sacrament.

[15] Cf. *Summa*, IIIa, q. 69, a. 10.

[16] Loc. cit.

[17] Cf. Ibid, q. 63, a. 3.

[18] Cf. Mura, *Le Corps Mystique du Christ*, Volume II, Chapters 2 and 3.

Father Boulanger says: "Grace communicates this form to us, which is a participation in the Godhead. Character gives us something of his physiognomy and of his power as Word Incarnate, and, by reproducing in miniature the great marvel of the hypostatic union, authorizes and explains the famous definition: The Christian is another Christ."[19]

Because the Christian is configured to Christ by the baptismal character he must live by his divine life through sanctifying grace. Character is a call to the supernatural life, to an ever more intense life. Every grace afterwards granted to the Christian, even to the most sublime graces of the mystical life, is but the flowering of the seed deposited in the soul by baptism, the consequence of the first incorporation accomplished at the baptismal founts.

For baptism is not a transitory sacrament; it is a permanent reality by reason of the indelible character it imprints on the soul, a reality by which the Christian must live, of which he must be-come ever more conscious, which he must nurture and develop. To live a Christian life, in short, consists in living one's baptism, living ones incorporation into Christ, living as a member of Christ, acting under his influence, after his example, and under his impulsion, as a continuation of the divine-human life he lived on earth and that he continues to live in heaven.

Who, therefore, can fail to see the immense scope of this first sacrament in the formation of the Mystical Christ, the primordial role that it plays in the constitution of its supernatural unity?

Everything comes to us through baptism, because it is our first contact with Christ, a contact that opens up the current of grace between him and ourselves. Baptism engrafts us on the sacred Vine, Christ, thus making us commune in the life, virtue, and holiness of Jesus. From that moment on, all the supernatural and divine riches of Christ belong to us in a certain respect. In the words of Haugg: "Incorporation into Christ [through baptism] is thus the canal of graces that flow from the Head into the members. Everything that Christ is ours: his kingship, his priesthood, his pastoral office. What he is, we become."[20]

Holy Baptism is an inexpressible gift, for which we cannot repeat too often the heartfelt gratitude of the Apostle Paul: "Thanks be to God for his unspeakable gift" (2 Cor. 9:15). The best way we can express this gratitude is by living the grace of our baptism.

---

[19] French translation of die *Summa*, "Baptism" (Paris: Editions des Jeunes) Appendix II, 351.
[20] *Wir sind dein Leib*, 154–55.

Precious as this gift is, however, Jesus has given us something better. He has made available to us in his Sacrament of the Altar a means of still closer union with himself.

Union through the Eucharist

Impelled by the love that consumes him, our Lord seeks to unite himself to us in every manner possible. It is of the nature of love to unite those who love one another; and to attain its ends love is inventive in the extreme. Our Lord found a surprising means of uniting himself to his faithful: the Holy Eucharist.

This divine sacrament does not merely transmit to us the action and the power of Jesus, his grace, his supernatural motions. It gives us the Author of grace himself, the Savior in person, physically present under the sacramental species, who, through Communion, makes our hearts his dwelling and his temple, and gives himself to us as the food of our souls.

The Holy Eucharist is the sacrament of union from three points of view:

First, it gives us sacramental union with Jesus who has become the guest of our souls through his Real Presence. As long as the sacramental species continue in existence, we are united to him in a loving embrace; we hold him against our heart more intimately than we ever could those dearest to us, for we possess him within ourselves as in a living and conscious tabernacle.

Moreover, the divine sacrament unites the faithful among themselves, as they kneel at the same sacred banquet. A study of the origins of Christianity shows us that reception of the Holy Eucharist has been called Communion less because of our union with our Lord than because of the fact of our common union with our brothers in Christ Jesus. In fact, the same spiritual bread is given to all, and our Lord really forms the divine connecting link among all those who receive his sacred Body. That is why the Apostle said to the Corinthians: "Because the bread is one, we though many, are one body, all of us who partake of the one bread" (1 Cor. 10:17).[21]

The Eucharist is the sacrament of union because its fruit, its sacramental grace, is charity, the divine charity that unites us to God and to our brothers.

Did not our Lord say: "He who eats my flesh, and drinks my blood, abides in me and I in him" (John 6:57)? This reciprocal immanence is not produced

---

[21] It is wise to pay close attention to the meaning of this verse which, in the Vulgate, is equivocal. In the sentence *"Quoniam unus panis, unum corpus multi sumus,"* there are two propositions, one subordinate to the other: "Because *one* is bread, we are all but a *single* Body."

by the fact that we possess in our hearts the Eucharistic species, for if it is because of the species that Christ abides in us, how can we say that we abide in Christ? Furthermore, how could the Eucharistic presence, which ceases with the sacramental species, explain the stable and continuous permanence of which the Savior speaks? Thus the question here can concern only the union produced by charity, which is the first effect of the Holy Eucharist. Charity makes of God the permanent guest of our souls, as Jesus said to his disciples: "If anyone love me ... my Father will love him, and we will come to him and make our abode with him" (John 14:23). Thus it is that the Beloved Disciple attributes to charity the effect that Jesus said was the result of the Eucharistic feast: "He who abides in love abides in God, and God in him" (1 John 4:16).

Since this is the specific fruit of the Eucharist, we can understand why St. Thomas, in dealing with this divine sacrament, constantly assigns as an effect of the Eucharist our incorporation into Christ, our union with the other members of the Church. The Angelic Doctor says that this sacrament signifies "ecclesiastical unity, in which men are aggregated through this Sacrament; and in this respect it is called Communion. . . . For Damascene says that it is called Communion because we communicate with Christ through it, both because we partake of his flesh and Godhead, and because we communicate with and are united to one another through it."[22]

We can understand also how St. Augustine could declare that children who die after baptism, without having received Holy Communion, are not totally deprived of the benefits of the Eucharist. For if participating in this sacrament of love is to become a member of the Mystical Body of Jesus, baptism on the other hand already incorporates us into Christ and is, therefore, an anticipation of the Eucharist, whose fruit it gives to us.

The Eucharist is necessary to salvation, in a certain way, through a necessity of means, as the Angelic Doctor explains:

> The reality of the sacrament [the *res sacramenti*] is the unity of the Mystical Body, without which there can be no salvation; for there is no entering into salvation outside the Church, just as in the time of the deluge there was none outside the Ark, which denotes the Church, . . . And it has been said above (q. 68, a. 2), that before receiving a sacrament, the reality of the sacrament can be had through the very desire of receiving the sacrament . . . By baptism a man is ordained to the Eucharist, and therefore from the fact of children being baptized, they are destined by the Church to

---

[22] *Summa*, IIIa, q. 73, a. 4.

the Eucharist; and just as they believe through the Church's faith, so they desire the Eucharist through the Church's intention, and, as a result, receive its reality.[23]

This remarkable text gives us an understanding of the mystery of the Church, which exists entirely as a function of the Eucharist, for the Eucharist, and through the Eucharist. Father Sertillanges must have found inspiration from this passage when he wrote his beautiful pages on the Eucharist in relation to the Church. The relationship is so close that the author went so far as to establish a kind of "identity between the Eucharist and the Church." Let us understand it well: the identity is dynamic and virtual, inasmuch as the Sacrament of the Altar nourishes and increases the life of the Church and strengthens the unity of the Mystical Body.

Christ depends upon his Mystical Body, says Father Sertillanges; thus we cannot be united to Christ without being united to his Mystical Body, and to his Mystical Body as it is, as a social entity.

To quote him directly:

> Few Christians think of that. They see Eucharistic love especially in its sentimental form, with effects in the moral order. But the unity to be established among us is something much more precious, more concrete, and more conformable to our nature, which is a social nature. It is a functional unity, a unity of organization, it is life in a real society. And this society is the Church. Thus, we come back to the beautiful but so little known doctrine of St. Thomas Aquinas, that the fruit of the Eucharist is the unity of the Mystical Body of Christ; in other words, the very substance of our religious constitution.[24]

True, this doctrine is little known. However, more and more attention is being paid to it, and the dogma of the Mystical Body will acclimate it anew among the Christian faithful by bringing them back to the thought of St. Paul, which is at the very heart of Christian dogma.

Father Sertillanges goes on to say:

> We may seem to be splitting hairs when we speak in this way. We are only expressing one of the most profound and delicate aspects of Catholic theology. Fundamentally there is an identity between the Eucharist and the Church inasmuch as charity, the specific effect of the Eucharist, contains the Powerhouse of all other forms of charity and dominates them all. Now

---

[23] Ibid., a. 4.
[24] Article in *La Vie Spirituelle* (September, 1934).

this essentially Eucharistic charity is also essentially ecclesiastic, that is, it unites us into a Church. All of its other effects derive from this fact. We might think that the opposite is true, and that the Church is founded on love because each one first draws from Christ individual effects that are afterwards socialized. But that would be a purely Protestant conception.[25]

These words are exact, hard as they may seem. The mysteries of Christ all tend to achieve the mystical unity of the faithful, "*that he might gather into one the children of God who were scattered abroad*" (John 11:52). The passion of Christ, the supreme mystery that we encounter at the altar, was willed— St. John tells us—"that he might gather into one the children of God who were scattered abroad." (John 11:52).[26] Thus Eucharistic Communion must rekindle in the souls of the faithful the sentiment of their divine solidarity in Christ, a profound sense of union with all their brothers in the faith, a sentiment of powerful, tender, devoted, and efficacious love, that leads them to will and to procure, each for his part, the divine good of the entire Mystical Body.

During Holy Communion and under the influence of Eucharistic grace the saints, the founders of Orders, conceived the plans for the great works they were to accomplish for the good of the Church. In their thanksgivings, in their intimate contact with the divine Savior, many men of works received the inspiration for institutions of zeal and charity whose benefit continues to be felt throughout the Mystical Body.

To quote Father Sertillanges again:

> We must therefore conceive that the communicant, in order to obtain the individual effects of the sacrament, must commune with the group (that is to say, the whole Church), by communing with Christ as he is, Christ the universal Man, "the first born among many brethren," by accepting love and returning it in accordance with the intention of creative Love, as an organic law heavy with the whole of religious organization, and by extension, of Christian civilization. That is no small matter. And it is in this that the primacy of the Eucharist shines forth at the center of the whole Catholic system.[27]

---

[25] Art. cit.

[26] The words "children of God" refer to the Gentiles whom the Gospel here distinguishes from the Jews: "*non pro gente (sua) tantum*." A beautiful name given to the pagans in anticipation, says Abbé Fillion. "They are the sons of God in potency, until they become such in reality" (cf. his *Comment. de saint Jean*).

[27] *La Vie Spirituelle, loc. cit.* The expression "Catholic system" may sound a bit profane, but the beauty of the idea makes us overlook this flaw.

From this we can see to what degree Holy Communion, thus understood, broadens the perspectives of our faith and becomes fruitful for the good of Christian society for the support and growth of the whole Christ.

The unity of the Mystical Body is not only produced by the Eucharist as its specific effect; it is also represented and symbolized by the twofold substance that serves as the matter of the Sacrament, according to the classical teaching of St. Cyprian[28] and of St. Augustine.[29] Bread, formed from many grains of wheat crushed by the millstone, and wine resulting from the fusion of the many grapes crushed under the winepress, both signify the union of the faithful in the Body of Christ and the prerequisite condition for this union—death to nature and the renouncement of self.

Abbé Anger in his *Doctrine du Corps mystique* says:

> This symbolism of the grains has nothing sacramental about it. To the remote and accommodating aptitude of the species for symbolizing the union of the members of the Mystical Body, *outside any relation to the Body and Blood of Jesus*,[30] there has not been added any positive volition of Christ specifically choosing them for this purpose ... But what follows remains true: this symbolism can be suggested by the composition of the species, by certain words of Christ himself. Besides, it can be very useful to open up minds to the profound signification of the Eucharist, to make clear that the purpose of the Eucharist is not only to bring Jesus Christ within us, but that it has a more extensive, more universal significance, a truly social significance.[31]

The symbolism is sufficiently based on the nature of things to allow St. Thomas—who develops his doctrine so cautiously and is so careful to avoid any disputable theological concept—to mention it without any restrictive clause as one of the reasons that justify the choice of the Eucharistic species.[32]

We see the central place Holy Communion holds in the Christian life and in the divine economy of our sanctification and salvation. The end of the whole plan of Providence is to form the Body of Christ, to unite us to

---

[28] Cf. St. Cyprian, *Ep. ad Magnun*, n. 6, *PL* 3:1142.

[29] Cf. St. Augustine, Tract. 26, *in Joan.*, n. 17.

[30] The italics are ours. It should be noted that the sacred species remain signs in relation to the total effect of the Eucharist and therefore to the union of the faithful in Christ. But this last signification is indirect and is verified only on the basis of the relationship of the species to the Body and Blood of Christ, through which the unity of the Mystical Body is realized. On the symbolism of the sacramental species, cf. de la Taille, *Myst. fidei*, Eluc. 43.

[31] Part II, Chapter 2, Article 3.

[32] Cf. *Summa*, IIIa, q. 74, a. 1; q. 79, a. 1 (4th effect).

Christ, and Holy Communion is the supreme means of accomplishing this spiritual incorporation to our Savior. As Abbé Anger also says:

> To commune with Christ is to commune with the Church; it is to be united through Christ to all the members of the Mystical Body in the measure that they themselves are united to the Head. Consequently it is to be united to the saints in heaven, and above all to the Blessed Virgin, to the souls in purgatory, to one's brothers on earth, and most particularly to those who are, under Christ, the visible heads of the Church (CORPS ECCLESIASTIQUE): the pope and the bishops. Whence the utility of Communion in acquiring the Catholic spirit, the Catholic sense. Whence also the necessity for communicants to make their sentiments with respect to their neighbor harmonize with the charity symbolized in this sacrament.[33]

How clearly do the Eucharistic decrees of St. Pius X, when seen in this light, reveal themselves to us as an unparalleled blessing, as a stimulant of the highest order in promoting the supernatural life, in accomplishing the work of our union to Christ and of our union in Christ, and in hastening the consummation of the Mystical Body!

The Other Sacraments in Their Relationship to the Eucharist

The Holy Eucharist constitutes the sacrament of union par excellence, the sacrament of communion, the efficacious rite of the mystical unity between Christ and his members.

And yet the other sacraments are not devoid of this unifying virtue of the principal sacrament, for they are, as it were, its extension and development. All of them without exception prepare or complement the action of the Holy Eucharist. Each one, according to a particular mode and according to its own grace, its sacramental grace, strengthens our union with Jesus, a union realized in its perfection by the sacrament of the altar.

That is what the *Catechism of the Council of Trent* teaches when it says: "[Pastors will in some degree] show what an abundance and profusion of all goods are contained in those sacred mysteries [of the Eucharist] if, having explained the efficacy and nature of all the sacraments, they compare the Eucharist to a fountain, the other sacraments to rivulets. For the Holy Eucharist is truly and necessarily to be called the fountain of all graces,

---

[33] *Op. cit.*, Article 4.

containing, as it does, after an admirable manner, the fountain itself of celestial gifts and graces, and the author of all the Sacraments, Christ our Lord, from whom, as from its source, is derived whatever of goodness and perfection the other sacraments possess."[34]

The last reason for the universal influence of the Eucharist through the other sacraments is that every supernatural good comes to us from God through the humanity of Christ immolated on the cross; every grace is a fruit of the redemptive Sacrifice. Now the Victim of the cross is present on the altar in the divine Sacrament of the Eucharist.

Father de la Taille says:

> The vital influx descends from the divine nature into the human nature assumed [by the Word]. But by the nature assumed he reaches us. We cleave to this human nature, we are united and pressed to this sacred Humanity in its entirety, not only to the soul of Christ, but also to his Body, quickened by the soul, and through it bringing life to our souls. Thus, in the order of grace we are simply an increase in the Lord's Humanity.[35]

Nowhere is this union and this vital adherence to the sacred Humanity of our Savior more perfect than in sacramental Communion. In the Host lies every principle of life and holiness for us. And the other sacraments simply prepare and dispose souls for the perfect union which takes place at the banquet of love and of Eucharistic Communion.[36]

This dependence of the various sources of grace upon the Eucharist becomes still clearer if we consider the Sacrament of the Altar as food, as the spiritual nourishment of our souls. Every sacrament gives grace, and every grace gives life to or increases the life already existing in the soul. It follows that every sacrament in some way feeds our spiritual life, and hence depends on the Eucharist. It is true even of baptism, which brings us forth in Christ. For birth depends upon preceding nutrition, on the divine nutrition of the whole Church of which St. Thomas speaks,[37] and which, by nurturing the life of the mystical Spouse makes her spiritually fruitful in bringing forth souls to grace.

Father Sertillanges also shows us the solidarity of all the sacraments with the Eucharist, considered as *spiritual* food. In referring to the Eucharistic discourse of Jesus, he says:

---

[34] English translation by McHugh and Callan (New York: Joseph F. Wagner, Inc., 1958), 241–42.

[35] *Mysterium fidei*, Eluc. 34, Conclusion.

[36] Cf. ibid., Eluc. 47 and 48.

[37] Cf. *Summa*, IIIa, q. 73, a. 3.

The mystical food in question here is indeed general in its nature. It is not purely a matter of preservation, such as is required when one is grown, when one has an effort to make or a loss to repair. It is needed quite as much in order to be born, or to bring forth, and for everything that concerns life, since the living Bread which is here spoken of, the bread "come down from heaven" who is Christ, gives us everything. . . .

What more can the other sacraments do? There is no room for anything else. I do not say there is no room for their intervention, for they can collaborate. I say there is no room for their independence.

With regard to the sacraments individually, we can easily see that baptism, confirmation, penance, and extreme unction are only preparations or specialized aids in relation to the general life-giving effect that the Eucharist can lay claim to of itself. It is only with regard to the social sacraments, namely holy orders and matrimony, that the relationship is more delicate.[38]

A few words will suffice to bring out the nature of this relationship in each of the sacraments.

Baptism: St. Thomas has pointed out the essential dependence of baptism with regard to the sacrament of ecclesiastical unity. There is no grace or salvation except through incorporation into Christ, through aggregation with the Church which is his fulfillment. Incorporation is accomplished in a perfect manner in the Sacrament of the Altar that unites us directly to our Head and binds us to the source of all grace. But the very desire to receive the Host already brings about a spiritual communion between man and Christ. (The Church conceives and forms this desire for the newborn that she brings forth to divine life.)

In being born of God through grace, the baptized Christian becomes a member of Christ in whom resides the whole of divine life. Since Adam's sin, outside of Christ there is no life, and there is no salvation except in him. To become a member of Jesus Christ, however, to share in his life, is to commune with his sacred Humanity; it is to commune with his divine mysteries through which supernatural life flows into our souls. This spiritual communion, as we have said, wins for us the firstfruits of the Eucharist, until such time as sacramental Communion gives them to us in plenitude.

Confirmation: Confirmation strengthens the effects of baptism by making the baptized Christian a spiritual adult, strong with the power of the Holy Spirit to fight against the enemies of the Church and to defend the integrity of the Mystical Body. It is a more perfect incorporation, in which the

---

[38] Article in *La Vie Spirituelle, loc. cit.*

influence of the most perfect of the sacraments makes its influence equally felt, the action of the Head present in the Host.

Moreover, the Holy Spirit, whom the confirmed Christian receives in a new effusion, is the Spirit of Jesus, the one who transforms the soul into the likeness of Christ in Holy Communion.

The principal effect of the Eucharist is to kindle in our souls the ardors of divine, unifying charity, so efficacious for the building up of the Body of Christ. But is not the Holy Spirit, the personified love of the Father and of the Son, the principal author of this divine fire in the Christian soul and in the Church as a whole? "The charity of God," says St. Paul, "is poured forth in our hearts by the Holy Spirit who has been given to us" (Rom. 5:5).

The divine Spirit acts more efficaciously in our souls through Holy Communion than in any other manner, because in Communion we receive the sacred Humanity of Christ, where the Holy Spirit abides as in his favorite dwelling and pours out the fullness of his grace and love. Through confirmation, however, the divine Paraclete anticipates in a sense the personal visit of Jesus in our souls, communicating to us in advance its benefits, which are the fruits of the passion of Christ. And he prepares us to receive the God of the Host with a more perfectly disposed soul, a soul that has become more spiritualized and better acquainted with such an eminent Guest. Indeed, who is better prepared to understand the mystery of the altar and to be at one with Jesus in the sacrament of his love than he who has already received the Spirit of Jesus through the sacrament of confirmation?[39]

Penance: Penance is also bound to the Holy Eucharist by strong ties of dependence. It repairs the losses of life caused by sin. True, Eucharistic union, incorporation into Jesus, is of itself permanent, at least insofar as spiritual union is the fruit of the Host. Even though it is permanent by nature, however, it can be compromised and ruined by an act of rebellion against the Spirit of grace who rules us, it can be destroyed by a mortal sin. The means of restoring the bond of vital union is the sacrament of penance.

The sacrament incorporates us into the Victim of Calvary, immolated on the cross and presented again on the altar of the Church "for the remission of sins." It applies to us the virtue of the Host, that our unworthiness does not allow us to receive sacramentally. It bathes us spiritually in the precious Blood of the divine Lamb, which also fills the cup of the Eucharistic Sacrifice.

---

[39] Cf. Mura, *Le Corps Mystique du Christ*, Volume II, Part II, Chapter 20, on confirmation in the Christian life.

Extreme Unction: This sacrament completes what penance has begun, by wiping out the last traces of sin in the Christian soul. It unites us to the dying Jesus Christ, making us die completely to the world and to sin and placing us in the hands of God.[40] It is the *In manus tuas* of Jesus on the cross, repeated in us his members and bestowing upon us in our supreme hour the holy dispositions of our sacred Head: a state of total abandonment into the hands of God, and of total separation from all created things in order to make us belong to God alone. In this respect, extreme unction is also, in its own way, the sacrament of the death of Christ, subordinate to the Eucharist which, according to the formula of St. Thomas, is *the perfect sacrament of the Passion.*[41]

Holy Orders: Holy orders was instituted in order to give the Mystical Body its social organization, its hierarchical ordering, by giving it visible heads and ministers. In all of its degrees holy orders remains dependent upon the Sacrament of the Altar, transmitting its virtue to those who receive its various characters. "Everybody knows that all the functions of the hierarchy, diverse as they may be, are at the service of the priesthood, and that the priesthood in its turn is totally at the service of the Eucharist. The reason is that the Eucharist is the very center of the social life [of the Church] and the point of departure of all her operations."[42]

Matrimony: The dependence of all the sacraments on the Eucharist appears lastly in the sacrament of matrimony itself, although at first sight the relationship seems less evident. We should call to mind here the beautiful doctrine of St. Paul concerning the lofty significance of the conjugal union between Christians.[43] The union of husband and wife symbolizes for the faithful the union of Christ and the Church, of Christ who loved his Church and who delivered himself up for her in order to purify her and to unite her to himself here on earth in a transforming love, and later in the consummation of glory. But what is the supreme sacrament of the union of Jesus with the Church, if not the Eucharist? What more certain pledge of glorious consummation, of divine viaticum in the journey to heaven, than the Sacrament of the Altar? And in the measure that it expresses this mystical union, the communion of the Church with the immolated Victim

---

[40] Cf. *Summa*, Suppl., q. 29, a. 8; q. 30, a. 1.

[41] Cf. *Summa*, IIIa, q. 73, a. 5 ad 2. A beautiful illustration, a lived application of this doctrine is to be found in the life of Condren, receiving extreme unction in the spirit of union to the dying Jesus Christ. Cf. Brémond, *Hist. litt. du sentiment religieux en France*, III, 415 ff.

[42] Sertillanges, *loc. cit.*

[43] Cf. Chapter IV above; Chapter II, 17–18.

of the altar, matrimony also transmits to Christian spouses the graces of sanctification and of incorporation into Christ, which they need in their particular vocation.

Thus the mystical septenary of the sacraments is centered in its entirety around the ineffable Sacrament of the Altar, through which is accomplished and consummated the union of our souls and bodies with Jesus, and thanks to which the divine organism of the total Christ, of the Head and members, is built up and perfected in its supernatural unity.

CHAPTER X

Union through Efficient Causality

J esus is our head, the Head of the mystical organism whose members we are. Through baptism he has incorporated us into himself. Through the Eucharist he has consummated our union with him. The function of the head, St. Thomas tells us, is to move the other members, and to govern their activity through the faculties of perception and of movement situated within it. Likewise, Christ "has the power of bestowing grace on all the members of the Church, according to John 1:16: 'Of his fullness we have all received.'"[1]

If we belong to Christ, if we have become his members, it is so that he may act within us and deploy in our souls the power of his sanctifying virtue. If he loves us and delivered himself up for us, he did so in order to purify us and to make us holy and without spot through the efficacy of his precious Blood.

Our Lord is not content to love with a sterile love. He acts upon our souls; he infuses into his members the supernatural sap of grace. And thus he accomplishes the parable of the vine whose vinestock he is and whose branches we are (cf. John 15:1 ff.). Here, however, we must give analogy its proper place. Vital influx in the strict sense is an immanent action accomplished within a subject, within a person. It demands a strict continuity between the part that gives and the part that receives, between the part that moves and the part that is moved. Now between Jesus and us there is no substantial continuity, since there exists a distinction of persons. Consequently the supernatural influences that our Lord exercises on our souls are not strictly immanent, and are called "vital" only in an analogical manner, according to an analogy of proportion.[2]

---

[1] *Summa*, IIIa, q. 8, a. 1.

[2] The fact remains, however, that in each individual, in each faithful considered as a distinct person, the life of grace is an immanent and vital activity in the strict sense of the word.

In fact, by reason of this secret action of Jesus in our souls we are totally dependent upon him in the order of grace, in the same way that the members of the natural body are dependent upon the vital impulses that originate in the head. All good movements, all salutary thoughts, all the motions of grace come to us from our divine Head, who gives the impetus to our entire supernatural activity. Without him we can do nothing, as he himself has assured us (cf. John 15:5). No doubt, when our Lord acts within us he is not dispensing us from acting on our own part. But there is no salutary work of which he is not the initiator and principal author.

This truth of faith gives the doctrine of the Mystical Body a special importance and an eminently practical value for our spiritual life. It stimulates our trust in Jesus, our spirit of abandonment to his life-giving influence, and our generous cooperation with his salutary impulses. Therefore it is important that we make a careful study of its nature and manifestations in the life of the Mystical Body.

Through his sacred Humanity our Lord produces in us the effects of grace and of sanctification. Therefore, it is as man that Jesus is constituted our Head and the principle of our supernatural life. St. Augustine teaches this truth in his commentary on the Gospel of St. John. In commenting on our Savior's words, "I am the true vine, you are the branches," he writes: "The vine and its branches have the same nature. So too, our Lord, being of a different nature from ours inasmuch as he is God, became man so that he might, through his human nature, become the vine and we its branches."[3]

Through its union to the Word, the Humanity of our divine Savior has become, as the Fathers say, the organ of the Divinity, in order to accomplish all the works of power and of grace that infinite Goodness accomplishes among us. The Humanity of Christ is, as we have said, the *universal sacrament* of our sanctification, the sensible and efficacious sign of all grace,[4] of all holiness, the visible and palpable coating of divine power, of which all the other sacraments are but the instruments.

The Angelic Doctor is the one who compares our sacraments to the mystery of the Word Incarnate, insofar as the material reality united to the sacramental words is a figure of and an imitation of the union of human nature with the Word of God in the unity of a single Person. [5] Jesus is a subsistent and permanent sacrament of sanctification, because each of the

---

[3] *In Joan. XV.*
[4] As we know, this is the definition of the word "sacrament."
[5] *In Joan. XV.*

actions of his sacred Humanity, the least of his movements, looks, sighs, has been and remains the active principle and efficient cause of grace and virtue.

St. Thomas often refers to this principle of the life-giving influences of the sacred Humanity of Christ, and applies it successively to each of the mysteries of our Lord's life. The baptism of Jesus sanctified the waters and endowed them with the purifying power that they communicate to us through the sacrament of regeneration.[6] If he willed to be tempted, it was in order to overcome our temptations through his own.[7] All the sufferings of his divine passion heal and quicken our souls.[8] His death makes us die to sin.[9] His resurrection is the cause of our bodily and spiritual resurrection.[10] His glorious ascension is the principle of our complete redemption and ultimate salvation, by obtaining our entrance into heaven.[11]

In truth, everything in Jesus is holy and sanctifying. In the measure that we unite ourselves to the sacred Humanity of our Savior, that we incorporate ourselves through faith into the various mysteries of his life, we receive the life-giving influences that pour in on all sides from this universal source of sanctification.

Among the revelations made to St. Mechtilde, there is one that confirms and illustrates this truth magnificently. In the *Book of Special Grace*, it is recorded:

> The Lord having called her to him, placed his divine hands upon the hands of his spouse, so as to give her all the labor and all the works of his sacred Humanity. He then placed his most gentle eyes on the eyes of his beloved, and thus communicated to her the merit of his holy looks and of the abundant tears he had shed. Through the contact of his ears, He gave her all the operations of his divine hearing, and through the contact of his crimson lips all his words of praise, of thanksgiving, and prayer, and even of his public discourses, to make up for her negligences. Finally, he united his most gentle heart to the heart of his beloved, applied to it the fruit of all his meditation, devotion, and love, and enriched her heart with all the treasures of his.
>
> Then this soul, totally incorporated into Christ Jesus, melted like wax under the influence of fire and received the seal of the divine likeness. It was in this manner that this blessed one became one with her Beloved.[12]

---

[6] *Summa*, IIIa, q. 39, a. 1.

[7] Ibid., q. 41, a. 1.

[8] Ibid., q. 48, a. 6, and q. 49, a. 1.

[9] Ibid.., q. 50, a. 6.

[10] Ibid., q. 56, aa. 1, 2, ff.

[11] Ibid., q. 57, a. 6.

[12] *The Book of Special Grace*, Part I, Chapter 1.

Clearly, the author of this account relates the communications of grace, which Jesus gave his servant through the channel of his sacred Humanity, to the doctrine of the Mystical Body. Jesus as Head of the Mystical Body is the one who possesses in plenitude the divine life that he infuses into us. He became man in order to sanctify our humanity. The sacred flesh that he assumed is completely imbued with divine virtualities, and each of his senses, each of his organs, projects into our being supernatural gifts that mold us to the likeness of our divine Savior. This is the truth of the matter.

But how can we understand this sanctifying influence of the human nature of Jesus? Is not grace produced by God alone, as the exclusive privilege of the divine nature? Does the creature really become the efficient cause of our sanctification? Do we really receive the vital influx, the deifying action of the most sacred Humanity of the Savior, or is it not a matter of mere images, a metaphorical way of speaking, to express the meritorious value and the efficacious intercession that our Lord offers up for us to his Father?

No, it is not merely through a moral action, through an indirect influence of his all-powerful prayer, that Jesus obtains divine life for us. He transfuses and produces this supernatural life in our souls through a true causality.

Certainly, God always remains the principal cause of grace, for every effect must proceed from a cause of the same nature. Deification, the participation in the divine nature that grace confers on us can proceed, in the last analysis, only from the one who is God through his essence.[13] In this capacity Christ himself, as the Word of God, is the principal author of our interior sanctification, in union with the Father and the Holy Spirit. But the sacred Humanity of Jesus shares the honor of sanctifying our souls, as the instrument of the Godhead.

There is no contradiction in the fact that a creature, and even a purely corporeal being, should produce, through the power of God that fills it, supernatural works such as the sanctification of souls. Do we not see quite frequently in the material world that a very imperfect instrument guided by a skillful hand can produce marvelous effects and accomplish works far above its own perfection and native power? The painter's brush, of itself, can do no more than trace formless marks devoid of order and beauty. But let the hand of a Raphael or a Murillo grasp this puny instrument; then the activity and genius of the artist will flow into the brush and cause it to produce an incomparable masterpiece, a "Transfiguration," an "Immaculate Conception," that will be admired through the centuries.

---

[13] Cf. *Summa*, Ia-IIae, q. 112, a. 1.

The same holds true for the supernatural order in which God in his infinite condescension toward man has deigned to use means proportioned to our sensible nature in conferring upon us the wonderful gift of his grace. He has deigned to call material creatures to the signal honor of cooperating as instruments in the work of our sanctification. And yet the distance between corporeal nature and the supernatural reality that is grace is far greater than that between the artist's brush and the masterpiece he produces. Nonetheless the Spirit of God, the author of all holiness, fills these weak and powerless beings and raises them above themselves to the point of communicating his own sanctifying power to them during the time they are subject to his influence. That is what he does every day through the channels of grace we call "sacraments."

Now what God does for inanimate beings, could he fail to do for a rational nature, the most perfect, the holiest of all, the one that most closely resembles his infinite perfection, namely, the human nature of his Word? Personally united to the Son of God, this eminently holy nature has been constituted the necessary intermediary of every supernatural good. The human nature of Christ is the canal, joined to the infinite ocean of the Godhead, that pours the life-giving waters of grace into our souls. According to a hallowed expression, it is *the conjoined instrument of the Word, his inseparable organ*, in every work of salvation.

The Gospel shows us in a striking way the supernatural power of the sacred Humanity of Christ in the accomplishment of miraculous works. Jesus himself compares his power as a miracle worker to his power to forgive sins and sanctify souls. The one can, therefore, help us to understand the other, for both are beyond the powers of nature left to itself.

Listen to St. Mark's account of the cure of the woman suffering from the hemorrhage:

> And there was a woman who for twelve years had had a hemorrhage.... Hearing about Jesus, she came up behind him in the crowd and touched his cloak. For she said, "If I touch but his cloak, I shall be saved." And at once the flow of her blood was dried up, and she felt in her body that she was healed of her affliction. And Jesus, instantly perceiving in himself that power had gone forth from him, turned to the crowd, and said, "Who touched my cloak?" And his disciples said to him, "Thou seest the crowd pressing upon thee, and dost thou say, "Who touched me?" And he was looking around to see her who had done this (Mark 5:25–32).

In this account, St. Luke is more explicit and has our Lord himself speak the words used by St. Mark regarding this miraculous power. In answer to St. Peter's words: "Master, the crowds throng and press upon thee," Jesus answered insistently: "Someone touched me; for I perceived that power had gone forth from me" (Luke 8:45–46).

There is certainly a question of a divine power here, but one whose instrument and vehicle is the sacred Humanity of Christ. Obviously there is no question in this merciful intervention of our Savior of the power to sanctify. But for Jesus, the healing of bodies and souls is all one, as he himself made clear in another circumstance.

One day our Lord was preaching at Capharnaum in someone's home:

> They came, bringing to him a paralytic, carried by four. And since they could not bring him to Jesus because of the crowd, they stripped off the roof where he was, and having made an opening, they let down the pallet on which the paralytic was lying. And Jesus, seeing their faith, said to the paralytic, "Son, thy sins are forgiven thee."
>
> Now some of the Scribes were sitting there and reasoning in their hearts, "Why does this man speak thus? He blasphemes. Who can forgive sins, but only God?" And at once Jesus, knowing in his spirit that they so reasoned within themselves, said to them, "Why are you arguing these things in your hearts? Which is easier, to say to the paralytic, 'Thy sins are forgiven thee,' or to say, 'Arise, and take up thy pallet, and walk'? But that you may know that the Son of Man has power on earth to forgive sins"—he said to the paralytic—"I say to thee, arise, take up thy pallet, and go to thy house." And immediately he arose and, taking up his pallet, went forth in the sight of all, so that they were all amazed, and glorified God, saying, "Never did we see the like" (Mark 2:3–12).

To forgive sins is to give grace. The former necessarily implies the latter. With equal facility Jesus sanctifies souls through grace and restores health to bodies, for a power goes forth from him that deifies. His sacred flesh is life-giving, as the Council of Ephesus expresses it: "If anyone does not confess that the flesh of the Lord is life-giving ... and belongs to the Word of God ... [who] has power to give life to all things, let him be anathema."[14]

The hypostatic union has penetrated the soul and the body of Christ the Redeemer with the plenary power of the Godhead, and deifies all who approach it with faith. In the words of St. Cyril of Alexandria: "The flesh of Jesus receives from the Godhead a power that heals. From the fact that

---

[14] Denziger, n. 123.

the Word has inhabited this flesh, he associates it with his life-giving work, and makes it life-giving just as he himself is life-giving by nature."[15]

St. Thomas merely repeats the teaching of the Fathers in equivalent terms when he speaks of the instrumental power of the sacred Humanity of Jesus. He says: "To give grace or the Holy Ghost belongs to Christ as he is God, authoritatively [as the author of grace]; but instrumentally it belongs also to him as man, inasmuch as his manhood is the instrument of his Godhead."[16] In another passage he says: "Although Christ did not suffer as God, nevertheless his flesh is the instrument of the Godhead, and hence it is that his Passion has a kind of divine power of casting out sin."[17]

But in what manner does Jesus exercise the power of sanctification? Every instrument acts under the impulsion and motion of the principal agent. By exercising its own activity it subordinates itself to the superior action of the one who moves and impels it. The effect it produces, while corresponding to its power as an instrument, nonetheless exceeds it and shares in the very perfection of the artisan who applies it to his work.

When this work is called grace, God alone is the artisan and he acts by simple volition, by a command that proceeds from his all-powerful will. God speaks and everything is made; he commands and all things are created (cf. Ps. 148:5). Between God's supremely efficacious command and the production of the effect, is there room for the intervention of a subordinate, instrumental activity? Yes; and it is precisely the divine command, the operative word of God that passes through the organ chosen by him to accomplish his work.

In his ineffable goodness, God has chosen to join us to his divine life. He needs only to speak and the thing is done. And he does speak, but through his Word Incarnate. He sanctifies us, but through the Humanity of his Son. His will that deifies us passes through the human will of the God-Man, and this human will of Jesus is actualized and expressed by commands whose efficacy is felt by every creature. To the deaf and dumb spirit, Jesus said: "I command thee, go out of him and enter him no more" (Mark 9:24), and the possessed child was liberated. He commanded the sea imperatively to be calm, and the raging waters obeyed. "Receive the Holy Spirit," he said to his apostles as he breathed upon them, "whose sins you shall forgive, they are forgiven" (John 20:23). And at the Last Supper he said: "This is my Body,

---

[15] *In Joan.*
[16] *Summa*, IIIa, q. 8, a. 1 ad 1.
[17] Ibid, q. 49, a. 1 ad 1.

this is my Blood which shall be shed for you" (cf. Luke 22:19–20). The power of his words effects what he has willed and commanded in the disciples and in the bread and the wine. This efficacy is not directly perceptible to the senses in the two latter cases; but it is guaranteed by the miraculous works that have preceded it.

The command of Jesus is efficacious because it simply transmits the command of God himself, whose supreme power it channels. We can form a more exact idea of this manner of acting through an efficacious command if we meditate upon the profound words of St. Thomas, explaining how God can communicate the power to work miracles to a creature:

> God works miracles by his command alone. Now we see that the divine command reaches the inferior or human spirits through the means of superior or angelic spirits. . . . In this way, through angelic or human spirits, God's command can [likewise] reach corporeal creatures in such a way that through them the divine command is in a certain way presented to nature [by a transmission that shares in the very efficacy of the divine command]. And thus men and angels act in a certain way as the instruments of divine power. . . .

Then, passing from the working of miracles to the production of grace, St. Thomas concludes: "There is nothing surprising in that, since God likewise makes use of corporeal creatures for the justification of souls as is apparent in the sacraments."[18]

How much greater, therefore, is the power of the sacred Humanity of Jesus in the production of grace. All power is given to him in heaven and on earth for the salvation of his elect—the members of his Mystical Body. He orders and disposes all the sanctifying effects God wills to produce on

---

[18] *De Pot.*, q. VI, a. 4. St. Thomas often refers to this notion of the instrumental causality of grace with regard to the doctrine of the sacraments. And Christ, we know, is the Sacrament par excellence, the living and universally efficacious Sign of all grace and sanctification. The Angelic Doctor often affirms, especially in the *Summa*, that this action of the sacraments is a causality by way of sign, but an efficacious sign which, by exercising its own activity, produces the effect willed by God the principal agent.

Now the sacramental sign is an order, a divine command, a creative word, a productive word, filled with the efficacy of God who pronounces it through Christ by means of his minister: *He commanded and they were created*. Referring to the Eucharistic Consecration, St. Thomas writes: "Since these words are uttered in the person of Christ, it is through his command that they receive their instrumental power from him, just as his other deeds and sayings derive their salutary power instrumentally" (IIIa, q.78, a. 4. Cf. *ibid.*, ad 3; IIIa, q. 63, a. 1, *in corp. ad finem; ibid.*, ad 2; a. 4 c. and ad 1, ad 2, and ad 3).

It is true that the sign in itself is purely intentional, a being of reason, an *ens rationis*. But inasmuch as this rational ordering of the sign to its effect proceeds from the efficacious will of Christ and from the fact of its institution by Christ, it elicits within the sign itself the power of God and of Christ. The sign ceases being purely intentional and becomes physically efficacious, and the material reality that expresses the sanctifying will of Jesus is filled with the divine power of Jesus that produces grace. Thus, the causality of the divine sign may be called not simply intentional, not simply physical or ontological, but intentional-physical.

earth. He commands when he speaks. He orders and commands also when he suffers and dies, for all his actions and sufferings are willed and ordered by him for our salvation, and receive from this commanding will, subject to his Godhead, a divine efficacy to save and to sanctify. Thus all the works of Christ are sacraments of salvation that prolong and particularize the one Sacrament that is the Incarnation of the Word.

As Father Bouesse writes:

> It is from the first instant of the Incarnation that we must date the exercise of the instrumental causality of Christ's Humanity in the work of our salvation.... From that moment, the human will of the Savior, instrumentally imbued with divine power, was in a state of perfect activity and command of all the operations of the sacred Humanity and all the operations of the instruments of this sacred Humanity, according to the sanctifying and glorifying ends of the Incarnation.[19]

We can understand now how the very contact of Jesus' body healed bodies and sanctified souls, how his divine touch restored to health the woman suffering from the loss of blood and returned Magdalene to grace. When anyone approached Jesus with faith, communication was established with a divine Generator that was charged with every supernatural virtuality. Furthermore, this divine power was not limited to those who approached Jesus during his life on earth. It continues to extend its operative efficacy to all who, through the centuries, will ever unite themselves to him and be incorporated into him through baptism, or at least through faith.

Father Bouesse also says in the same article:

> We must conceive of the instrumental causality of Christ's human will just as we must conceive of the causality of the divine will. The mobility and chronology of his works do not change the eternal immobility of the will of God. The initial will of the soul of Christ, the instrument of the divine power ... exercises an immobile activity in the perpetual motion received from God ... According to the plan of divine Wisdom, perfectly accepted by the obedient will of the Servant of God (Christ), the actions and passions of the Savior, each at its own hour, participate in the wonderful power of his human will. Each one at its hour realizes the divine effects in whose production the following have concurred: God as the principal cause, the human will of Christ as the primary instrumental cause, the psychological and corporeal powers of Christ as secondary instrumental causes ....[20]

---

[19] *Revue Thomiste* (May–June, 1934), 381–380 (order of pages inverted).
[20] *Loc. cit.*

In speaking of the passion of our Lord, St. Thomas compares its salutary influence on all the generations to come to the action of a pharmacist who today prepares a remedy to which everyone can have recourse in the future for all sorts of ailments.[21]

The sacred Humanity of Jesus, our divine Physician, is itself the salutary remedy, the universal specific, prepared during the course of his mortal life, and especially during his Passion, in which he placed all the salutary power of all the mysteries of his life and death. This supremely efficacious virtue is applied to us every time the conditions established by the will of God are established, that is to say, as often as we turn with faith and love to the Source of grace, every time we establish vital contact and allow our divine Head to exercise his action as Savior over us.

This salutary action of Jesus upon us seems impossible at first glance, because of the distance separating us from his sacred Humanity. Let us not forget, however, that between the cause and the effect produced there is no need at all for corporeal contact; a virtual contact suffices. Light and heat come from the sun to the earth without hindrance, pouring life and joy into all creatures. Our divine Sun is much more intimately present to us than is the physical sun to our planet, bringing his beneficial influences to the depths of our souls. For, as the Angelic Doctor says, the divine power that makes use of the Humanity of Christ as an instrument "is in touch with all places and times; and such virtual contact suffices for its efficiency."[22]

This beneficent action upon souls who know the gift of God never ceases. Such souls submit their every activity and their whole life, all their undertakings and sufferings to the life-giving influence of the divine Redeemer. They live their incorporation into Christ through a continual union with Jesus in the various mysteries of his life, uniting themselves to his actions and to his divine circumstances, whose salutary power quickens and sanctifies their own actions and the corresponding conditions of their existence.

Such was the understanding of Venerable Marie Celeste, the chosen soul who was a great source of inspiration to St. Alphonsus de Liguori. She used to say to her divine Spouse, with complete confidence and familiarity:

> I am united to thy virtue, and all the virtues that I possess receive strength and courage by quenching their thirst at the very pure spring of the merit of thy excellent virtues with which thy heavenly Father has adorned me. I feel thy heroic humility, thy divine purity, thy perfect and longsuffering

[21] Cf. *Summa*, IIIa, q. 49, a. 1 ad 3.
[22] Ibid., q. 56, a. 1 ad 3.

patience, and thy infinite charity, clothing my nakedness. Union with thy will unites me with thy heavenly Father, in whom I am glorified by thee, my one treasure. In thee I am loved by the heavenly Father.[23]

Privileged souls have understood and practiced in an eminent degree what must be the all of Christian life, the life of Christ in us through union with his life-giving mysteries and through submission to his influences. They have carried out the program that Jesus bequeathed to his apostles as he was about to leave them:

Abide in me, and I in you. . . . He who abides in me, and I in him, he bears much fruit (John 15:4–5).

Thus, we see more and more clearly the nature of the union that it has pleased our Savior to contract with us by becoming our Head and making us members of his Mystical Body. And we have not yet catalogued all the secrets of his love, which are given over to the perfecting of this union.

[23] Favre, *Vie de la Vén. Marie-Céleste Crostarosa*, 372.

CHAPTER XI

Union in the Holy Spirit, the Soul of the Mystical Body

I n a living organism, whatever its nature, more than a head and members constitute the body by their harmonious ordering. There is also an internal and hidden principle from which its life and movement proceed. In the case of an organism endowed with intellectual or spiritual life, a spirit quickens and governs all the members, including the head. The first principle of life, the spirit that activates and quickens the whole, is what is called the soul. In the Mystical Body this soul is the Holy Spirit, the Spirit of Christ Jesus (cf. Acts 16:7), who has also become the Spirit of all the faithful.

This conclusion, which is contained at least virtually in the New Testament, is taught explicitly by patristic Tradition and by the great theologians of the Middle Ages. But is the argument decisive? Is not theology subject to progress? In the analogy of the Body by which St. Paul translated the reality of our union with Christ our Head, can we not express with greater precision some of its constitutive elements, notably the one that is called the life-giving principle or soul of the total Christ? If, since the sixteenth century several writers have preferred, in opposition to the overwhelming trend of Tradition, to consider sanctifying grace as the soul of the Mystical Body, does this not indicate theological progress, a useful clarification worthy of general acceptance?[1] It does not seem so, for even if we agree with the analogy, even if we accept the essential difference between the soul of a natural organism and that of the supernatural organism which is the Mystical Body, sanctifying grace does not fulfill the requisite conditions to entitle it to be called the soul of the Church or of the whole

[1] This is the concept set forth in *Collectanea Mechlinensia* for May, 1935, by His Excellency Carton de Wiart, in an article evaluating with gracious approval the present study of the Mystical Body. His Excellency later accepted the doctrine here set forth.

Christ. The Holy Spirit, on the other hand, by reason of the role he plays in the supernatural society of the faithful, deserves this title attributed to him by the great Doctors of the Church in their commentaries on St. Paul.

Using the above remarks as a prelude, we can quite naturally divide into two parts the reasons why the Holy Spirit can rightly be called the soul of the Mystical Body: the reasons of authority drawn from Tradition and from Scripture, which are primordial in all questions relating to faith; the reasons theology furnishes to explain and to justify the attribution of the name "soul of the Mystical Body" to the Holy Spirit, in preference to sanctifying grace.

Testimony of Scripture and Tradition

Anyone who has read the New Testament, especially the Acts of the Apostles and the epistles of St. Paul and of St. John, is struck by the predominant role there attributed to the life-giving Spirit in the whole life of the Church and in that of her divine Head, Christ Jesus.

For St. Paul, the Holy Spirit is the Spirit of the Son: "God has sent the Spirit of his Son" (Gal. 4:6). He is the Spirit of Christ Jesus—"the Spirit of Jesus" (Acts 16:7) in the words of St. Luke. He is the Spirit of Jesus because Jesus sends him to us: "the Advocate . . . whom I will send you" (John 15:26). He is the Spirit of Jesus also because his sacred Humanity is his temple and his favorite dwelling, where he deploys his life-giving action in plenitude. As St. Luke tells us: "Jesus, full of the Holy Spirit, returned from the Jordan, and was led by the Spirit about the desert" (Luke 4:1). After his forty-days' fast, it was also "in the power of the Spirit" (Luke 4:14) that he returned into Galilee. When he afterwards entered the synagogue of Nazareth, he read a passage of Isaias, and then applied to himself these words of the Prophet: "The Spirit of the Lord is upon me because he has anointed me to bring good news to the poor he has sent me" (Luke 4:18; cf. Isa. 61:1ff.). John the Baptist had received no other sign than that by which to recognize the promised Messias: "He upon whom thou wilt see the Spirit descending, and abiding upon him, he it is who baptizes with the Holy Spirit" (John 1:33).

If Jesus, the Head of the predestined, the Head of the Mystical Body, possesses in plenitude the Spirit of the seven gifts (cf. Is. 11:1–3), it is necessary that all his members receive a communication of this Spirit from him, in order that all of them may be united in one Spirit of life and holiness, according to the words of the Angelic Doctor: "The Spirit of Unity is poured into us through Christ."[2] Thus we see the divine Spirit at the beginning of every interior and exterior activity of the Church.

The Spirit presides over the choice of the apostles (cf. Acts 13:2); he establishes the bishops to govern the Church of God (cf. Acts 20:28); he enlightens minds and enables them to penetrate divine truths (cf. John 14:26; 16:13); and he warms hearts with the fires of divine charity (cf. Rom. 5:5). All the virtues are the fruit of his profound action within souls (cf. Gal. 5:22). He sanctifies and regenerates the children of God in baptism (cf. Tit. 3:5); he infuses into them the filial sense that makes them cry to God: "Abba, Father!" (cf. Gal. 4:6; Rom. 8:15), for he is the Spirit of the Son, who is poured from the Head into the members. Anyone who does not possess this Spirit does not belong to Christ (cf. Rom. 8:9), since the members of the same Body have been the same Spirit.

Scripture reveals the Holy Spirit to us as a principle of unity and of life in the living whole which is the Mystical Body. Through the Holy Spirit the various parts of this divine organism are made one:

> Now there are varieties of gifts, but the same Spirit....To one through the Spirit is given the utterance of wisdom; and to another the utterance of knowledge, according to the same Spirit; to another the gift of healing, in the one Spirit; to another prophecy; to another the distinguishing of spirits....But all these things are the work of one and the same Spirit, who allots to everyone according as he will" (1 Cor. 12:4–11).

This unity in the Holy Spirit originates in baptism, in the very act of our incorporation into Christ: "For in one Spirit we were all baptized into one body, whether Jews or Gentiles, whether slaves or free" (1 Cor. 12:13).

The Holy Spirit, being the source of the unity of the Mystical Body, is also the principle of its life. Does not St. Paul call him "the Spirit of life" (Rom. 8:2)? We would have to review the entire eighth chapter of his Epistle to the Romans in order to understand to what degree everything that lives in Christ lives only through the Holy Spirit. The life of the soul, quickened by his breath, and later on the life of the body resuscitated by his power (cf. Rom. 8:11)—everything in the supernatural activity of the members of Christ is attributable to him. He is the secret principle of our prayer (cf. Rom. 8:26–27); he forms the interior man within us (cf. Eph. 3:16); he makes us walk from glory to glory in our progressive configuration to

---

[2] *In Rom. XII*, lect. 2ª

Christ (cf. 2 Cor. 3:18). The whole Church, formed by his influence, under the auspices of Mary, on Pentecost, is moved by his action, consoled by the sentiment of his inward presence (cf. Acts 9:31), until the day of her perfect union with Christ, for whom she yearns under the impulsion of the Spirit (cf. Rom. 8:23).

All of these indications from Scripture show us the Holy Spirit as the Spirit of Christ poured into his Mystical Body to quicken it with his divine life. They make of him the soul of the Mystical Christ. Indeed, the Fathers understood these passages from the Sacred Books in this way.

St. Gregory Nazianzen writes: "We are all one Body in Christ; and while all the members do not have the same operation, none the less they become a single thing, united as they are by the same Spirit in Christ."[3] Likewise, St. Athanasius says: "We are all considered as having become one in the Word and in the Father, because within us dwells the Spirit of the Word who abides in the Father."[4]

St. John Chrysostom, commenting upon the Epistle to the Ephesians, asks himself this question with regard to "the unity of the Spirit" (Eph. 4:3) recommended by the Apostle: "What is the unity of the Spirit?" In answer to his own question, he says:

> Just as in one body there is only one spirit (a soul), that keeps all things united even if they belong to different members, so is it here. For the Spirit is given to unite those who were divided by diversity of race and custom. Henceforth, the old man and the young man, the poor man and the rich man, the child and the adolescent, woman and man, and the souls of all are but one thing.[5]

More than anyone else, St. Augustine insists on this doctrine and returns to it, in many passages of his works, with a precision that leaves nothing to be desired. In his Sermon 268, he speaks of the soul of the Mystical Body in these terms, which have the clarity of a definition: "What our spirit, that is our soul, is to our members, the Holy Spirit is to the members of Christ, to the Body of Christ which is the Church."[6] The analogy of the soul applied to the Holy Spirit, however, is conceived by St. Augustine not precisely from the point of view of the substantial form united to matter, but far more from the point of view of the vital action and of the interior impulsion that

---

[3] *Oratio*, 32ª.
[4] *Oratio*, 3ª
[5] *In Epist, ed Eph*. IV, homil. 9
[6] *Serm*. 268, n. a.

the soul exercises on the members of the body. Moreover, that is how it is conceived by all the Fathers and Doctors who expose the doctrine. Certain authors who have failed to notice this distinction have fallen into insoluble difficulties on the subject. Here is what the great Bishop of Hippo says:

> If you want to have the Holy Spirit, listen to this, my brothers. Our spirit, the one by which each man possesses life, is called the soul . . . and you see what the soul does in the body. It quickens all the members. It sees through the eyes, hears through the ears, smells through the nose, speaks through the tongue; through the hands it works, and through the feet it walks. It is present in all the members, giving life to all, and giving to each its proper function.
>
> The same is true of the Church of God. In certain saints she works miracles, in other saints she preaches the truth; in some she preserves virginity, in others she observes conjugal sanctity. In some she accomplishes one thing, in others, something else. Each of the members has his own work, but the life of all is the same. What the soul is to the body, the Holy Spirit is to the Body of Christ which is the Church. The Holy Spirit accomplishes in the Church as a whole what the soul accomplishes in the diverse members of a single body.[7]

From this precise doctrine, St. Augustine draws the important conclusion that in order to possess the Holy Spirit, the Spirit of Christ, we must belong to the Body of Christ, we must be a part of the Church of Christ. This conclusion is now expressed by theology in the axiom: *Outside the Church, there is no salvation.* St. Augustine says:

> Let the faithful become the Body of Christ, if they wish to live by the Spirit of Christ. Brethren, understand what I am saying: you who are a man have a spirit and a body; but does your spirit live by your body, or does your body live by your spirit? . . . What does every living man answer? Certainly, it is my body that live by my spirit. Do you too want to live by the Spirit of Christ? Abide in the Body of Christ. Does my body live by your spirit? It is by my spirit that my body lives, just as your body lives by your spirit. The Body of Christ can live only by the Spirit of Christ.[8]

A little further on, in his Discourse 27 on the Gospel of St. John, the great Doctor completes his thought. Starting with the text, "It is the spirit that gives life" (John 6:64), he makes the following commentary:

---

[7] *Serm.* 267.
[8] *In Joan.*, tract. 26, n. 13.

It is the spirit that gives life, for it is the spirit that makes the members alive. It makes alive only the members it finds in the body that it quickens. For how can the spirit that is in you, O man, and by which you are a man, quicken a member that might be separated from your flesh? When I say your spirit, I mean your soul. Now your soul quickens only the members that are in your body. Separate one from the rest, and it will cease being quickened by your soul, for it will no longer belong to the unity of your body. Let us therefore love unity and fear separation. The greatest evil that the Christian must fear is to find himself separated from the Body of Christ. For if he is separated from the Body of Christ, he is no longer a member of Christ. And in ceasing to be a member of Christ, he is no longer quickened by his Spirit. "But," the Apostle says, "if anyone does not have the Spirit of Christ, he does not belong to Christ" (Rom. 8:9).[9]

It will be noted in passing that for St. Augustine the soul of the Church does not overflow her Body, and it would thus be impossible to belong to the soul of the Church without belonging to her Body at least in *voto*, through an implicit desire that every sincere soul, in grace with God, necessarily possesses. Any separation between the soul and the Body of the Church, even though partial, must be abandoned as incorrect. As Abbé Journet rightly remarks: "Such a manner of distinguishing the soul and the Body of the Church is without foundation in the authentic documents of the Magisterium,[10] it appears to be influenced by the Protestant conception of the spiritual Church distinct from the visible Church, and it is dangerous to use it."[11]

Without saying precisely that the soul and the Body of the Church are coextensive[12]—for one can belong to the Body without being quickened by the grace of the Holy Spirit, and St. Augustine speaks of rotten members who still adhere to the Body but will nevertheless be cut off from it[13]—we must declare with the Doctor of Hippo that the soul of the Church does not extend beyond her Body, and quickens only those that are in some manner attached to the unity of the Body. The necessity of belonging to the Body of the Church in order to be saved is of the same nature as the universal necessity of baptism, and flows directly from it. Since the specific effect of baptism is to incorporate us into the visible Church of Christ, we cannot get along without incorporation any more than we can get along without baptism. But just as we can receive the effect of baptism through a desire

---

[9] *In Joan.*, tract. 27, 6.

[10] Reference to the article "Église," in the *Dictionnaire de théologie catholique*, col. 2166, by Dublanchy.

[11] L'Église, issue "de la hiérarchie," *La Vie Spirituelle*, Supplement (May, 1934), 71 ff.

[12] Ibid., 70, 74, note.

[13] Cf. *In Joan.*, tract. 26, 13.

that is at least implicit, likewise we can enjoy the benefit of incorporation and of the life-giving influences of the soul of the total Christ through adhering in desire, *in voto*, to the unity of the Mystical Body.

The doctrine concerning the soul of the Mystical Body, which St. Augustine held up in opposition to the schismatics of his own time, was taken up again by the Doctors who came after him.[14] St. Gregory expresses himself in this way: "Just as there is but one soul that quickens the different members of the Body, so one Holy Spirit quickens and illumines the entire Church.... The heretic does not live by this Spirit, nor does the schismatic, nor he who has been excommunicated, for they do not belong to the Body of Christ. The Church possesses this life-giving Spirit, because she adheres inseparably to her Head, Christ."

Hugh of St. Victor, taking up the thought of St. Paul, tells us that the Holy Spirit becomes the life-giving principle of the Mystical Body only by flowing from the Head, Christ, into us who are his members. "Just as the spirit of man, through the head, extends its life-giving power to the members, so the Holy Spirit through Christ descends into Christians. For Christ is the Head, the Christian is his member. The head is one and the members are many; a single body is composed of the head and the members, and possesses one spirit."[15]

St. Albert the Great, commenting on the Master of the Sentences, writes: "There can be a communion of saints only through the Holy Spirit who unifies and quickens the whole Body."[16] Clearly, the analogy of the soul of the Mystical Body always is based upon the action of the Holy Spirit, who unifies and quickens the whole Church.

It is said that St. Thomas strayed from the common mode of expression when he spoke of the Holy Spirit as the heart of the Mystical Body. True, he did write in his *Summa*: "The head has a manifest pre-eminence over the other exterior members; but the heart has a certain hidden influence. And hence the Holy Ghost is likened to the heart, since he invisibly quickens and unifies the Church; but Christ is likened to the head in his visible nature in which man is set over man."[17]

---

[14] On this question one will find many passages both from the Greek and Latin Fathers in two tracts edited by Rev. P. Tromp, S.J., *De Spir. S. Anima Corporis myst: I. E Patribus grecis; II. E Patribus latinis.*

[15] *Lib. de Sacr*, Volume II, Part II, Chapter 1.

[16] Book IV, d. 24, a. 1.

[17] *Summa*, IIIa, q. 8, a. 1 ad 3.

Even though St. Thomas makes use here of the analogy of the heart to answer a particular objection, it is more usual for him to speak of the Holy Spirit as the soul of the Mystical Body.[18] Moreover, the analogy of the heart, considered as an interior and hidden principle of life, is very close in meaning to that of the soul, the primary source of life, and may be considered as its equivalent. St. Thomas also warns us in this same article (ad 2) not to take too literally the metaphorical expressions by which we express supernatural realities, and especially that of the Mystical Body.

Therefore, without giving any undue attention to this particular passage of St. Thomas, we shall give preference to other passages among the writings of the Angelic Doctor, in which the Holy Spirit is presented in his role as the life-giving Spirit or soul of the total Christ. Toward the end of the *Secunda Secundae*, a few questions before the text that we have just discussed, St. Thomas answers in the following way an objection against the unity of the Church, drawn from the diversity of her functions:

> Just as in the natural body the various members are held together in unity by the power of the quickening spirit, and are dissociated from one another as soon as that spirit departs, so too in the Church's body the peace of the various members is preserved by the power of the Holy Spirit, who quickens the body of the Church, as stated in John 6:64. Hence, the Apostle says in Ephesians 4:3: "careful to preserve the unity of the Spirit in the bond of peace."[19]

In a more concise manner the holy Doctor expresses the same doctrine in his commentary on the Epistle to the Colossians: "Just as the unity of the body is realized by the unity of the soul, so the Church is one through the unity of the Spirit, according to this text: 'one body, and one Spirit.'"[20]

In his explanation of the Epistle to the Romans, he says with reference to the verse: "If anyone does not have the Spirit of Christ, he does not belong to Christ" (Rom. 8:9): "As there is no member of the body that is not quickened by the spirit of the same body, so there exists no member of Christ who does not have the Spirit of Christ."[21]

---

[18] In another portion of the works of St. Thomas, the analogy of the heart is insinuated in a more discreet and almost indecisive way, with the possibility of a different application of this expression to the divinity of Christ: "The heart is a hidden member, whereas the head is a visible member; therefore it is possible to designate as the heart the divinity of Christ or of the Holy Spirit . . ." (*De Verit.*, q. 29, a. 4 ad 7).

[19] *Summa*, IIa-IIae, q. 183, a. 2 ad 3.

[20] *In Col. 1*, Lect. 5

[21] *In Rom.* VIII, lect. 2.

In his *Commentary on the Sentences*, St. Thomas had already treated of the same question at greater length. Explaining the nature of the mysterious unity of the Mystical Body, he wrote:

> In the natural body there is a fourfold union of members: the first according to their conformity of nature...; the second by reason of their being joined together by nerves and joints...; the third inasmuch as the vital spirit and strength flow through the whole body; the fourth, finally, inasmuch as all the members receive their perfection from the soul that is one and the same in the whole body. These four kinds of union are found in the Mystical Body: the first, by reason of the fact that the members have the same specific or generic nature; the second, through their being joined together in one faith, and thereby in a single object of faith; the third, inasmuch as they are quickened by grace and charity; the fourth union is confirmed inasmuch as the Holy Spirit resides in all the members, he who is the ultimate and principal perfection of the whole Mystical Body, just as the soul is of the natural body.[22]

Obviously the Angelic Doctor does not deny that grace has its role to play in the unification of the total Christ. But he does not want grace to be called the soul of the Mystical Body, because this function belongs to the Holy Spirit as the "last complement"[23] of the mystical members of Christ.

These are the more significant testimonies from Tradition pointing to the Holy Spirit as the soul of the Mystical Body. It is the doctrine followed even today by a great many authors, especially since the study of the Mystical Body has been restored to a place of honor.[24] On the other hand, several of those who consider sanctifying grace as the soul of the Church are merely following a habit of language accredited by a few theologians since the sixteenth century, rather than offering any carefully thought-out doctrine of their own.[25]

---

[22] Book III, d. 13, q. 2, a. 2, sol. 2.

[23] Ibid., ad 1.

[24] In this connection we might cite Volume I of Father Sertillanges' work on the Church, *L'Eglise*; Bishop d'Herbigny's two-volume work, *De Ecclesia*; Father Fernand Prat's *The Theology of Saint Paul*; Father Hurtevant's *De L'unité de L'Eglisé du Christ*; Father Arintero, Father Jürgensmeier, etc. Such was also the position taken by Cardinal Franzelin, as seen in his posthumous work, *De Ecclesia*, and by Father Hurter in his *Compendium* of theology as well as in Volume XXVII of his Patristic library.

[25] Thus, for example, Father Muncunill, in his *Tractatus de Christi Ecclesia* (Barcelona, 1914), in speaking of the body and soul of the Church cites texts known by St. Augustine and by Origen; then he concludes in a most unexpected manner—and without the shadow of an argument: "Although Origen and St. Augustine did not speak of sanctifying grace and of the infused virtues, which perform the function of a soul in the members of the Church, and consequently in the Church herself, at least they did not exclude them. But they mentioned the Word [this is true of Origen] and the Holy Spirit, who, with the Father, are the principle of all satisfaction, because that fitted in better with the conclusion they intended to prove, namely,

Theological Exposition

The scholastic teaching is that the soul is the formal cause, the informing principle of the human organism. It is an internal and constitutive principle of every living being. The Holy Spirit is not an informing principle of the Church. He is the efficient cause, acting from without, but not the substantial form of the total Christ. It would seem, therefore, that he cannot be called the soul of the Mystical Body.

Sanctifying grace on the other hand, whether considered by itself or together with charity and the other virtues, appears to realize the conditions required by the concept of the soul. It is truly the formal cause of our supernatural being; it makes us godlike, children of God and brothers of Christ by an interior reality inherent in the substance of the soul. At the same time it is the first principle of our divine life, the source of all the supernatural activity of the members of Christ. What does it lack to justify its being called the soul of the total Christ? This is the substance of the argument on which the contrary opinion is founded.

The question is further asked why—if we do not want to condemn traditional teaching or be accused of rashness in falsely opposing so many illustrious Doctors—we cannot accept what they say about the Holy Spirit as the soul of the Mystical Body and also add the ideas more recent authors have said concerning sanctifying grace and the other principles of unity of the Church. What would prevent us from attributing two souls to the Church, an uncreated soul which is the Holy Spirit, and a created soul which is grace, charity, and every other analogous principle?[26]

What are we to think of this explanation? First, we must note that we cannot attribute two souls to the Mystical Body without falsifying the analogy of the Mystical Body with the natural body. If every living being can have only one soul, is it not fitting—barring an indication to the contrary in Scripture or in Tradition—to maintain the oneness of the life-giving principle in our analysis and designation of the elements that constitute the mystical Christ? If we disregard this rule of language, are we not in

---

the perfect unity of the Church through the unity of body and soul" (*op. cit., c. 1, a. v, th. 2*). Starting from such an exegesis, it would seem that one can reach any conclusion one pleases.

[26] This is the position, among others, taken by Abbé Journet in his remarkable articles published in *La Vie Spirituelle*, Supplement (May–July–August–September, 1934), as well as in his article on the doctrine of Cajetan concerning the soul of the Church, which appeared in the *Revue Thomiste* (November, 1934–February, 1935). Fundamentally, however, his disagreement with us is more verbal than real. Cf. likewise his studies in *Nova et Vetera* (1936, and April–June, 1946).

danger of distorting the very doctrine of the Mystical Body, or at least of rendering it less clear and intelligible?

A second consideration is that the soul is not just an indifferent principle of life or activity, but a universal and primary principle, upon which depends the vital activity of the whole body. Such is not the case of sanctifying grace in the total Christ. Jurisdiction, the power of orders, the ecclesiastical magisterium, do not depend on sanctifying grace, as the Church was obliged to define against the error of the Hussites. On the contrary, grace normally flows from the power of orders, and therefore presupposes that the Church has already been constituted and is in possession of her essential principle, her soul. It follows that grace is not and cannot be called the soul of the Mystical Body.

Certain authors who maintain the traditional doctrine that we are defending further point out that sanctifying grace is undoubtedly a principle of spiritual life for each member of Christ taken individually, but that it is not a common principle of supernatural life for the Mystical Body as a whole. The grace of Peter is not that of Paul, nor a fortiori is it the grace of the whole Church.

This argument holds good, if we consider the grace of each one individually, quite apart from any dependence upon the grace of the Head from which it flows. It should be noted, however, that this point of view is incomplete. The grace of each member of the faithful is a participation of the grace of Christ, and reciprocally the grace of Christ contains virtually the grace of all his members. Seen in this light, the grace of the Head is in a certain sense a common grace that quickens each of the members of Christ.

But then, cannot this grace of Christ and of his members, considered in this dynamic unity, be called the soul of the Mystical Body? This grace, which assumes in each of the baptized "the perfect and plenary modalities that it had in the soul of the Savior"[27] as Abbé Journet says so well, and which therefore forms the Mystical Body in the likeness of its divine Head, is it not the life-giving principle of the whole supernatural organism?

To answer this question fully and to safeguard the portion of truth that these observations contain, we shall first make three points that will throw light on the problem and establish the traditional doctrine on more solid ground.

1. Everything that is a formal cause in the total Christ is not by that fact the soul of the Mystical Body. Indeed, the formal cause implies above all

---

[27] *La Vie Spirituelle*, Supplement (May, 1934), 67.

two things: (1) a perfecting of the subject informed by the cause, either in the order of substance or of first being, or in the order of accidents or of second being; (2) a principle of unity inasmuch as the integrating parts of the subject thus perfected are brought together and unified, at least in a certain order, under a single form. The notion of soul also includes the idea of a principle of life, and in addition of the primary principle of this life in the organism which it quickens.

2. *There can be several formal principles in an organic whole, but there can be only one soul.* There can be several forms, for to the primary perfection brought by the substantial form can be added many others of the accidental order. The soul, for its part, must be unique, for it denotes the ultimate formality of the living being which gives it its specific degree of being, its proper place in the scale of the living. And just as a single being cannot belong to two species, so also it cannot have two souls.

3. *In a social organism, and notably in the Mystical Body, there can be a common form or soul only in an analogical sense.* The reason for this is that the formal cause is bound up with a subject that is numerically one. The same form cannot inform several actually distinct subjects. The same is true of the notion of soul which, in its ordinary acceptation, is always an informing principle. But at the same time that it is a formal cause, the soul is also a principle of life, an efficient cause of immanent activity. In the rational being, it is the source of knowledge, of volition, and of love. It follows that in the analogical acceptation of the word soul, we may retain only the second element separated from the first. In other words, we may designate as the soul the principle of life, of knowledge, and of love, even though it is not, in the strict sense, a form of the organism that it quickens. If, moreover, this life-giving principle is immanent in the body that it animates, intimately present within it by a certain indwelling which does not go as far as information in the strict sense—that is, the indwelling that Scripture attributes to the Blessed Trinity and by appropriation to the Holy Spirit—then the notion of soul will apply even more aptly to this principle of divine life, intimately present in the subject that it vivifies.

Now that these principles have been stated, let us consider their application. Grace and charity (and likewise the jurisdictional orientation of the Church of which Abbé Journet rightly speaks) constitute a certain common form of the members of Christ. The form is not numerically one, for each Christian possesses an infused virtue of faith, a virtue of charity, numerically distinct from that of the other members of Christ. Nevertheless, the supernatural habitus of the different individuals are unified in a common root, as St. Thomas says: *conveniunt in radice una*.[28] The grace and charity in each one proceeds from the same sanctifying Spirit and tends to the same object, which is known through faith and loved through charity. The Angelic Doctor also says:

> The root of operation is the very object from which it receives its specifica-
> tion. That is why, inasmuch as the same object is believed and loved by all,
> the faith and charity of all are thereby unified in a root that is numerically
> one, not only in the primary root that is the Holy Spirit (as the efficient
> principle), but also in the proximate root which is the proper object [of
> these operations].[29]

Sanctifying grace, and consequently sacramental grace, and the virtues of faith, hope, and charity can be called formal causes of ecclesiastical unity. Very probably this is what is understood by most of those who consider grace as the soul of the Mystical Body.[30] Concerning this idea, no disagreement nor divergence is possible. However, it is not fitting to call these principles of unity the soul of the Church. The soul is not just an ordinary formal element of organic unity, but the ultimate principle, the prime root of unity, the original cause of all the movements, of all the activities of the living organism. And in the Mystical Body this role belongs to the Holy Spirit alone.

St. Thomas, in the passage just cited, compares grace and charity to the vital energies poured into the organism and receiving their ultimate formality from the soul, likewise, grace and the activity of the theological virtues depend upon the Holy Spirit, who gives to the members of Christ their ultimate form and their final complement: "*Ita omnia membra Corporis*

---

[28] Cf. *Commentary on the Sentences*, Book III, d. 13, q. 2, a. 2, sol. 2, ad 1.

[29] *Loc. cit.*

[30] This is particularly clear in the article that Abbé Journet has devoted to this question in *Revue Thomiste* of November, 1934, 266 ff. The diverse elements that he includes in the created soul of the Church are as many internal causes of ecclesiastical unity, but they are not the ultimate principle of life and of unity which must be called the soul of the Church in the strict sense.

Moreover, we must beware of interpreting the doctrine of this article devoted to Cajetan, as if Cajetan himself professed the distinction between the created soul and the uncreated soul of the Church. The great commentator on St. Thomas speaks, in the passages quoted, of the unity of the Church and of the various principles of unity. Therefore, the author of the article in *L'Ami du Clergé* (September 12, 1935), 579, col. 2, was wrong when he wrote in a footnote: Cajetan rightly distinguished the uncreated soul of the Church as being the Holy Spirit by appropriation, and the created soul as grace and charity communicated principally through the sacraments. Cf. in the special number of the *Revue Thomiste* (Nov.,1934), dedicated to Cajetan ..." This distinction and this terminology are Abbé Journet's, in his interpretation of Cajetan's doctrine.

mystici habent pro ultimo complemento Spiritum, qui est unus numero in omnibus."[31]

While grace and charity cannot be called the soul of the total Christ, the Holy Spirit is rightly given this denomination. In fact, the soul fulfills a twofold function with reference to the body. First it gives it unity of nature, and makes of its diverse parts a single whole. The instant the soul leaves the body, there is disintegration, decomposition, the complete destruction of the organism. As long as the soul is present, it gives order, harmony, and beauty to the members. Once it has departed, the body is nothing but a chaotic mass of formless elements. Secondly, the soul gives the body movement, heat, and life; and we recognize that the soul has left the body when the latter is inert, penetrated with the frigidity of death.

The Holy Spirit likewise exercises this twofold function with relation to the Mystical Body which is the Church. He gives it unity and communicates movement and life to it.

He is the *principle of unity*. It is he who produces and preserves the threefold unity of the Church: unity of faith, unity of love, and unity of government.

The Holy Spirit, the soul of the Church, produces and maintains *the unity of faith*. Did not our Lord call him "the Spirit of truth" (John 14:17; 15:26), of the common truth to which we adhere through faith? It was to the Holy Spirit that Jesus bequeathed the mission of completing the instruction of the apostles through the completion of Revelation: "When he, the Spirit of truth, has come, he will teach you all the truth" (John 16:13).

Unity of love or of communion is therefore even more clearly an effect of the action of the Holy Spirit. For he is Love in person and the principle of love. The tongues of fire that appeared on Pentecost over the heads of the disciples symbolized the fire of charity that he then kindled in the souls of those who belonged to him, and that he does not cease to nourish in the hearts of the faithful. Do we not repeat often the prayer: "Come, O Holy Ghost, fill the hearts of thy faithful, and kindle in them the fire of Thy love"?[32]

Unity of government, established by our Lord in the person of Peter and of the apostles for the maintenance of the common faith and of the communion of love, is, like the two other forms of unity, a blessing bestowed by the Holy Spirit. Thus we see St. Peter reprimanding Ananias and Sapphira

---

[31] *Op. cit*, ad I *et in corp.*
[32] Antiphon, *Veni, Sancte Spiritus.*

for having acted fraudulently in his regard, and by this very fact having lied to the Holy Spirit (cf. Acts 5:3–9). To fail in loyalty toward ecclesiastical authority amounts to a lack of sincerity toward the Spirit of truth. St. Paul, in addressing his exhortations to the priests and bishops of Ephesus, reminded them that it was the Holy Spirit who had placed them in charge of the flock of the faithful: "Take heed to yourselves and to the whole flock in which the Holy Spirit has placed you as bishops, to rule the Church of God . . ." (Acts 20:28).

This same Spirit is the soul of the teaching body of the Church, the inspirer of the holy councils. It is he who guides the deliberations of these solemn assemblies despite the intrigues and schemes of the human mind. It is he who guides the supreme Pastor in the determination of infallible truth, as well as in the government of the Church, and in piloting Peter's bark toward the shores of the heavenly homeland.

Not only is the Holy Spirit the principle of unity, he is also the wellspring of life for the whole Mystical Body. We have only to refer to the scriptural passages cited above, to meditate upon the beautiful prayers that the sacred liturgy in its hymns, sequences, and antiphons addresses to the Holy Spirit *"giver of life,"*[33] and we shall understand to what point the divine Paraclete is the *Spirit of life* (cf. Rom. 8:2), the principle of every grace.

Whether grace comes to us through the sacraments or outside of them, it is always to the Holy Spirit that it is attributed. In baptism, we are "born again of water and the Spirit" (John 3:5). We are confirmed and inured for the struggle by the Spirit of fortitude. The Holy Eucharist sanctifies us only through the life-giving power of the Spirit of life. And when, in the Sacrament of the Altar, Jesus immolates himself and perpetuates his sacrifice of Calvary, he does so always through the power of the Holy Spirit. For, according to the Apostle's teaching, it was through the Holy Spirit that Christ "offered himself unblemished unto God" (Heb. 9:14).

The remission of sins is also granted us through the purifying operation of the divine Spirit, and our Lord gave his apostles the ineffable power to remit sins only after he had breathed into them his spirit of grace, saying: "Receive the Holy Spirit, whose sins you shall forgive, they are forgiven them; and whose sins you shall retain, they are retained" (John 20:22–23).

[33] Nicene Creed.

The sacrament of holy orders is still more directly under the influence of the divine Sanctifier, since, through the priesthood almost all the other sacraments are applied to us. The diaconate is specifically conferred under the invocation of the heavenly Paraclete. The pontiff says to the one who has been elected to the sanctuary: "*Accipe Spiritum Sanctum ad robur*— Receive the Holy Spirit unto power and fortitude, to resist the devil and his temptations." And in the ordination to the priesthood all of the prayers call down upon the candidates "the blessing of the Holy Spirit," "the Spirit of the seven gifts," "the Spirit of holiness."[34]

The life-giving influence of the Spirit of love is not confined to or circumscribed by the application of the sacraments. His unlimited power goes far beyond them and touches us in many ways, enlightening our minds, inspiring and stimulating our wills. These are the actual graces which, on the road to salvation, dispel the darkness of our ignorance, sustain our weakness and make up for our many deficiencies. To obey more promptly the motions of grace, the impulsions of the divine Paraclete, we have been endowed in baptism with the receptive powers that are the gifts of the Holy Spirit. Thanks to them, our souls are inclined, as it were naturally, in the direction of the wind of divine inspirations.[35]

It is primarily in the souls of the perfect, in the mystics, that the gifts of the Holy Spirit are seen and felt. These souls, docile to grace, are under the habitual guidance of the divine Spirit and form the chosen segment of the Mystical Body.

Thus the Holy Spirit reveals himself to us in Scripture, in the liturgy, and in the very life of the Church as the universal principal of life and of unity. St. Thomas aptly sums up the whole action of the Holy Spirit in the words: "*Spiritus Sanctus invisibiliter Ecclesiam vivificat et unit*"—"the Holy Ghost . . . invisibly quickens and unifies the Church."[36] For this reason the designation "soul of the Mystical Body" properly applies to the Holy Spirit, and to him alone.

It is true that the Holy Spirit is not received in the Mystical Body after the manner of a substantial form, united to matter as its act. His specific effect, his quickening action remains in the line of efficient causality. Peter Lombard erred by identifying the Holy Spirit with the habitual grace that adorns our souls and abides in them as a permanent form. This would be a

---

[34] The *Pontifical of Ordinations.*
[35] St. Thomas uses the word "connaturaliter" in this connection. Cf. *Summa,* IIa-IIae, q. 45, a. 2.
[36] *Summa,* IIIa, q.8, a. 1 ad 3.

new hypostatic union, even a union according to nature (*unio in natura*), which is absolutely repugnant to the supreme perfection of God. The Spirit of sanctification remains distinct from our personality.

As we have indicated above, the notion of the soul of the Church as applied to the Holy Spirit is primarily analogical. Even from the point of view of this inwardness, of this intimate union of form with matter, however, the Holy Spirit retains a certain resemblance with our soul. He does not act on the members of the Mystical Body after the manner of a cause that is entirely outside of us, in the sense that the sun makes plants grow. On the contrary, he resides within the depths of our souls, he dwells in us like a most gentle Guest,[37] he fills our souls and all our faculties with his life-giving action. This idea is the beautiful dogma of the indwelling of the Blessed Trinity in the souls of the just, an integral part of the doctrine of the Holy Spirit as the soul of the Church.

We know the texts in which St. Paul teaches the Christians of his time the truth concerning the indwelling of the Holy Spirit. "Do you not know," he asks them "that you are the temple of God and that the Spirit of God dwells in you?" (I Cor. 3:16; cf. I Cor. 6:19.) In this passage the Apostle designates not only each particular individual, but also and primarily the Church as a whole as the sanctuary of God. "In [Christ] the whole structure is closely fitted together and grows into a temple holy in the Lord; in him you too are being built together into a dwelling place for God in the Spirit" (Eph. 2:21–22).

We can see already what this intimate and friendly presence of God within us adds to the simple exterior action. To dwell is not merely to be present in a certain place; rather it means to be with someone, to converse with him, to communicate oneself to him through knowledge and love. When God dwells in a soul, he gives himself to it as the object of its possession. St. Thomas says: "We are said to possess only what we can freely use or enjoy."[38] "God is not merely in the soul the way he is present in every creature through his immensity or the way he is in the stone or insect into which he continually infuses being. He is with the soul like a friend who gives himself; he is in it as the principle and the term of its interior and godlike life, as the object of its supernatural knowledge (through faith here on earth and through the beatific vision in heaven) and of its love of charity. In the words of St. Thomas: "God is said to be present as the object known is in the knower and the beloved in the lover."[39]

---

[37] Cf. the verse *Dulcis hospes animae*, in the Sequence of Pentecost.
[38] *Summa*, Ia, q. 43, a. 3
[39] *Loc. cit.*

Nor should we think that the presence of faith and love is a purely objective presence, after the manner in which every object known and loved becomes present to us. "The Holy Ghost is possessed by man and dwells within him, in the very gift itself of sanctifying grace [to which faith and charity are related]."[40] God himself, substantially present in the sanctified soul, offers himself to it to be known and loved. [41]Residing in the most secret center of our being, and as it were at the very root of our faculties, he quickens everything from within and gives life and grace to every activity that does not withdraw from his influence to remain on the purely natural level. He truly becomes the soul of our soul, and the soul of the whole Church.

This is what the dogma of the indwelling adds to the reality of the universal action of the Holy Spirit in the faithful, in order to justify more perfectly his title as the soul of the mystical Christ which traditional doctrine attributes to him.

Abbé Journet writes:

> It is the indwelling of the Blessed Trinity which gives the Church the perfection of her supernatural being and unity. . . . The uncreated Person of the Holy Spirit, because it thus dwells mysteriously in the Church, deserves once more to be called the soul of the Church, but this time in a more excellent manner than before [when the Holy Spirit was considered merely as the efficient cause of ecclesiastical unity]; let us say in a strict manner, but one that is analogical and supereminent.[42]

It is analogical because the intimate presence that the grace of the indwelling of God brings to the Church and to the just souls does not make of this God of love, who is the source of our divine life, the form of our being[43] the way our human soul informs our body. It is supereminent also, inasmuch as supernatural realities incomparably surpass natural realities in excellence and in perfection.

Such is the theological justification and explanation of the name "soul of the Church" or "soul of the Mystical Body of Jesus Christ," which Tradition commonly attributes to the Holy Spirit.

These same theological reasons seem to demand that we reserve for the Holy Spirit alone this attribution and role as soul and life-giving principle,

---

[40] *Loc. cit.*

[41] [41]Cf. on the nature of this divine presence, the article by Rev. Garrigou-Lagrange and Rev. A. Gardeil, "La Structure de l'Âme," *Revue Thomiste*, (November, 1928) Part III.

[42] *La Vie Spirituelle* (September, 1934), 73–74.

[43] We also believe that the term "formal cause of the Church" which the same author attributes to the Holy Spirit should be avoided as leading to confusion. Cf. *loc. cit.*

to the exclusion of every other supernatural reality, and in particular sanctifying grace.

However, still another question remains to be solved: How can the universal influence of the divine Spirit, the soul of the Mystical Body, be reconciled and harmonized with the life-giving action that we have recognized in Christ the Head? If Christ is the efficient cause of all of our supernatural activity, what is left for the Holy Spirit to do? And if the divine Spirit really quickens all the members of the Mystical Body, how can we attribute to Jesus a life-giving role in their regard?

When we look at things correctly, these two influences—far from being mutually exclusive—are reciprocal. Thus, in the human organism, the dominant role of the head over the body does not exclude the part played by the soul, but requires and necessarily presupposes it. For the head owes to the soul the fact that it lives and acts upon the totality of the members.

To make this doctrine even clearer, let us distinguish the two natures in Christ. When the divinity of the Word is in question, then the action of Jesus is one and the same action, one and the same life-giving influence, as that of the Holy Spirit. In the Blessed Trinity, the three Persons have but one operation, just as they have but one nature which is common to the Father, to the Son, and to the Holy Spirit. Whatever the Father does, his Word and his Spirit of Love do in unison with him through a single act. And it is only by appropriation[44] that we attribute to the Holy Spirit the effects of grace produced in the Mystical Body. From this point of view there is no difficulty.

But when we speak of the influence of Christ the Head, usually we refer to the sanctifying action of his Humanity, inasmuch as St. Thomas and St. Augustine have taught that the Word of God became our Head only when he became man. Now the life-giving action of the Humanity of Jesus is subordinate to that of the Holy Spirit, just as the action of an instrument is subordinate to that of the artisan, of the principal agent. When Jesus sanctifies us, it is the Holy Spirit who, through the canal of his sacred Humanity, communicates grace to us. When our sacred Head gives us divine life, he transmits to us the influx of the Spirit of life whom he possesses in plenitude. His sacred wounds, his precious Blood, the mysteries of his

---

[44] In the Trinitarian dogma, appropriation extends from the special attribution to one of the divine Persons of a perfection common to the entire Trinity. This attribution is founded on a resemblance between the perfection thus attributed and a strictly personal property. Thus it is the property of the Father to be the Principle of the Son and, together with the Son, the Principle of the Holy Spirit. By appropriation we likewise attribute to the Father in preference to the other Persons the role of being the creative principle of all beings, although creation is common to the three divine Persons. Likewise, we attribute to the Holy Spirit, who proceeds by way of love, all the works of love and of grace.

divine life, exercise their beneficial influences on our souls, but through the power and under the action of the Word and of the Holy Spirit.[45]

For this reason St. Paul uses, alternatively and almost with the same meaning, two expressions that are common to him: *in Christo Jesu and in Spiritu*. Everything that is done in Christ and under the influence of our divine Head is done also in the Holy Spirit, the soul of the total Christ. As Dom Gréa writes:

> The operations of the Spirit in the Church have no other object than those of the Son; and he does not come, through his mission, as some heretics have claimed,[46] to do a new work that is different from the work of Christ. Christ and the Spirit together accomplish the wonders of the Church's one life. The Spirit pours into the Church the life of Christ himself, and not life other than that of Christ.[47]

His Holiness Pope Pius XII recapitulates this teaching in the following terms which, in confirming the doctrine exposed in this chapter, provide the best possible conclusion to it:

> To this Spirit of Christ, also, as to an invisible principle is to be ascribed the fact that all the parts of the Body are joined one with the other and with their exalted Head; for he is entire in the Head, entire in the Body, and entire in each of the members. To the members he is present and assists them in proportion to their various duties and offices, and the greater or less degree of spiritual health which they enjoy.

It is he who through his heavenly grace is the principle of every supernatural act in all parts of the Body. . . . This presence and activity of the Spirit of Jesus Christ is tersely and vigorously described by Our predecessor of immortal memory Leo XIII in his encyclical letter *Divinum Illud* in these words: "Let it suffice to say that, as Christ is the Head of the Church, so is the Holy Spirit her soul."[48]

---

[45] St. Athanasius speaks of this dependence of Jesus upon the action of the Holy Spirit in one of his discourses against the Arians, at the same time that he is striving to establish the perfect equality and consubstantiality of the Son with the Holy Spirit. "The Lord [Jesus] who gives the Spirit is shown to us as receiving the unction of the Holy Spirit; he did not hesitate, when there was need, to proclaim himself inferior to the Holy Spirit according to his human nature. To the Jews who accused him of driving out demons through Beelzebub, He said: . . . 'I cast out devils by the Spirit of God.' These words must be understood to refer to his Humanity, which did not have, of itself, either the capacity or the power to drive out demons, without the help of the Holy Spirit" (Second Discourse against the Arians).

[46] Montanus, Manes, and others.

[47] *De l'Église et de sa divine constitution*, Book I, Chapter 5.

[48] Encyclical, *Mystici Corporis*, June 29, 1943, Vatican Translation (National Catholic Welfare Conference, Washington, D.C.).

CHAPTER XII

Union in Christ, the Exemplary Cause

When an artist is contemplating the creation of a masterpiece he first fixes in his mind the master idea that will govern the execution of his entire project. If he is a painter, he will first conceive the principal personage who will occupy the central place in his picture and toward whom all the other parts of his work will converge. If he is a composer, a melodic phrase, a musical motif of particular power will emerge in his imagination, capable of giving life to every movement of a great work and of uniting its different parts in perfect harmony.

The greatest masterpiece in the world was the creation of the mystical unity of the total Christ, which the Wisdom of God, the supreme Artist, conceived from all eternity. In this design of love the good God also had a master idea, an Exemplar on which he modeled and formed in advance in his creative thought all the other elements of his work. The divine Exemplar to which all the predestined will be conformed (cf. Rom. 8:29), the image that all the children of God are to reproduce in themselves under pain of being excluded from the divine plan and cut off from the unity of the Mystical Body, is the only-begotten Son made man (cf. Rom. 8:29)—Christ Jesus, the prototype of all holiness for the elect of God.

Since it is a unifying principle of prime importance in its own order (the order of intention), the exemplary cause will therefore also project its light on the mystery of the unity of Christ. To show its nature and role in the constitution of the Mystical Body, we shall distinguish two aspects in the divine Exemplar which is Christ the Head. Jesus, the Word Incarnate, is the model of the members of his Mystical Body, both as God and as man. As God, he is the Son to whom we are configured by the grace of our adopted sonship. As man, he is the Holy One par excellence, whose life and virtues must be reproduced in various ways in each of our human lives.

Christ our Exemplar in His Divine Nature

The Apostle tells us that God has predestined us to be conformed to the image of his Son. He explains this conformity, this exemplarity by adding, "that he should be the first-born among many brethren" (Rom. 8:29). It is as the only-begotten Son of the Father that Christ our beloved Head is primarily our model. His divine Sonship is the archetype of our situation as children of God, and it is to this unique Sonship that our baptismal grace, our grace of incorporation into Christ, configures us.

Through the divine entity, the supernatural reality created in us by baptism and now called sanctifying grace by us, we are truly born of God (cf. John 1:13), as St. John says. We are born of God, not as equals but after the likeness of the only-begotten Son. St. Peter spoke of this grace as a partaking of the divine nature (cf. 2 Peter 1:4), and the Beloved Disciple called it "the seed of God" (cf. 1 John 3:9). Participants of the divine nature, capable thereby of godlike operations, we are in very truth adopted sons of the Father, images or living copies of the one who is the Son by nature, Christ.

In order to better understand this splendid configuration to the Son of God through the grace of our baptism, we shall take up again and analyze the definition that the Prince of the apostles gives of it when he calls it a participation in the divine nature.

Nature, according to philosophy, is the essence of a thing considered as the intrinsic principle of operations. Divine nature, therefore, is the Godhead considered as the principle of the operations attributable to God alone: operations of knowledge and operations of volition or of love. Through his divine knowledge God knows himself perfectly and sees, in an immediate and beatific vision, the infinite perfection of his Godhead. Through his divine volition and love, God loves his infinite goodness and his ineffable beauty with a supreme love. It is an admirable life, hidden in the depths of the Trinity, and toward which no creature would ever have dared to raise a scrutinizing glance.

Sanctifying grace, the divine seed deposited in our souls, renders us capable in a certain measure of this divine life and of these Godlike operations. Through it, in fact, we are destined to see God as he sees himself and to love him as he loves himself. "For," St. John tells us, "we shall see him just as he is" (1 John 3:2). We shall see him eternally "face to face" (1 Cor. 13:12). And our love, proportioned to this eminent and divine knowledge, will resemble the knowledge of God himself. Even here on earth we bear in our souls, through grace, the seed of divine life.

To say it is a seed is not enough. For godlike life is not delayed until the day of our entrance into glory. Even here on earth we begin to live it; the Angelic Doctor tells us this with a boldness of expression that is all the more remarkable in view of his rigorous theological precision. On several occasions he has said that grace is the beginning of glory in us: "For grace is nothing else than a beginning of glory in us."[1] Glory will merely bring the life of grace to its normal consummation. But even the beginning of glory makes us understand better even now the nature and the excellence of sanctifying grace, by showing us all that the divine seed holds in the way of supernatural riches and virtualities.

Father Garrigou-Lagrange says:

> If we wish to understand the nature of the seed contained in the acorn, we must consider this nature in its perfect state in the fully developed oak. In the same way, if we wish to know the life of grace, we must contemplate it in its supreme development; in glory which is its consummation. Fundamentally the life of grace and the life of glory are the same supernatural life, the same charity, with two differences. Here on earth God is known only in the obscurity of faith, not in the clarity of vision. In addition, we hope to possess God in an inadmissible manner; but as long as we are on earth we can lose him through our own fault. In spite of these two differences, it is the same life.[2]

Faith itself, despite its darkness, faith which flows in a direct line from grace just as the branch springs from the trunk, is already an anticipation of and a priming for the beatific vision, as the Angelic Doctor assures us. Thus we see that the gift of faith is essentially supernatural, and requires an infused light. For our natural activity can never raise itself up to the point of grasping the object of faith as it is in itself but only as we can express it in our human language.

St. Thomas writes:

> Eternal life consists in the full knowledge of God, according to the doctrine of Christ in St. John: "Eternal life is to know thee [Father], the one true God, and him whom thou has sent, Jesus Christ." This supernatural knowledge, therefore, must have a beginning within us, and this comes about through faith, which holds as certain and believes through an infused light things that surpass our natural knowledge.[3]

---

[1] *Summa*, IIa-IIe, q. 24, a. 3 ad 2.

[2] *Christian Perfection and Contemplation* (St. Louis: B. Herder Book Co., 1937), 121.

[3] *De Verit.*, q. 14, a. 2.

Grace, together with the theological virtues that proceed from it, makes us really like to God (cf. 1 John 3:2) and participants of the divine nature. To have this God-likeness, this participation of the divine nature, is therefore to be truly the children of him who communicates it to us. Consequently our sonship is not simply a name but a divine reality, as St. John affirms in his first epistle: "Behold what manner of love the Father has bestowed upon us, that we should be called children of God" (1 John 3:1).

Our divine sonship, however, is purely adoptive. Jesus alone is the Son of the Father by nature; it is he who communicates to us this quality of children of God by taking us as his brothers. Jesus is the image of the Father and the brightness of his glory (cf. Heb. 1:3). We who are adopted sons must be, as it were, the complements of Jesus in the substantial glory that he renders to his Father. That is our whole vocation, our predestination, as St. Paul has told us: "For those whom he has foreknown he has also predestined to become conformed to the image of his Son, that he should be the first-born among many brethren" (Rom. 8:29).

This admirable and divine solidarity makes us enter into communion with the rights and the condition of the only-begotten Son of the Father, our divine Exemplar and our older brother.

This sublime dignity, the incomparable beauty of sanctifying grace, draws down upon us the love of the heavenly Father, and makes us worthy of the same love with which the Father loves his only-begotten Son. The God of mercy sometimes reveals this to a few of his privileged children. To one of his faithful souls, he said one day:

> When I call thee my dear and most beloved spouse, with so many titles and honors, with pure embraces and kisses so full of sweetness, when I clothe thee with incomparable beauty, I do all these things to my Christ in thy soul. When I say to thee: My friend, most pure spouse, the only and beautiful one of my heart, I am really saying these things to thee, but I say them first of all to him who is the life of thy being and through whom thy soul is my spouse. It is through union with him that every soul is my one, my beautiful, and my dear spouse.[4]

Sanctifying grace gives the soul this supernatural beauty, this conformity with the beloved Son of the Father, and wins for it the ineffable tenderness that the most loving Father shows to his adopted children. Grace enables

---

[4] Words addressed to the Venerable Marie-Céleste, Foundress of the Redemptoristines. Cf. Fabre, *La Ven. Marie-Céleste Crostarosa*, 73.

the soul to cry out with fiery fervor and with divine enthusiasm when speaking to the Word made flesh: "O my adored ideal! O life of my life, O divine form of my being, O my eternal name, O my perfection, O my glory, O my Jesus!"[5]

The form of my being! Sanctifying grace which comes to us from Christ does indeed unite all the members of the Mystical Body in a common form. We must note once again, however, that there does not exist in all the souls of the faithful taken together a single grace that is numerically one and bears the same relationship to the mystical Christ that the soul does to the body. The sanctifying grace of the various members is one in a certain respect only by its conformity to a unique Exemplar, only by its vital dependence upon a single source, Christ the Head and the Holy Spirit who acts through his Humanity.

It is with these refinements and clarifications that we can speak of the unity of the Mystical Body through sanctifying grace as a formal cause. Grace is an accidental cause at the most, added to our substantial being to deify it and make it capable of Godlike operations.

There is another supernatural reality which, together with sanctifying grace, prepares the way for the unity of the Mystical Body, and contributes to configuring our souls to that of the Word Incarnate: the sacramental character. We have written about it at greater length elsewhere when we spoke on the subject of the priesthood, whose formal principle is character.[6] But we must at least mention it here, to point out the role that it plays in the constitution of the Mystical Body.

When we spoke of the sacrament of regeneration, we remarked that the baptismal character configures us to the priesthood of Christ. The same holds true of the character of confirmation, and how much more of the character that the sacrament of holy orders impresses upon the souls of Christ's ministers. The specific effect of sacramental character is to impress upon the Christian the likeness of Christ the Priest, by deputing and qualifying him for the exercise of divine worship, in union with Christ his Head.

Grace likewise configures us to Christ, as we have just seen, but in a different manner. Following St. Thomas, Canon Cuttaz writes: "Character configures, assimilates the Christian to Christ not by a likeness of nature—as

[5] Bishop Gay, *Elevations*, Volume II, Elevation 121.
[6] Cf Mura, E., *Le Corps Mystique du Christ*, Volume II, Chapter 20.

does sanctifying grace—but through a likeness of function, of deputation, of power, inasmuch as it is a participation in the priesthood of Christ."[7]

Likeness of nature and likeness of function—these terms correctly distinguish and exactly define each of the two configurations to Christ. Sanctifying grace makes us resemble Christ in his divine nature, of which grace is an ineffable participation. Sacramental character, by making us share in a certain measure the priestly power of Christ, configures us to the mystery of the hypostatic union of Jesus, which constitutes him Priest and Mediator.

Indeed, in the mystery of the Incarnation, the Word of God, by uniting himself to human nature in the unity of his Person, sanctified and consecrated this most sacred Humanity by the unction of the Godhead, for the perfect worship of the infinite Majesty of God. As Father Héris says:

> Just as the hypostatic union consecrated Christ and deputed him to the most perfect form of worship possible, so does the character consecrate a man and enable him to take part in this same perfect worship of Jesus. The character is as it were a derivation from the substantial consecration of the hypostatic union. Man's acts of worship are of value only insofar as they reproduce those of Christ. It is in view of giving them this value that the character confers a consecration on man that is derived from and linked up with our Savior's substantial consecration.[8]

This is the explanation of St. Thomas' words: "*Christi sacerdotio configurantur fideles secundum sacramentales characteres*"—"The faithful are likened to the priesthood of Christ by reason of the sacramental characters."[9] Here another resemblance between the members of the Mystical Body and their Head is brought to light, a resemblance that conforms the faithful to their divine Exemplar and unites them, as in a common form, in a proportional participation of the dignity and functions of Christ the Priest.

We say this participation is proportional, for while sanctifying grace is the same in all the faithful—although it grows in different degrees—sacramental character establishes a whole hierarchy among the members of the Church. For the power conferred by baptism is one thing, that conferred by confirmation is another, and still higher is the power of holy orders with its various degrees, as we have shown elsewhere.[10] Thus, at the same time that

---

[7] *Les Effets du baptême*, Chapter 1.
[8] *The Mystery of Christ*. (Westminster, Md.: The Newman Press, 1950), 156.
[9] *Summa*, IIIa, q. 63, a. 3.
[10] Cf. Mura, *Le Corps Mystique du Christ*, Volume II, Chapter 20.

character unites us in Christ, it establishes among us those differences that are necessary for the diversity of the members within a single organism.

Christ our Model in His Human Nature

Although Christ is our Exemplar according to his divinity by reason of his condition as the only-begotten Son of the Father, he is also our Exemplar in his most sacred Humanity. For this reason the Word came from heaven to earth, so that he might be the visible and palpable model of the virtues we must reproduce in ourselves and of the various states through which we must pass.

Our virtues, our holiness, must be strictly Christian holiness and Christian virtues, the holiness and the virtues of Christ within us. God could have disposed things differently. The perfection that Adam possessed in his state of innocence was not in fact a Christian perfection, because it was not yet related to Christ as the principle and Exemplar of holiness. But from the instant of original sin, there was no longer any virtue that was not Christian in a certain way. St. Paul showed that Moses was happy to share in the reproach of Christ (cf. Heb. 11:26). After Jesus appeared on earth, he became in a much more striking way the one Exemplar and the exclusive criterion of all perfection.

The reproduction of the divine model, even in his Humanity, is presented to us under two different forms, for the Christian must resemble Christ in his exterior mysteries, and he must also resemble him in his virtues and interior dispositions.

First, the Christian life is a reproduction of the exterior mysteries and of the acts of Jesus Christ. As Monsieur Olier writes:

> We are all obliged to be conformable to Jesus Christ. St. Paul teaches us this when he says that God has predestined us to be conformable to the image of his Son. Now this conformity consists first of all in resembling him in his exterior mysteries, which have been, as it were, sacraments of the interior mysteries that he was to work in the souls of men. Thus, just as our Lord was crucified outwardly, we must be crucified inwardly. Just as he died outwardly, we must die inwardly. Just as he was buried outwardly, we must be buried inwardly. And this interior life, expressed by exterior mysteries and by the graces acquired by these same mysteries, must exist in all men, since they were merited for all."[11]

---

[11] *Introduction à la vie chrétienne*, Chapter 2.

The living expression of the mysteries of Jesus in the Christian soul belongs so intimately to the essence of Christianity that it is, as it were, the very core of all the sacraments. Indeed, these sacred rites are but a symbolic and divinely efficacious reproduction of the life, death, and resurrection of Jesus, as we have shown elsewhere in discussing baptism.[12]

But there is another reproduction of the life of Christ, a natural consequence of the preceding one. This is the imitation of his virtues, according to the words he addressed to his disciples: "Learn from me, for I am meek and humble of heart" (Matt. 11:29).

Monsieur Olier also says:

> The second conformity we must have with Jesus Christ is with his interior attitudes in his mysteries, so that our souls may be made conformable in their sentiments and inward dispositions not only with the externals of the mysteries, as we have seen, but also with the interior dispositions and sentiments that our Lord had in these same mysteries.
>
> Christian life consists specifically in this, that the Christian live inwardly by the operation of the Spirit, the way Jesus Christ lived. Otherwise, there is no perfect unity or conformity. And to this we are called by our Lord, since he wants us to live, through the operation of the Holy Spirit, a life of union with him that is as truly one as that which the Father and the Son live within themselves.[13]

It follows that this imitation of Jesus Christ is a principle of unity, and hence gives to all Christians a common spiritual physiognomy, a family resemblance that points to them as belonging to Christ. It had to be so, for we cannot conceive of an organism composed of heterogeneous parts, nor can we engraft a branch on any but a tree of the same species unless we are to produce a monstrous and sterile composite. How much truer is it, therefore, that eternal Wisdom could not realize the masterpiece of the mystical Christ by an ill-assorted assemblage of dissimilar parts.

God the Father wants all of us to attain to a supernatural perfection of the same kind, since he has called all of us to constitute a single divine organism. In the formation of this Mystical Body, however, he first established the Head, the consummate model of all virtue and holiness, and it is after his example that all must be formed who want to be united to him as his members.

---

[12] Cf. Mura, *Le Corps Mystique du Christ*, Volume II, Chapter 12.
[13] *Introduction à la vie chrétienne*, Chapter 3. Cf. John 17:22.

The saints, those eminent members of the Mystical Body, have understood and realized within themselves this principle of Christian life and this norm of holiness: whence the fervent study of the Gospel; whence the cult to "the interior of Jesus Christ," which was particularly dear to our great spiritual leaders of the seventeenth century. St. Vincent de Paul, the greatest glory of this school of holiness, sees everything through the life and the examples of our Lord. Speaking of the vocation to the apostolic life, he expresses himself in this way:

> Are we not blessed to express the vocation of Jesus Christ to the ignorant? O how blessed are those who give themselves to God in the right way, to do what Jesus Christ did, and to practice after his example the virtues that he practiced: poverty, humility, patience, real for the glory of God and the salvation of souls! For thus they become the disciples of such a Master: they live purely by his spirit, and pour forth, together with the perfume of his life, the merit of his actions for the sanctification of souls.[14]

According to St. Vincent de Paul, everything in the Christian life must bear the imprint of the actions of Christ, everything must be marked with the stamp of his virtues. He counsels: "Let us honor the divine Master in the moderation of his behavior." When he wants to restore calm in a troubled soul, he says: "For God's sake, let your heart honor the tranquility of our Lord's." When he sends one of his followers upon an errand of charity, he gives him this rule of conduct: "When, therefore, you go and visit a sick person, it must be in union with and to honor a like action that our Lord performed upon earth." When he recommends the practice of silence to his sons, it is again in the same spirit: "The priests of the mission who are in the army . . . shall honor the silence of our Lord at the regular hours." Whatever task presents itself, he wants it to be acquitted in imitation of Jesus: "We must remember him in order to honor the state of his divine interior in these encounters."[15]

Nothing can give us a clearer idea of the imitation of Christ as the example lived by a saint.

Indeed there is great variety in the reproduction of the life of Christ in his members. One man may be drawn more to the mystery of his childhood, another will be more eager to reproduce his hidden life in Nazareth. One will prefer to follow the Savior in his apostolic journeys, preaching the

---

[14] Quoted in Maynard, *Vertus et doctrine spirituelle de saint Vincent de Paul,* Chapter 9, par. 11.

[15] Citations from H. Brémond, *Hist. litter. du sentiment religieux en France,* III, 253–54.

Gospel to the poor, calling sinners to himself, forgiving Magdalene and the adulterous woman. Another will devote himself to the meditation of the fathomless depths of his passion, in order to take part in his agony at Gethsemani and to drink with him the chalice of his humiliations and sufferings. Attention to a particular mystery of the life of Jesus, moreover, does not prevent us from gleaning the essentials in the other mysteries, just as the more assiduous practice of a specific virtue is no obstacle to the exercise of all the other virtues as the occasion arises.

The diversity in the manner the members of Christ imitate their common Exemplar adds to the beauty and harmony of the Mystical Body. Since the plenitude of perfection in the Person of our divine Savior cannot be reproduced in its entirety in each of his members, it flows into the totality of his Body and thus strengthens the unity of order that belongs strictly to the divine organism of the whole Christ.

Bishop Gay has expressed this entire doctrine concerning Christ in a magnificent Elevation on "Jesus, our divine ideal":

> This Word Incarnate is at once an idea and a will of God; he is what from all eternity God thinks and wants of us.... This voluntary thought of our Creator and Master is the law of our life. It is, first of all, what is common between God and us, the terrain of our mutual meeting, the place of his deifying operations and of our heavenly formation. Outside of that nothing is true for us, nothing is really useful, nothing is practical....
>
> This voluntary thought is manifested to us under many forms.... How adorable is this will! How salutary, beneficent, and beloved! It is living in this will, being molded by it, transformed into it, identified with it, that makes of us the Jesus that God wants us to be, and consequently a mode of the Word Incarnate. It is something divine that is made man; it is something invisible that appears ... an idea of God expressing itself outside of himself.[16]

This idea of God expressing himself *ad extra*, in the plenitude of the Christ that we are through grace, is precisely the exemplary idea of the Mystical Body, conceived in the image of Christ the Head. At the same time it is the ideal principle of its own unity.

---

[16] *Elevations*, Volume II, Elevation 121.

CHAPTER XIII

Moral Union in Faith and Charity

Moral union in Christ Jesus, a union of minds in faith and a union of hearts in divine charity—this is the last link that strengthens and perfects the mystical unity of all the members of Christ.

Predestined from all eternity in Christ the Son of God, conquered by his redemptive passion, gathered together in a single body by baptism and the Eucharist, quickened unceasingly by the influx of their divine Head and by his Spirit, and finally modeled after his likeness by the grace of adopted sonship, all the members of the mystical Christ must unite and fuse their intellects and wills in an identity of views and of sentiments. This is the urgent recommendation of St. Paul to the Philippians: "If, therefore, there is ... any fellowship in the Spirit [of Christ] ... fill up my joy by thinking alike, having the same charity, with one soul and one mind" (Phil. 2:1–2).

St. Thomas, commenting on St. Paul's words "one body and one Spirit" (Eph. 4:4), writes: "That is to say, you must have a fellowship of spirit, *unum spiritualem consensum*, through unity of faith and charity."[1]

Faith and charity are the essential principles of the supernatural harmony of souls in Christ, to which all the other virtues, both theological and moral, also contribute. The Apostle comes back again and again to the two dispositions necessary to maintain and strengthen the close union of minds and hearts in Christ. Let us follow him in clarifying the role of both faith and charity in the work of unification. We can deal with this subject rather briefly, for it offers no great difficulty with regard to the point of view which now concerns us.

---

[1] *In Eph. II*, lect. 1.

The Union of Minds through Faith

If there is any essential and constitutive mark of ecclesiastical unity, if there is an exterior and visible sign of belonging to the one Spouse of Christ, it is certainly the profession of a single faith, the proclamation of the same Creed. Revealed truth is as one and undivided as its Author, who is subsistent and immutable truth: *one Lord, one faith* (cf. Eph. 4:5).[2]

The reason for this is obvious. The divine life which Christ allows the members of his Mystical Body to share adapts itself to the needs of their human nature. It respects the order established by God among the faculties of man. Now, the first of these faculties is the intellect. The intellect governs all of human activity; it proposes to the will the object of its volition; it rules and moderates the exterior and interior senses; it determines the rule of action for the passions. Likewise, in the supernatural order, the activity of the members of Christ must be directed, unified, and coordinated by the light of faith: divine light shining in the human intellect.

Faith consummates the union of minds in their adherence to the same divine truths. To this end, it demands the submission of all intellects to the common magisterium of the Church. Indeed, God has not willed that the faithful should adhere inwardly to the same dogmas solely in the light of the Holy Spirit. This purely spiritual unity of the Mystical Body in the same faith would not have been sufficiently manifest, nor sufficiently conformed to the needs of human nature. On the contrary, he willed the union of all men in faith, founded on the teaching of a visible magisterium. Because of this St. Paul wrote to the Ephesians:

> [God] gave some men as apostles, and some as prophets, others again as evangelists, and others as pastors and teachers . . . *for building up the body of Christ, until we all attain to the unity of the faith* and of the deep knowledge of the Son of God . . . that we may be now no longer children, tossed to and fro and carried about by every wind of doctrine devised in the wickedness of men, in craftiness, according to the wiles of error. Rather are we to practice the truth in love, and so grow up in all things in him who is the head, Christ" (Eph. 4:11–15).

Divine faith in Christ the Redeemer not only consummates the unity of the Mystical Body in the present moment, but also unites the faithful of the

---

[2] We are not concerned here with everything that concerns the exercise of faith and charity. We need note only how these two virtues of faith and charity contribute to the constitution of the supernatural unity of the total Christ.

Old and New Covenants in Jesus our Head. In the beautiful eleventh chapter of his Epistle to the Hebrews, which deserves to be cited and commented upon in its entirety, St. Paul praises in magnificent terms the faith of the Patriarchs in the Messias to come. Here the events of the Old Testament appear to us as transfigured by this divine illumination that projects upon them the light of the future Redeemer, and as transposed by faith to the higher realm of supernatural realities. Here we see *the mystery of Christ* already filling up all the centuries that precede the Savior's coming. Even the Patriarchs, whose history the Apostle repeats to us, have been saved only by a spiritual incorporation into the total Christ, whose "going forth is from the beginning" (Mic. 5:2). All of them died in the faith, without having received the effect of the promises (concerning the Messias), but "beholding them afar off" (Heb. 11:13).

Note especially the beauty of verse 26, which shows us the Lawgiver of Israel already sharing the sufferings of Christ with the chosen people: "By faith Moses, when he was grown up, denied that he was a son of Pharaoh's daughter; choosing rather to be afflicted with the people of God than to have the enjoyment of sin for a time, esteeming the reproach of Christ greater riches than the treasures of the Egyptians" (Heb. 11:24–26).

Union with Christ through sufferings and persecutions— this is what the faith of the chosen people in the Head accomplished even then. This is what it realizes for all the saints of the Old Law, whom St. Paul enumerates in triumphal fashion in the following way:

> And what more shall I say? For time will fail me if I tell of Gideon, of Barac, of Samson, of Jephthe, of David and of Samuel and the prophets, who by faith conquered kingdoms, wrought justice, obtained promises, stopped the mouths of lions, quenched the violence of fire, escaped the edge of the sword, recovered strength from weakness, became valiant in battle, put to flight armies of aliens.

Women had their dead restored to them by resurrection. Others were tortured, refusing to accept release, that they might find a better resurrection. Others had experience of mockery and stripes, yes, even of chains and prisons. They were stoned, they were sawed asunder, they were tempted, they were put to death by the sword. They went about in sheepskins and goatskins, destitute, distressed, afflicted of whom the world was not worthy—wandering in deserts, mountains, caves, and holes in the earth.

And all these, though they had been approved by the testimony of faith, did not receive what was promised, for God had something better in view for us; so that they should not be perfected [and receive the grace of the Redemption] without us" (Heb. 11:32–40).

Thus divine faith establishes a bond of solidarity among us who have known Jesus Christ in his coming, and the faithful of the Old Law, who knew him in figures and promises. Today, as in days past, it is this faith that makes us cleave to Christ, share his reproach and live by his life: "*one body and one Spirit . . . one faith*" (Eph. 4:4–5).

But the union of minds in the truth prepares and evokes the union of hearts in charity. Faith blossoms forth in love! And the Apostle himself tells us that faith acts through charity: "*fides quae per charitatem operatur*" (Gal. 5:6).

The Union of Wills through Charity

"Charity unites not only one person to another with the bond of spiritual love, but also the whole Church in unity of spirit."[3] This maxim set forth by the Angelic Doctor truly describes the role of divine charity in the constitution of ecclesiastical unity, and the nature of the moral and spiritual bond that it establishes among the members of the Mystical Body. A union of spiritual affection, a bond of love, that ennobles and as it were penetrates with a sweet unction the juridical and social relations existing among the members of the Church.

But is this charity that we discover at the heart of the mystical unity of the total Christ absolutely essential to maintain unity? It might seem that it is not. Supremely useful in assuring the strong cohesion of the members of the Church, in strengthening it, and thus adding an accidental perfection to it, it might seem at first sight that charity could disappear without compromising the unity of the Church. Indeed, we know that many of her members live in the state of sin, and yet are not cut off from the Body of the Church. Sin can banish charity from the soul without breaking the bond that binds it to the communion of the Church. Only schism and heresy bring about a rupture. This would seem to be a manifest proof that charity, useful and valuable as it may be, is not necessary to make the Church one and organically undivided.

---

[3] *Summa*, IIa-IIae, q. 39, a. 1

Several theologians, among them Bañez, have allowed themselves to be led into error by this specious argument, and have affirmed that charity brings only "an accidental perfection to the essential unity of the Church."[4] St. Thomas, however, sees so clearly the role of charity as the proximate principle of the unity of the Church that, to his mind, the sin of schism is a sin against charity.[5] He accepts as equivalent and synonymous the two expressions: "ecclesiastical unity" and "ecclesiastical charity."[6]

How can we reconcile this doctrine with the fact that a member of Christ can be deprived of charity? First we must note that the Church as a whole,[7] the Mystical Body in its noblest part, is always quickened by the Holy Spirit and by charity. This charity of the Body of the Church extends its influence to all her members, although in a different way to some than to others.

To those who are in the state of grace, charity communicates itself in a formal manner, inspiring in them a love of friendship for God and for their neighbor. To the others, it makes its influence felt at least through a few of its effects, and notably through the unifying power that preserves them in ecclesiastical unity. This is the substance of the solution suggested by Cajetan in his *Commentary on the Summa*.[8]

But how is union with the other faithful possible when charity, the principle of this union, is absent from a soul? How can the sinner, who no longer loves God nor his neighbor out of a motive of charity, remain united to his brothers precisely through the influence of charity? True, St. Thomas observes that ecclesiastical unity relates to the secondary object of charity which is neighbor, and not to the primary object of charity which is God.[9] But is not supernatural love of neighbor founded upon love of God?

To our way of thinking, the answer to this difficulty is to be found in a proportional application of the doctrine invoked for the question of attrition, which recognizes a genuine supernatural love of God and of neighbor that is inferior in degree to charity.[10] This is the love of benevolence that wills the good of the person loved, and not a simple love of concupiscence

---

[4] Ibid., q. 1, a. 10 ad 2. Cited from the article by Abbé Journet in the *Revue Thomiste* (November, 1934), 271–72.

[5] Cf. Ibid., q. 39, a. 1.

[6] Cf. Ibid., a. 1 ad 3; a. 2 ad 2 and ad 3.

[7] This does not mean in the majority of her members.

[8] Cf. *In IIa-IIae*, q. 39, a. 1. Cf. also Journet, the article in Revue Thomiste, cited above.

[9] Cf. *Summa*, IIa-IIae, q. 39, a. 2 ad 3.

[10] Cf. for example, Billuart, *De Sacr. Poenit.*, Dissert. IV, q. 7; also Pèrinelle, *De l'attrition d'après le Concile de Trente*.

which seeks its own good in the object loved. Moreover, it is a love that can remain in the sinner deprived of charity.

Now this love, of an inferior order even though it is good and supernatural, can maintain the essential union with the other members of the Mystical body in those who no longer possess the grace of charity. It makes them will the good of Catholic unity, the supernatural unity begun in baptism, founded on the same faith, and strengthened by the hope of the same goods. True, the love of benevolence cannot rise to the formal motive of charity, which is a love of friendship founded on the actual (at least initial) communication of the Good that is God himself. Nevertheless, love of benevolence remains, in a certain respect, under the influence of the charity that quickens the living members of the Church. It is inspired by a motive related to that of the love of supernatural friendship, and it can and must serve, in the designs of God, to restore to the sinner's soul the same charity that sin has driven out.

This explains the doctrine of St. Thomas who sees in ecclesiastical unity an effect of charity, an unformed effect, as Cajetan says, in those who no longer possess grace; a formed (FORMA) effect informed by charity in those who are in God's friendship.

Divine charity, the wellspring of spiritual unity, exercises its action and wields its unitive power in two ways: it joins all the faithful to Christ the Head through the bonds of love; and, as a consequence, it unites the faithful among themselves in Christ. Let us briefly illustrate each of these two points of view.

THE UNION OF THE FAITHFUL WITH CHRIST THEIR HEAD

Who can measure the incessant reciprocal interchange of love between Jesus and his faithful, and between the faithful and their lovable Savior? Jesus loves those who belong to him infinitely more than we can say. Have we not seen him shedding his Blood for his friends in the mystery of his passion, at a time when they were still far removed from him? (Cf. Rom. 5:6 ff.) And has he not given us the assurance that the most excellent proof of love is to give one's life for those one loves (cf. John 15:13)? Jesus gave his life with divine profusion; he poured it out through all the wounds of his sacred Body. Furthermore, so that there might be no mistake as to the principle which dictated this extraordinary prodigality, he chose to show us the source of his sublime devotion by allowing the soldier's lance to pierce his divine heart.

Jesus concentrates his generous love for each of the souls redeemed by his precious Blood and pours it out in a single deluge upon the whole Church, whom he calls his Spouse, his Immaculate One. For her he immolated himself out of love, according to the beautiful words of the Apostle: "Christ . . . loved the Church, and delivered himself up for her, that he might sanctify her that she might be holy and without blemish" (Eph. 5:25–27).

"Tradidit semetipsum pro ea"—"He delivered himself up for her!" Such is the mystery of love, the mystery of union between Jesus and redeemed humanity, the mystical covenant of God with men, prepared and won on Calvary, consummated at baptismal fonts (cf. Eph. 5:26), and destined to be consummated some day in the beatific love of our eternal homeland (cf. Apoc. 19:7).

This is the love of Jesus for his own, a love beyond measure, pushed to the utmost limit, even to sacred folly; for how can reason explain such liberality and such self-sacrifice?

The hearts of the faithful, of the lovers of Jesus, answer love with love. Only love explains the fidelity of Jesus' disciples in observing the law of righteousness, which were contrary to nature and to the enticements of the corrupt world. Only love explains the sacrifices, insane in the eyes of the world, of so many generous souls who leave their family, their native land, and their temporal future, in order to serve the divine Redeemer. Only love explains the heroic courage of the martyrs who, even in our own day, are shedding their blood for Christ the King in China, in Africa, and in Communist-dominated lands.

Who can describe the mystical embraces that charity kindles in seraphic souls, unknown to men, in the secret of the cloister or in the solitude of a humble home, sometimes even amid the noise of a heedless world or the pomp of a royal palace?

If the love of creatures is strong enough to make lovers live for one another, and so to speak, one in the other, each making his own the interests of the beloved and finding his happiness in procuring the good of the other, how much more does divine love bring about this mysterious fusion? Mystical terminology, following the inspired Canticle, has even adopted a term of striking realism, the melting of the soul, to express the reciprocal transfusion that love brings about. Spiritual lovers flow, in a certain respect, into the bosom of God.[11] The holy Curé of Ars, whose earthy style was full of images, used the language of the mystics—perhaps without knowing it—when he said that the saints had "*liquid hearts*," through the effect of divine charity.

We have to read through the pages of Christian hagiography to know to what point divine love makes a human heart beat in unison with the heart of Jesus. St. Teresa of Avila, from her earliest years, lived only for her beloved Savior, and under the impulsion of her love she slipped out of her father's house with her young brother, to go and preach to the Moors and win the palm of martyrdom. St. Francis of Assisi, through the virtue of his seraphic love, was transformed into the image of the divine Crucified. St. Joseph of Cupertino, St. Catherine of Siena, St. Magdalene of Pazzi, and many others lived in a continual ecstasy of love, passionately zealous for the glory and the kingdom of their beloved Savior.

Jesus himself has given us many examples of the mystical exchange of his heart for the hearts of his lovers, and in so doing has shown us the intimacy or identity of the life that charity establishes between him and those who belong to him.

As if the veils of faith did not exist, Christ and his Spouse exchange expressions of the most unitive love, which the consummation of glory will merely bring to its ultimate perfection.

This is the thought expressed by St. Augustine when he says:

> The whole Church, composed of all the faithful inasmuch as all are members of Christ, has her Head in heaven, whence he governs his Body. Although he is separated from it so far as vision is concerned, he is nonetheless united to it by charity.[12]

The life of love must be the life of all the faithful. A Christian without love is a dead branch, still attached to the tree that grew it but having lost its vital union with the trunk, and therefore no longer producing leaves, flowers, or fruit.

Thus Jesus, in the parable of the vine, counsels his disciples to abide in his love: "He who abides in me, and I in him, he bears much fruit. . . . Abide in my love" (John 15:5, 9).

Our faith now sees charity as a vital link, the principle of supernatural fruitfulness for the members of Christ united to their Head. In this way,

---

[11] Cf. *Summa*, Ia-IIa, q. 28. a. 5.

[12] *Enarr. in psalmos*, Ps. 56.1 *PL* 26:662.

from the point of view of love, of the moral union that charity creates between the Christian and Jesus, each one can already say, after St. Paul: "*To me to live is Christ*" (Phil. 1:21).

THE UNION OF THE FAITHFUL AMONG THEMSELVES

United to his divine Head through love, the Christian is likewise united to all the members of Christ. Fraternal charity harmonizes his life with those of the other faithful. Divine love governs the pulsations of the Mystical Body, and assures all baptized Christians of the community of sentiment, the unity of supernatural views of which the Apostle speaks to the Philippians: "*Thinking alike, having the same charity, with one soul and one mind*" (Phil. 2:2).

Does not the common interest of the community draw its citizens together? In the City of God, this common interest consists in the participation of all in the riches of God himself. That, according to St. Thomas, is the formal reason of charity.[13]

In civil society, whose immediate end consists in peace and temporal prosperity, the juridical bond ranks above the moral bond. Mutual love, whose necessity and importance must not be minimized, holds a somewhat secondary place. In the Church, on the contrary, the society of souls is ordered more to interior perfection than to purely external goods and benefits. In the Church, the Mystical Body of Christ and the assembly of the saints, the bond of love takes on a particular significance and constitutes among her members a power of cohesion and a unitive principle of the first order.

This bond of charity, however, is not merely interior and hidden. It tends to reveal itself to the eyes of men through expressions of Christian benevolence and mercy. Love then becomes the manifest and sensible sign of the supernatural bond that unites the faithful among themselves. For the Church, while visible in her social unity, is nevertheless a spiritual society, and in that respect escapes perception by the senses. Charity gives the world the means of recognizing the intimate and profound unity that binds the members of Christ together. Charity gives the Church the added aspect of visibility lacking to her by reason of her spiritual and interior character. This is what our Lord meant when he prayed to his Father for his disciples: "That all may be one, even as thou, Father, in me and I in thee; that they also may be one in us, that the world may believe that thou hast sent me"

---

[13] Cf. *Summa*, IIa-IIae, q. 25, a. 1.

(John 17:21); "By this will all men know that you are my disciples, if you have love for one another" (John 13:35).

In the supernatural order, to love our neighbor is also to love Christ. Jesus has designed to unite himself through his grace to each of our brothers. He lives in them just as he lives in our souls. And whatever we do to the least of those who belong to him, he considers as being done to himself. This is what gives fraternal charity such efficacy in consummating the union of all the faithful in Christ, in making us aware of the vital unity of all the members of Christ. To fail in this essential obligation is to sin against the unity of the Mystical Body and to belie our incorporation. If only all of us understood this sublime obligation of divine charity toward our brothers!

Dom Marmion writes:

> There are souls that seek God in Jesus Christ . . . but stop there. That is not sufficient: we must accept the Incarnation with all the consequences it involves: we must not let the gift of ourselves stop at Christ's own humanity but extend it to his Mystical Body. That is why—never forget this, for it is one of the most important points of the supernatural life—to abandon the least of our brethren is to abandon Christ himself; to succour one of them is to succour Christ in person. If anyone strikes one of your members, your eye or your arm, it is yourself they strike; in the same way, to touch one of the members of the Body of Christ is to touch Christ himself. . . . Now, in this, the supernatural reality that faith discovers to us is that Christ, in becoming incarnate, has mystically united himself to all humanity; not to accept and not to love all those who belong or who could belong to Christ by grace, is not to accept and not to love Christ himself.[14]

Love of Jesus and love of our neighbor in Jesus are substantially the same thing. This twofold love, which is the sign and practical consequence of our mystical unity in Christ, is also and above all its generative principle—so much so that the sacred liturgy sings this beautiful verse on Holy Thursday: "*Congregavit nos in unum Christi amor*"—"The love of Christ has gathered us together." And a little further on, it continues: "And let Christ our God dwell in the midst of us. Where charity and love are, there is God"—"*Ubi caritas et amor, Deus ibi est.*"[15]

———— • ————

The moral union of all the members of the Mystical Body, the community of sentiment and of affection that must reign in all the parts of a single

---

[14] *Christ, the Life of the Soul* (St. Louis: B. Herder Book Company, Md.), 328
[15] Antiphon 8, of the *Mandatum*, Holy Thursday.

supernatural organism, is guaranteed primarily by the virtue of charity. The two other theological virtues, however, tend, each in its own way, toward the same end of uniting souls, of harmonizing intellects, and of fusing wills into a fundamental identity of views and of aspirations.

First of all, faith harmonizes intellects in their adherence to the same truths, subjects them to the same beliefs and to an infallible common magisterium. The same Spirit of truth enlightens all the members of the Church, "until we all attain to the unity of the faith" (Eph. 4:13). A common rule determines the dogmas to which we must give our assent, "that we may be now no longer children, tossed to and fro and carried about by every wind of doctrine" (Eph. 4:14).

Hope, for its part, makes our faltering wills converge toward a common beatitude and guides the aspirations of our hearts toward the same infinite Good. The supernatural end of all the members of the total Christ is identical, and the means to attain it, namely the graces offered to us, are the same for all. In addition, through mutual aid and fraternal cooperation, we work in unison to fulfill our Christian vocation, for, as the Apostle tells us: "We have been called in one hope of our calling: (cf. Eph. 4:4).

Elsewhere in our study of the life of the Mystical Body, we discuss these theological virtues at greater length.[16] Let it suffice for the moment to point out their role and specific influence, which is concomitant with the role of charity and dependent upon it, in perfecting moral unity, the community of views through faith, the identity of aspirations through hope, that make of all the faithful a single mind and a single will, "one heart and one soul."

St. Augustine has summed up in one terse sentence the importance of the three theological virtues in constituting the unity of the Mystical Body. To the Christians gathered to hear him preach, he said: "We too are in his Body, if our faith in him is sincere, our hope firm, and our charity ardent. We are in his Body and we are his members—*Et nos in Corpore ipsius sumus, si tamen fides nostra sincera sit in illo, et spes certa, et caritas accensa.*"[17]

---

[16] Cf. Mura, *Le Corps Mystique du Christ*, Volume II, Chapter 14.
[17] *In ps.* 37, 6, *PL* 36:399.

CHAPTER XIV

The Mystical Person of Christ

We have now delved into the nature of the union, indeed into the oneness that exists between Christ and his saints as far as the mystery of divine life permits. Now we have the answer to the question we asked at the beginning of this work: How can Jesus form a single Mystical Body in union with us, his members?[1] Is it simply a moral union, or must we say it is a veritable physical union? In considering all the wonderful bonds by which God has joined our life to Christ's, we have seen that our union with Jesus is both physical and moral, and that neither of these terms exhausts the richness of the manifold relations which make of Christ and ourselves a single mystical Person.

A single mystical Person? Can we really use this term to describe the whole Christ? In doing so are we not in danger of distorting our theology of the Mystical Body by interpolating the notion of an inadmissible hypostatic union between Christ and his faithful? This is not the case at all. The term "mystical Person," which is very orthodox if we understand it rightly, is to be found in the writings of the Angelic Doctor himself. It merely synthesizes the totality of divine realities that our study has enabled us to discover in the mystery of the total Christ. In the present chapter we shall explain the meaning of the term "mystical Person," and stress its essentially analogical character. This will be the conclusion of our study of the principles that constitute the unity of the Mystical Body, and a general synthesis of the principles analyzed thus far.[2]

---

[1] Cf. above, Introduction, 10 ff.

[2] In so doing we are accepting the cordial invitation of Father Mersch (*Nouvelle Revue theologique*, March, 1935) to make our synthesis still more synthetic by reducing the seven principles analyzed to a single principle.

St. Thomas says: "The head and members are as one mystic person."[3] And further on he writes: "The whole Church, Christ's Mystical Body, is reckoned as one person with its head, which is Christ."[4] A single Person, a mystical Person—in what sense are we to take this? Philosophy teaches us that a person is a being that subsists in itself,[5] that is, a being that exists and acts of itself in an independent manner.[6] It is a being that possesses "to be" in an autonomous way, and thereby constitutes the ultimate subject of attribution.

Thus Peter is a person, whereas the soul of Peter is not a person any more than his body is, taken by itself. The reason for this is that Peter forms a complete whole that subsists in itself and possesses its own being, whereas his body does not subsist in itself, but only in the whole. And his soul, while it does subsist, is nonetheless ordered to the body so that it may communicate its own subsistence to it.

These brief notions will enable us to clarify the sense in which the total Christ can be called a single mystical Person. When applied to a divine subject, the concepts will lose the abstract quality that characterizes their technical presentation, in order to become the expression of realities of the highest spiritual interest.

The notion of the person can be reduced to two essential elements: the possession of an incommunicable being, and the fact that it is the ultimate term of attribution. First, the person possesses *incommunicability of being*. Because a given subject has its own being, or better still, because it is actually ordered to its own incommunicable being it is a person.[7] Therefore the sacred Humanity of Christ, which subsists not in itself but in the Word, is not a person; it belongs to the Person of the Word, and is hypostatically united (that is to say, personally united) to the Word of God.

---

[3] *Summa*, IIIa, q.48, a. 2 ad 1.

[4] Ibid., q. 49, a. 1

[5] According to the classical definition of Boethius: *Rationalis naturae individua substantia*; or, according to St. Thomas: *subsistens distinctum*.

[6] This is not to exclude the influx of an extrinsic efficient cause, namely God, but it does exclude an intrinsic being or principle of being, upon which the supposit or person would depend.

[7] We know that certain of St. Thomas' disciples identify *subsistence*, which constitutes the person, with substantial being (cf. Pègues, *Commentaire littéral de la Somme*, Part III, q. 2, a. 1); whereas for others who are in the majority, subsistence is distinguished from substantial being as the terminative act of the nature, which renders the nature proximately apt for its own being (cf. Hugon, Tract. dogm., Volume II, *de Verbo Inc.*, Sectio II, a. 2; Garrigou-Lagrange in the *Revue Thomiste* (March–April, 1933).

In the present study, we envisage personality only in an analogical manner, according to a certain resemblance of the mystical Christ with the physical person. We can, therefore, abstract from this final determination of the act of subsistence, of personality.

In addition, there is the fact that the person is the ultimate term of *all attributions*. This second essential mark of personality is the necessary consequence of autonomous subsistence. Whether I walk or rest, whether I think or love, whether I speak or act in any other way, everything I do proceeds from my person. My hand works, but it is I who am working. My eye sees, but it is I who am seeing. My mind meditates and my heart loves, but it is I, that is, my person, who meditate and who love. The same is true of both the human and divine operations of the Word Incarnate, all of which are attributed to the same physical Person, Jesus, at once God and man. When his Humanity suffers, it is Jesus who suffers. When his Godhead creates new souls, preserves and governs the world, it is Jesus who creates and preserves, it is Jesus who governs. He is the only-begotten Son who rests upon the Father's bosom and he is also the Child of Mary resting on his mother's breast, because he is the same divine Person, the Word eternal, who receives the divine nature from all eternity and who receives our human nature from his mother in time.

Since these are the distinctive marks of personality, the question again arises with regard to the Mystical Body: Can we say that Christ and his members form, supernaturally speaking, a single Person? Do we find in the divine Whole, that is, in the total Christ the two distinctive marks of the person which we have just enumerated?

First, do the Head and the members of the whole Christ have a common being, a common subsistence? And next, can we attribute to the same subject what Christ does and what his members do, the way we attribute to the same person what his head, hands, and feet do, and the way we attribute to Jesus the works of his Godhead and the actions of his most sacred Humanity?

Here we must be wary of the part played by analogy. Between Christ and his faithful there is no hypostatic union or substantial unity. There is no common *physical* personality extending through grace from the mystical Head to his members. Each of the members of the Mystical Body remains a distinct person in the order of being and of subsistence. Each one retains his own being, and in consequence remains the term of attribution of the works he performs.

Yet in the order of the accidental[8] and supernatural being given to us by grace, that which is not true in the order of substantial being is realized,

---

[8] We are referring here to predicamental accident which is opposed to substance, and not to predicable (or contingent) accident. No one should be shocked because we place the unity of the Mystical Body and of the mystical Person in the order of accidental being, as if the question here concerned some nondescript, superficial reality, something adventitious and contingent.

nonetheless, in a certain respect. The being of grace, the divine sonship which we have received from Christ the only-begotten Son of the Father, establishes us proportionally with relation to him, in the dependence of being and of operation in which the various parts of the same person are related to the whole. Indeed, certain authors have gone so far as to speak of a mystical subsistence of Christ and of his Church, assimilated to the subsistence of the Person of the Word Incarnate. This is the way Father Chardon expresses himself in his work, *The Cross of Jesus*:

> After this uncreated subsistence, communicated to the two natures united in the mystery of the Incarnation and in the principle of the adorable unity [of the Person of the Word Incarnate], which is the foundation of the Christian Religion, Jesus willed to establish another subsistence for his Church whose Head he is, so that he might thus be the Church's *supposit*[9] and mystical subsistence in the assembly of all the faithful which he unites as members into a single body through the means of grace. Now this grace, which is a most excellent participation in the divine nature, resides in Jesus Christ as in its dwelling, and flows from him into the souls whom it pleases him to choose, just as the vigor of the body derives from the head and is communicated to each of the members in accordance with its rank.[10]

This mystical subsistence, daring as the expression may seem,[11] signifies nothing but the multiple union that divine grace establishes between Christ and the members of the Church, a dependence of being and of operation *similar* (not identical) to that of the members with respect to the human

---

The grace of union with Christ is something very profound and interior, which penetrates the very substance of our souls—and even has repercussions upon our bodies, until the time of the *total immortality* of which St. Paul speaks (cf. 1 Cor. 15). This grace binds our souls to one another and to Christ, and causes a vital, supernatural, and very real flux from the Head into the members, a flux whose reality is physical or ontological, and which ennobles, transforms, and deifies our being and our actions.

The fact remains, however, that philosophically speaking— or better, theologically speaking—these realities are not of the substantial order, do not constitute a new substance or a new person that is *physically* one, *secundum esse simpliciter*. Now between substance and accident there is no possible middle ground, not only in the natural order but even speaking in absolute terms. In these problems theology does not repudiate the rigorous formulas whose mode of expression, if not their content, is provided by philosophy. And these categories of being, established by Aristotle, are but the precise formulation of natural and universally valid common sense, if it is true that the notion of being and the principle of contradiction are at the foundation of all science and all human knowledge whether natural or supernatural.

9   By this is meant the person, or better, the personality of the Church.

10   *La Croix de Jésus,* Chapter 1

11   For our part we would prefer that this expression were not used, for it can lead to confusion and distort certain ideas. The word subsistence has a meaning that is too precise, too profoundly hallowed in the theology of the Trinity and of the Incarnation, too exclusively reserved to signify an act that remains in the line of substance or of *esse primum*, to permit of transferring its meaning by analogy to the order of *esse secundum*, or of operation, which is the order of grace. The word *person*, which even in the natural order implies various analogical significations, does not present the same difficulty, and will be better understood in this derived sense of "mystical Person" in which St. Thomas uses it.

person and to the head that governs it. Let us listen once again to Father Chardon's theological realism:

> Just as the nerves, which have their origin in the head, are the links between the various parts of the body with the head; just as, without the nerves, each part would remain lifeless, would not participate in the life of the informing soul, and thus separated from the whole would be inept for any use; so Jesus Christ, pouring his grace and his charity into holy souls, unites them among themselves in order to make of them, in union with himself, but a single Body whose Head he is, and in order to give them a life that is not human but divine, not natural but mystical. As if this was still not enough, he infuses his divine Spirit into them, so that in all truth they may become not so much his venerable members as one and the same with him by participation, and what is more, *a single person* mystically, and a single Jesus Christ by imitation.[12]

Jesus himself proclaimed a single Person and a single Jesus Christ when he said to Paul who was pursuing Christians on the road to Damascus: "Saul, Saul, why dost thou persecute me? . . .

I am Jesus whom thou art persecuting" (Acts 9:4–5).

In the mystical Christ we find analogically realized through sanctifying grace the two essential marks of personality: (1) the total Christ possesses a being in common with the Head and his members; (2) we can attribute to the whole Christ and to his Head the actions and sufferings of the members as such.

Community of being: Jesus and his faithful do not possess the same being by nature, according to which each one subsists in himself. However, they do possess the same being of grace.[13] Although this being of grace is completely accidental (as opposed to substantial) and although it is added to our personal being, it does place us in a state of intimate dependence upon Jesus Christ in our entire supernatural activity.

> Since grace, which is the principle of adoption within us, is the *same* grace which in its infinite abundance subsists in Jesus Christ in the Person of the Word,[14] we can see more clearly than daylight how it is that through grace

---

[12] Chardon, *loc. cit.*

[13] Not numerically the same, but the same by way of origin inasmuch as the grace of the members flows from the plenary grace of Christ the Head.

[14] *The same:* This is not to be understood as identity with the created grace of Christ, and still less as identity with his divine Sonship, to which Father Chardon seems to be referring here. But it is to be understood as being the same in the sense of footnote 13, above, that is, through the dependence of our Grace of filial adoption in its origin upon the created grace of Christ in the first place, and then upon the supernatural

Jesus is the subsistence of his Mystical Body, and how it is that through the bonds of this grace which flows from him as the Head we are united as dependent members to the principal member, in order to form in him but a single mystical person, and to form with Jesus but a single Jesus mystically.[15]

"*Through grace Jesus is the subsistence of his Mystical Body.*" This statement by Father Chardon deserves our close attention, for it suggests a luminous comparison. The grace that resides in Christ and that is, in a certain respect, poured upon us his members is called, theologically speaking, *capital grace*, or the grace of the Head as Head. Christ possesses another grace called the "grace of union," which is none other than the Godhead of the Word communicating itself and uniting itself hypostatically to his sacred Humanity in the unity of a single Person. Just as the grace of union makes a single *physical* Person out of the Humanity and the Godhead of the Word Incarnate, so also capital grace makes of Christ and his members a single *mystical* Person. Despite the profound difference between the two kinds of union, there exists a real analogy and a harmonious proportion between them. The Word made flesh, considered alone in his twofold nature, constitutes only one Person in the strictly physical or ontological order. This is the effect of the grace of union. The same Word Incarnate, with all the faithful that he has mystically united to himself in a community of supernatural life [that is, the life of grace common to sanctified souls and to the sacred Humanity], allows the faithful to retain their own personality, their own natural subsistence, their independent physical being. But in a higher order, in the order of supernatural and divine life, he forms a single mystical Person with them. This is the effect of capital grace. Thus is verified in the total Christ, in an analogical manner, the first characteristic of the person.

Together with a certain community of supernatural being, the grace of adoption also gives us, in the mystical Person of the total Christ, the close solidarity that permits us to attribute to Jesus all the acts of his faithful who are his members through grace. With regard to the principle of juridical unity, we have already spoken of the community of merits and virtuous works, thanks to which Christ becomes the subject of attribution of the

Sonship of the Word, the first and exemplary source of our adoption through grace. We must speak of all this with extreme precision and with great circumspection if we do not want to distort radically the doctrine of the Mystical Body.

[15] Chardon, *op. cit,* end of Chapter 2.

operations of his members.[16] Christ continues to grow in his faithful until the day of his final perfection.

To quote Father Chardon again:

> It is in this sense that Jesus is born in us, that he is a child with the beginners, that he gains strength and grows, and finally receives his perfection in us. It is in this sense that the incomparable Apostle accomplishes in his flesh, for Holy Church, what is lacking in the sufferings of Jesus (cf. Col. 1:24). Now it is very true that nothing can be lacking in the flesh of Jesus for the end of our salvation; the justice of God has taken from it more than a sufficient amount of suffering to make satisfaction. . . . But even though nothing is lacking of the sufferings of Jesus as Head of the Church, something is still lacking of the sufferings of the members of the Body of the Church. St. Paul, as a part of this Body, accomplishes not in the flesh of Jesus but in the flesh of Paul what is lacking in the sufferings of Jesus.[17]

Thus truly our supernatural activity, the fruit of the grace of Jesus and the work of his members, is attributable to him. We refer to the Head, to his praise and glory, the divine good that exists in his members. For without him, there would be no such good in them. Our holy actions prolong in a certain way his theandric activity, since in us Jesus continues to manifest the sanctifying efficacy of all the mysteries of his life here on earth. The whole life of the Church is the consequence and the mystical prolongation of the divino-human life of Christ the Redeemer. Once again, let us listen to the words of Father Chardon:

> Even though the life of Jesus, when considered absolutely in itself, is not our natural life, nevertheless, by reason of the mystical subsistence that he communicates to us through grace, which unites us as members of a Body to our Head, his life becomes our life, his Spirit becomes the Spirit of our spirit, and his merits begin to belong to us. And when he is hungry and thirsty with us and takes our other miseries upon himself (cf. Matt. 25:35 ff.), we rise again and take our places in him in heaven, and we put on his glory.[18]

We can understand now the precise meaning that we must give to this expression, "the mystical Person," and also what we must exclude from it. The notion of the mystical Person expresses and synthesizes all the principles

---

[16] Cf. Chapter VII above, 73 ff.

[17] *Op. cit.,* Chapter 3.

[18] *Loc. cit.*

of the union of Christ with his members which we have analyzed in detail in the preceding chapters.

But it is to the principle of *efficient causality* above all the others that we must relate the formation of the total Christ. Thus we will see clarified and brought to completion the notion of the vital and sanctifying influence of Christ the Head upon his members, by the synthesis of the various constitutive elements of the Mystical Body already discussed in Chapter VI.

To say that we form a single mystical person with Jesus signifies primarily that Christ wraps us in his sanctifying action; that he secretly infuses his divine life of grace and love into us at every moment; that, like the vinestock of the vine, he communicates to us his supernatural sap, to make us "bear much fruit" of virtue and holiness.

This action of Christ, whose primary source is in his divine nature and in the influx of the Holy Spirit, reaches us through his most sacred Humanity, through his precious and life-giving Blood which, like a river of life, flows through and floods all the members of the Mystical Body. Thanks to this unceasing action of Jesus, the Church becomes the complement and the "fullness of Christ," as the Angelic Doctor explains to us in his commentary on the Epistle to the Colossians. He says: "The Church is called the fullness of Christ because everything that is virtually contained in Christ is realized in a certain way in the members of the Church. For all the spiritual senses, the gifts, and everything that can exist in the Church is found superabundantly in Christ, and flows from him into the members of the Church and is completed in them."[19]

"*Omnia virtute continentur in Christo!*" These precise words of St. Thomas sum up the doctrine of the present chapter and bring out the central point of the theology of the Mystical Body outlined in the preceding chapters. They will provide a conclusion to what we have already said.

At the end of this analysis we will have a better understanding, to the extent that our feeble intellect can grasp the ineffable, the supernatural grandeurs of this grace of incorporation which makes of all of us a single mystical Christ. We now know what this hidden sacrament, this hidden mystery is, that St. Paul was commanded to make known to the nations (cf. Eph. 3:19; Col. 1:27). We at least glimpse something of the "unsearchable riches of Christ" which we share through our vital union with the Savior of our souls.

---

[19] *In Epist. Coloss.*

If we the members of Christ want to take cognizance, in a spirit of faith and love, of this divine solidarity that makes us integral parts of the mystical Person of Christ, we must consent joyously and without reservation to this total vital dependence of the members with respect to their Head. We must renounce the undue autonomy that human nature and original sin make us cling to avidly throughout our natural and even our supernatural activity. Finally we must, by truly living by Christ and by his grace, suffer, through total abnegation, the spiritual *diminutio capitis* that effectively subordinates us in all things to our true and only Head, Christ.

In another work we shall show how we can realize in our daily lives this renouncement of our personality, this subordination of our being and of our activity to the kingdom of grace and to the vital influence of our sacred Head.[20]

Now that we have seen wherein the unity of the Mystical Body consists, we must still understand in greater detail the many parts that compose it. We have made a synthesis of the divine realities that concur in the constitution of this supernatural organism. We must now analyze the various elements that are united and hierarchized in the total Christ. This will be our concern in the following chapters, the first of which will deal with the Head, and the others with the members of the Mystical Body.

[20] Cf. Mura, *Le Corps Mystique du Christ*, Volume II.

ARTICLE II

THE VARIOUS PARTS
OF THE MYSTICAL BODY:
THE HEAD AND THE MEMBERS

CHAPTER XV

The Head of the Mystical Body

The principal part of an organism, of a human body, the part that attracts our attention from the first because it dominates the others and ranks above them in dignity and perfection, is the head. Likewise, in the Mystical Body the Head first deserves our attention and our pious consideration. The sacred Head of the mystical organism, as St. Paul has told us, is Jesus our Savior, the Word Incarnate, the Son of God clothed in our infirm nature.

Indeed, the Incarnation of the divine Word is the prerequisite and the primary principle of our incorporation into Jesus. Through it likewise, Christ has been constituted the Head of the Mystical Body. The eternal Son of the Father became like us in order to make us like him. He took on our nature in order to give us his. He united himself to his creature through the close bond of the hypostatic union, he gathered up in himself the whole of creation. And according to the expression of St. Paul he made himself its living recapitulation,[1] in order thus to hierarchize all things under his divine personality, to infuse his divine life into "every man who comes into the world" (John 1:19), and to offer up in the name of all men praise of his heavenly Father.

Through the Incarnation, extremes are brought together in the "one Mediator between God and men, himself man, Christ Jesus" (1 Tim. 2:5). For, as St. Leo the Great says in his first Christmas sermon: "Lowliness is united to Majesty, weakness to Power, mortality to that which is eternal."[2] Therein lies the origin of our mystical union with Christ, according to the words of the same Doctor in another of his sermons: "Because, just as the Lord became our flesh through his birth, so we have become his flesh

[1] Cf. Eph. 1:10: "to re-establish all things in Christ . . ."
[2] *Sermo I de Nativ.*, 2.

in being reborn. That is why we are his members, and the temples of the Holy Spirit."[3]

The union of the two natures in the Person of the Word was willed by the wisdom of God so that Jesus, God and man, might become our way to the Father, our divine Intermediary and our Head. According to the present plan of divine Providence, his Godhead alone would not have harmoniously accomplished the work of our salvation and of our sanctification, nor would it have become the Head of redeemed humanity. It was necessary that the Son of God put on our nature, take our humanity upon himself and become our brother, united to us by ties of blood and by a community of suffering, so that he might be our elder brother (cf. Rom. 8:29), and so that we might share in his divine Sonship and be incorporated into him in the unity of a single supernatural organism.

It is through his human nature, therefore, that Jesus is the Head of the Mystical Body. We must analyze in detail, however, all of the perfection that the title of Head implies.

St. Thomas remarks that the head possesses a threefold preeminence over the other members of the body: (1) a pre-eminence of order: it occupies the first place in the body; (2) a pre-eminence of perfection: in the head are gathered all the senses, all the perceptive and appetitive faculties of the body; (3) a pre-eminence of influence: the head moves and governs all the members by means of the motor nerves.[4]

This threefold pre-eminence is realized, having due regard for proportion, in Christ the Savior, inasmuch as he is the Head of the Mystical Body. Let us study attentively the prerogatives of our divine and adored Head. From them we receive all our perfection as members of his Mystical Body.

Pre-eminence of Order

Christ is at the summit of all creation, for, as St. Paul tells us: "He . . . is the beginning, the first-born from the dead, that in all things he may have the first place"—"*ut sit ipse in omnibus primatum tenens*" (Col. 1:18).

Jesus, the Son of God by nature, is the first of all creatures by reason of his Incarnation in his sacred Humanity. He is first not in the order of time, but according to a priority of intention.

---

[3] *Sermo III de Nativ.,* 5.

[4] Cf. *Summa*, IIIa, q. 8, a. 1. Cf. also *in Ep. ad Col. 1*, lect. 5; *ad Eph. I*, lect. 8; *De Verit.*, q. 29, a. 4.

When God brought forth creatures out of nothingness, Jesus filled his Creator's mind. From the beginning, all created things were ordered to the glory of the Word Incarnate. The eternal Father had set him at the head of the hierarchy of all created beings, which are all destined to reflect his perfections and to sing his praises. This is priority in the order of final causality.

Are we to conclude from this that the sole determinant of Christ's coming upon earth was the primacy of order and of glory that results from the Word's becoming man? Was the Incarnation decreed in order to give the created universe a Head, abstracting from all specific circumstances? St. Thomas does not think so. In the actual dispensation of divine Providence, the Word of God *"for us men and for our salvation* came down from heaven."[5] It was to save man from sin that the Son of God deigned to abase himself in our humanity and to take upon himself our misery and our infirmities.

True, Jesus is Head not only of redeemed humanity but also of the angels who remained faithful to him. God, says St. Paul, set Christ "at his right hand in heaven, above every Principality and Power and Virtue and Domination" (Eph. 1:21). It would seem, therefore, that although his Incarnation was motivated in part by the salvation of man, its first reason for being, sufficient in itself, was the will of the Father to constitute him Head of all men and angels.

And yet St. Paul, in the very texts that exalt the primacy of Christ above the angelic choirs, always relates the absolute kingship of our Head to the work of the Redemption. In the passage just cited, the Apostle says that it was by his resurrection, by his triumph over death that Jesus won his dominion over all creatures (cf. Eph. 1:20). And again in his Letter to the Colossians, he says that it was "through the blood of his cross" (Col. 1:20) that Christ made peace, whether on the earth or in the heavens, reconciling to himself both angels and men by making reparation for the sins that kept the latter far from the kingdom of heaven.

Christ the Head, therefore, is essentially a Savior. In honoring his primacy, we glorify his merciful Redemption; and the claims to his sovereignty are inscribed in his divine members in letters of blood, engraved in his hands and feet by the sharp nails that attached him to the cross.

His very name indicates the reason which determined his coming among us. His Father could have given him a name that was a direct expression of his universal Kingship. He did not will to do so, because the plans of his

---

[5] The Nicene Creed.

providence would not have found adequate expression in such a name. He called him Jesus, that is to say Savior, for that is his reason for being and as it were his definition.

Jesus came to become our Victim, the Host of propitiation immolated on the cross for our sins. From the moment of his entry into this world, he declared his intention through the lips of the Psalmist, as St. Paul tells us: "Therefore, in coming into the world, [Christ] says, Sacrifice and oblation thou wouldst not, but a body thou hast fitted to me: . . . Behold, I come . . . to do thy will, O God" (Heb. 10:5–7; Ps. 7–8). And the Apostle adds: "It is in this 'will' that we have been sanctified through the offering of the body of Jesus Christ" (Heb. 10:10).

Jesus, therefore, is essentially a Savior; hence under present conditions his coming among men was determined by the merciful goodness that impelled him to redeem us from the domination of the devil. He himself told us so in these words: "I have not come to call the just, but sinners, to repentance" (Luke 5:32). Thus St. Augustine, in his conviction that it was sin that earned the Savior for us, cries out with surprising boldness: "*O Felix culpa!* O happy fault, that merited such a Redeemer for us!" And the Church makes this astonishing exclamation her own by inserting it into her liturgical prayer, at the Exultet of the Easter Vigil.

The glory of Christ the Savior is not thereby subordinated to the service of men; on the contrary, the salvation of humanity is subordinated to the triumph of Jesus. Through the Redemption and through his victory over hell and over sin our Lord conquers the primacy that the Father has destined for him from all eternity. The glory of Christ was to be the glory of a conqueror, and his universal Kingship was to be a priestly Kingship, because his bloody immolation on Calvary was to be the foundation of the reign without end announced to Mary by the angel on the day of the Incarnation (cf. Luke 1:32–33).[6]

Through the Redemption our Lord obtained the pre-eminence of order that places him above every creature. For the heavenly Father foresaw the fall of the human race and permitted it only in order to restore his work in a more admirable way, to make the glory of his Word shine forth more brilliantly in our Redemption. It is as if a great king sent his son on a distant and arduous military expedition to subdue a revolting people and win them

---

[6] The glory of God and of Christ thus remains first in the order of final causality. The permission of the fall and the salvation of the human race by way of Redemption possess priority in the divine plan only according to the order of material causality, that is, of the conditions of fact under which the mystery of the Incarnation and the universal primacy of Christ were to be fulfilled.

to his service, in order to make the power and wisdom of the heir to the throne more apparent. In the same way Jesus, the born-Savior of the human race, by winning us to the loving and freely accepted service of his Father, whose sweet and beneficent rule we had rejected, manifests the gentle power of his charitable action. And thus we ourselves become the glorious trophy of his victory even as we acclaim our divine Conqueror.

Pre-eminence of Perfection

The primacy of order which Christ the Redeemer possesses evokes as its necessary consequence a pre-eminence of perfection, which makes him the masterpiece of the entire created world. Indeed, God, infinite Wisdom, could never order the more perfect to the less perfect. Hence the one whom he establishes as the principle of the universal order must by that very fact possess the plenitude of every greatness, of every excellence, of every perfection. St. Paul says this to the Colossians: "For it has pleased God the Father that in him all his fullness should dwell . . . that in all things he may have the first place" (Col. 1:19, 18).

Therefore Jesus shines forth to the eyes of our faith as a king "arrayed in majesty" (Ps. 92:1). And the Church joins the Psalmist in exalting him as the fairest of the sons of men, who goes forth in glory and majesty (cf. Ps. 44:3–5). Christ, our divine Head, possesses in his most sacred Humanity all the gifts of nature and of grace that a creature can possess. Let us first say a few words about his natural perfections, and then consider his supernatural excellences at greater leisure.

Jesus received the most perfect human nature conceivable, both with regard to his body and with regard to his soul. His body, formed from a virginal substance, is the work of the Holy Spirit. What more is there to say? While second causes can fail in their operations and inevitably inject some of their native imperfection in their productions, God, who is the first and indefectible agent, can produce only a perfect work. The Body of Christ, the fruit of the Blessed Virgin through the Spirit, is a wonder of nature. Its delicate complexion, the perfection of all its senses, the beauty of its features, exceed anything the sensible world has ever known.

Furthermore, the sacred Body is completely spiritualized by its contact with the Godhead. In Jesus' Body, matter is the transparent crystal through which the perfections of his most holy soul can be seen in the open. This fragile substance, which in us is subject to so many forms of deterioration,

171

has become in Christ subsistent purity and the generator of all purity: *"Quem cum amavero, casta sum; cum tetigero, munda sum; cum accepero, virgo sum"*—"When I love him, I am chaste; when I touch him, I am pure; when I receive him, I remain a virgin."[7] Such are the words that Holy Mother Church places on the lips of St, Agnes.

Is it not the Body of Jesus that we adore in the Host of the altar, that the Church exalts in the solemnization of Corpus Christi, and which, when received in Holy Communion, is a seed of virginity and chastity—"the corn of the elect, and wine springing forth virgins" (Zach. 9:17)?

What then can we say of the purely natural perfections of Jesus' soul? It was for his soul that the Holy Spirit formed his most perfect body. There is always a proportion and commensurateness between Jesus' Body and soul. His soul, therefore, is the most perfect conceivable. If we want to form even a remote idea of its excellences—of his intellect which was far above that of any genius, of the strength of his will and the goodness of his heart—we must scour the world to see what comparable perfections it has produced. We must seek out the most eminent exponent of wisdom, such as a St. Augustine or a St. Thomas, an exemplar of the gentlest and most powerful love, such as St. Francis de Sales or St. Catherine of Siena, and then make a mental leap far beyond them to attain some idea of Christ's supereminent perfection. Even then the very comparison might seem blasphemy. And we shall have to be content in the end with honoring by our silence and by avowing our ignorance what is lacking in our conception. With the inspired Psalmist, we shall say: *"Tibi silentium laus"*—"Silence is praise of thee" (Ps. 64:1).

If this is true of the natural perfections of Jesus, what of his supernatural perfections! In his human nature per se, Jesus was not superior to the children of Adam. But through the supernatural gifts which enrich his sacred Humanity, Christ surpasses even the angels, perfect as they may be.

The spiritual riches of our beloved Savior may be summed up under three principal categories: his plenitude of grace; his infinite knowledge; his boundless power. As St. John has said: "We have seen the glory of the Word, full of grace and truth" (cf. John 1:14). These words show the first two prerogatives of Christ, prerogatives which are wholly interior and which perfect the substance of his soul and his faculties of knowing and willing. "He was mighty in work and word"—*"potens opere et sermone"* (cf. Luke 24:19), says St. Luke. We shall deal a little later with the third supernatural

---

[7] Office of St. Agnes, Matins.

perfection of Jesus, which relates to his action on the external world and to his primacy of influence. For the present let us speak of the plenitude of grace in Jesus and of his infinite wisdom.

THE GRACE OF CHRIST

Who can search the ineffable depths of Christ's grace? Scarcely can we stammer a few words about it, since even the angels discover unfathomable mysteries in it (cf. 1 Pet. 1:12). Moreover, this grace is manifold. It is divided, in accordance with the threefold sanctity of Jesus, into grace of union or substantial grace, the habitual grace of accidental holiness inherent in Christ, and finally into capital or communicative grace, which sanctifies the members of his Mystical Body.

The grace of union constitutes the very essence of the mystery of the Incarnation. It is the hypostatic union of the human nature of Jesus with the Person of the divine Word. Through this grace of union, the sacred Humanity subsisting in the Word acquires infinite excellence and dignity. Christ's Humanity becomes more than the temple of God, it becomes God's "thing." indissolubly united to the divine nature. It is more than the spouse of the Word, it is the nature of the Word, who, through it, becomes true man just as he is true God.

Through the grace of union, the sacred Humanity is worthy of the adoration and homage reserved for the supreme Majesty of God alone. Through it also, each of the acts of Jesus obtains an infinite value. His prayers, his sufferings, each beat of his Sacred Heart have the value of the actions of a God, since they belong to a divine Person.

Habitual or sanctifying grace is present in Jesus in all its fullness. How could we receive it from him unless he himself were filled with it? *"Of his fullness we have all received"* (John 1:16).

Sanctifying grace, a sharing in the divine nature, is the seed and root of the beatific vision. Now our Lord, from the instant of his virginal conception in the womb of Mary, had a clear and supremely perfect vision of the divine Essence. From that same moment, therefore, he possessed sanctifying grace in the greatest measure conceivable, and hence in a measure that was infinite.[8]

The effect of sanctifying grace is to deify our souls, to make us, as St. Peter says, "partakers of the divine nature" (2 Pet. 1:4). This grace necessarily adorned the soul of Jesus. It is true that through the hypostatic union the

---

[8] Cf. *Summa*, IIIa, q. 7, 4. 2.

sacred humanity receives more than an accidental participation in the divine nature, it subsists in the Word; therefore Jesus the man is God by an identity of Person. However, the two natures remain completely distinct, and the human nature of the Savior is not intrinsically changed, perfected, or elevated by the fact of this union. Sanctifying grace, which accomplishes this assimilation of the creature to God was, therefore, indispensable to the soul of Christ in order that it might be worthy of union with the Word. In this light, sanctifying grace appears to us a natural efflorescence of the hypostatic union, its necessary consequence.

Sanctifying grace is never found in a soul without the complete retinue of all the supernatural *habitus*, namely, the infused virtues and the gifts of the Holy Spirit. The reason for this is that grace sanctifies only the substance of the soul in which it resides, whereas the faculties of the soul are supernaturalized by the virtues and the gifts. The former are given us so that we may *act* divinely, and the second are given us so that we may easily *receive* the impulsions of the Holy Spirit, that is, actual graces. Jesus necessarily possessed both kinds of supernatural perfections in the highest possible degree. He possessed all the virtues with the exception of faith, which is incompatible with the beatific vision, and with the exception also of hope, which is incompatible with the possession of God. All of his actions were holy and godlike, proceeding from the infused virtues, the habitual principles of our supernatural activity.

Jesus likewise possessed the fullness of the gifts of the Holy Spirit. The divine Spirit guided the Savior in all things and governed his soul with perfect liberty. The Gospel has shown him to us, led by the Spirit into the desert to begin his forty-day' fast (cf. Luke 4:1–2). Our Savior also applied to himself the following words of Isaias: "The Spirit of the Lord is upon me because he has anointed me; to bring good news to the poor he has sent me, to proclaim to the captives release, and sight to the blind; to set at liberty the oppressed . . ." (Luke 4:18–19).

To these first two graces is joined a third within the soul of Christ: *capital grace*. This new prerogative constitutes the sacred Humanity of Jesus, inasmuch as it is the conjoined instrument of the Word, the universal principle of the supernatural gifts distributed among men, and in a certain measure even among the angels. Like the holy oil that anointed the head of Aaron and ran down upon his garments imbuing them with its perfume (cf. Ps. 132), the grace of our Head, the Anointed of the Lord, is poured out upon all of us to fill us with "the fragrance of Christ" (2 Cor. 2:15).

Whatever supernatural gift we receive comes to us through our Lord Jesus Christ. Whatever grace we desire we must implore of him, for he is the throne of grace: "Let us therefore draw near with confidence to the throne of grace" (Heb. 4:16).

However, we must note that Christ's capital grace is substantially identical with the sanctifying grace that adorns his soul, as the Angelic Doctor teaches.[9] The distinction between them is a distinction of reason, for the habitual grace of our Lord differs from the habitual grace of others. In others, habitual grace sanctifies only the individual person in which it dwells; but in Christ, habitual grace not only sanctifies his sacred Humanity but is also the source from which the saving waters of grace and all heavenly gifts spring up in our souls.

This is the first crown that adorns the brow of our beloved Head. It is a crown of grace and of holiness. The second is a crown of perfect and in a certain respect infinite knowledge.

THE KNOWLEDGE OF JESUS

The Apostle tells us that in our divine Savior "are hidden all the treasures of wisdom and knowledge" (Col. 2:3). This fullness of knowledge belongs by right to the Head of the Mystical Body, for it is in the head that all the faculties of perfection within an organism are localized. Through the sight of the external world the head directs the other members in their operations. Our divine Lord, therefore, possesses a knowledge worthy of his role as Head, a knowledge that is infinite.

Furthermore, just as the grace of Jesus is threefold, so is his human knowledge. He possesses the knowledge of vision, or what is known as the beatific vision; he possesses infused knowledge, or knowledge of the angelic order; and he possesses acquired or strictly human knowledge. This threefold knowledge gives the soul of our Lord all the kinds of knowledge and all the modes of knowledge that any created intellect can have. It makes of his blessed soul, as it were, an ocean of light in which the universality of created beings is reflected.

Through his knowledge of vision, the interior gaze of Christ Jesus, excellently strengthened by an unequalled light of glory, plunges into the abyss of the Godhead and is ineffably intoxicated by the contemplation of the infinite perfections of God. He sees this ravishing Beauty "as it is" (John 3:2); Beauty that is the happiness of God himself. In the intuitive vision

---

[9] Ibid., q. 8, a. 5.

of the divine Essence Jesus knows everything that relates to his mission as Redeemer, that is, everything that exists or is ever to exist. Jesus knows us in the mirror of the Godhead incomparably better than we can know ourselves. He sees the least of our acts, our good desires, our love, as well as our sorrows, our temptations, our failures, and our sins. Otherwise how could he be our Savior, expiate our sins fittingly, and bring us succor in all our needs?

Christ is the Head of the whole supernatural world, the author of the salvation of men, and the perfecter of the beatitude of the angelic spirits. But how could he perform this role if he did not know in detail everything that concerns each of those who is subject to him?

Nevertheless, this science of vision of Christ the Savior, for all its universality, does not exclude the other modes of knowledge that occur in creatures. The fullness of Christ's perfection and his role as Head do not admit of his being deprived of any of the ways of knowing that the angels and men possess. That is why Jesus possesses both infused knowledge and acquired knowledge. Infused knowledge is that which comes through intelligible species or images impressed by God himself upon the created intellect. The angels have no other natural knowledge than this, and souls separated from their bodies, souls that have reached the ultimate term, likewise possess this form of knowledge. Therefore it properly belongs to the soul of Christ which was *in statu termini*, that is, in the condition of those who have reached the end of their lives, although in his mortal and passible body he was still *in statu viae*, a wayfarer traveling toward the term of perfect beatitude, that is to say, toward impassibility and immortality.

With regard to acquired knowledge, which belongs properly to men, Jesus must have had it and must have willed to have it so that he might be like us in all things. The experimental knowledge of the senses and the abstract knowledge that the intellect obtains from the objects presented to it by the imagination, in Christ attain a summit of perfection that they will reach in no other man. For, as we have said, the soul of Christ is the most perfect that has ever or will ever exist. Moreover, this third form of knowledge is not supernatural; we would have dealt with it above under the natural perfections of the sacred Humanity if the analogy had not required us to present everything that relates to the knowledge of Jesus in a single picture.

The first two forms of Jesus' knowledge—his knowledge of vision and his infused knowledge possessed their ultimate perfection from the very beginning. The same does not hold true for his acquired knowledge. In Jesus as in every other man, acquired knowledge had a beginning, gradually made progress, and finally reached consummation. In this respect it was possible for our Savior to resemble us, for this resemblance was no impediment to the fullness of knowledge that he possessed in other ways.

We have spoken only of Christ's knowledge as man, of his created knowledge. It goes without saying that as God his is an absolutely infinite and strictly divine knowledge, which is common to the Father and to the Son. Indeed, the various forms of knowledge in Jesus' soul are but diverse participations in this comprehensive intellection of God.

PRIMACY OF INFLUENCE

After pre-eminence of order and pre-eminence of perfection, St. Thomas attributes a third primacy to the Head, which is conformable with the ordering of the human organism: a primacy of influence. Christ has power over all the members of his Mystical Body to accomplish in them everything he wants and everything that their common supernatural end requires.

Elsewhere we have developed at length the question of the action of Jesus on his members.[10] We shall mention it here briefly in order to give a complete over-all view of the perfections and prerogatives of our divine Savior in his capacity as Head of the divine organism.

The power of Jesus extends over souls as well as over bodies. It embraces the whole spiritual world and the whole of corporeal nature. It extends principally over our souls, for through his Humanity, which is the instrument of his Godhead, Jesus transmits to our souls all the sanctifying influences that flow from his fullness of grace. It extends to our bodies, to which our Savior communicates even now something of his purity and holiness, especially through the Sacrament of his Body. It extends to our bodies, upon which Jesus will bestow resurrection and immortality on the last day. According to the words of St. Paul: "Christ has risen from the dead, the first-fruits of those who have fallen asleep. . . . For as in Adam all die, so in Christ all will be made to live" (1 Cor. 15:20–22).

Finally, Jesus exercises his power over all beings, over everything that lives or moves in nature, and over all the elements of the cosmic world, in order to produce, as he wills and according to the plans of divine Wisdom, all the miraculous changes that do not stem from the creative power. Only the power to create cannot be communicated to any creature. The Gospel shows us the unlimited power of Jesus over corporeal nature. Every creature

[10] Cf. Mura, *Le Corps Mystique du Christ*, Volume II.

obeys his voice. At his command the waves of the sea subside, the winds are calmed, bread is multiplied, water is changed into wine. He heals the sick, he raises up the dead, He commands all creatures, and the whole universe recognizes in him its Master and King. The devils dread his power and execute his orders.

Christ, therefore, is the Head in the most extensive sense of the term. He has all the perfections, all the excellences that the role demands. We have merely to enumerate succinctly his prerogatives and we shall find delight in contemplating them with love in mental prayer.

Now that we understand a little better the Head whose members we are, we shall glory in being so closely united to him. We must take advantage of this dignity, however, to conform our lives to the exigencies of such a noble condition. *Noblesse oblige.* The nobility that Christ confers upon us is of the highest quality, and the obligations it imposes upon us are all the more rigorous.

Having considered the Head of the Mystical Body, we must learn to know its members. This we shall strive to do in the following chapters.

CHAPTER XVI

The Members of the Mystical Body:
The Church Triumphant

A s the body is one and has many members . . . so also is it with Christ"
(1 Cor. 12:12). The multitude of members, with their diverse functions and unequal perfection belong to the very essence of the body. Some
members, closer to the head, receive life-giving influences more directly and
abundantly. Others are less closely linked with the head, with the principle
of all life and movement. Some contribute to the common good of the
organism in a universal and preponderant way, others play a more hidden
and less essential role in the general well-being.

In the Mystical Body of Christ also an admirable diversity of members
exists: some are closer and others farther removed from the sacred Head,
from whom—under the action of the Holy Spirit—all sanctifying influences are poured into this divine organism. Bound together by a thousand
mysterious bonds, and subordinated to the Head in a harmonious hierarchy,
they all interact upon one another in the communication and transmission
of the graces of light, of love, and of supernatural life.

In order to have an over-all idea of all of these integral parts of the whole
Christ, we shall consider them briefly one by one in the order of their
dignity, to the extent that it is given to us to know them, and according to
the degree and extent of the influences that they receive from their Head
or that they transmit to the members subordinate to them.

In the first place, we shall see the eminent place in the unity of the
Mystical Body held by the mother of our sacred Head. We cannot consider
her spouse, St. Joseph, apart from her because he was indissolubly united to
her in her maternal providence and was close to the Word made flesh. We

shall then point out the very eminent rank that belongs to the Precursor of Christ, the place reserved for the angels in the unity of the Mystical Body, and the relationship of the saints of the Church Triumphant to Christ and to his other members. Next we shall give our attention to the Church Suffering. Finally, we shall indicate the presence in the Church Militant of the different orders of the sacred hierarchy and the diverse categories of faithful or of other human beings whoever they may be, who are joined in a proximate or more remote manner to the unity of the total Christ, whose fullness encompasses all times and places.

Mary, the Heart of the Mystical Body

Above all the angels and saints there is a being of grace and beauty who is necessary to the integrity of the Mystical Body: the Blessed Virgin Mary, the mother of Christ and the mother of his members. Indeed Christ the Head, the one essential Mediator between God and men, did not need the help of any creature to communicate the superabundant life that he came to bring (cf. John 10:10). However, it was in the order of divine Wisdom that by the side of the new Adam a Woman was to take the place the ancient Eve had held by the side of the first head of the human race. Mary was to be the new Eve, like to Christ in all things (cf. Gen. 2:18), cooperating with him in the spiritual birth and nurturing of the children of God (cf. John 1:12),[11] the true mother of all the living (cf. Gen. 3:20).

The solid foundation of the Virgin Mother's role as the new Eve, which was the first dogma formulated by Marian theology in the primitive Church,[12] is to be found in a group of converging scriptural texts that relates to the central point of the economy of Revelation, namely, the great mystery of Christ the Redeemer. The texts range from the first chapters of Genesis to the vision of the Woman of the twelve stars seen by the Seer of Patmos (cf. Apoc. 12), from the prophetic message of Isaias concerning the virginal mother of the Emmanuel (cf. Is. 7:14), to its accomplishment in the virgin of Nazareth that St. Matthew bears witness to (cf. Matt. 1:18–25),

---

[11] Cf. St. Augustine, *De Sancta Virg, PL* 40:398.

[12] Cf. St. Justin, *Dialogue with Tryphon, PG* 6:710: "We say that the Son of God was made man through the Virgin, so that the disobedience instigated by the serpent might come to an end in the same way that it had begun. Eve, still an intact virgin, having conceived the word of the serpent, brought forth disobedience and death. The Virgin Mary, conceiving faith and joy, answered the Angel Gabriel who was bringing her the joyous tidings; and the coming of the Holy Spirit upon her, overshadowing her with the power of the Most High, assured her that the Holy One who would be born of her would be the Son of God. 'Fiat!' said she. 'Be it done to me according to thy word.'" Cf. also St. Irenaeus, *Adversus Haereses*, Lib. III, C. 72, PG, 7:958 I.

through the annunciations, the visitations, and the nativities narrated by St. Luke (cf. Luke 1 and 2), as well as the Marian scenes reported by St. John such as the wedding of Cana (cf. John 2:1–11) and the testament of Jesus on the cross (cf. John 19:25–27). Nor must we forget the deeply mysterious presence of Mary at the birth of the Church through the workings of the Holy Spirit (cf. Acts 1:14). Throughout this succession and concatenation of oracles and of prodigies, of prophetic announcements and of Messianic fulfillments, we see the unfolding and clarification—with the discretion proper to God in the communication of "the mysteries of the kingdom" (Matt. 13:11)—of the sublime mission reserved for the Woman blessed among all others (cf. Luke 1:28, 42), by the side of the One who is the Envoy (cf. Gen. 49:10),[13] the "Desired of all nations" (Agg. 2:8), and the "glory of Israel" (cf. Luke 2:32).[14]

We can only indicate here the deposit of Revelation concerning Mary the new Eve and companion of Christ the Redeemer in the entire work of salvation. Both exegesis and theology, taking up the teaching of the Fathers, now offer us solid explanations of this great truth.[15] The Magisterium of the Church, especially during these last few years, has placed great emphasis on the mediation of Mary dependent upon the universal and primary mediation of Christ. More than any other pontiff, St. Pius X, in his Encyclical *Ad diem illum*, has illustrated the role of the Virgin Mother, beginning with the twofold mystery of the Annunciation and Redemption. At the moment of the Incarnation, Mary conceived in her womb Christ and all his mystical members. On Calvary, she brought forth all the faithful through the merits of her compassion.

Referring to the Incarnation of the Word in the womb of the Virgin Mary, St. Pius X writes boldly: "Is not Mary the Mother of Christ? Therefore she is *our* Mother." On what is this conclusion based? Pius X finds it in the doctrine of the Mystical Body: "We, the many, are one body in Christ" (Rom. 12:5), he says, citing St. Paul. Likewise, in the same virginal womb of his most chaste mother, Christ assumed flesh and joined to himself a spiritual body composed of all those who would ever believe in him. Hence we can say that when she carried the Savior in her womb she also carried all

---

[13] Cf. also Is. 61:1; Luke 4:18; John 20:21.

[14] Cf. also Rom. 9:4–5.

[15] Cf. among others the substantial summary of Father Laurentin in his *Court Traité de Théologie Mariale*; Father Braun's *La Mère des Fidèles*; and above all the four series of conferences of the Société Française d'Études Mariales, under the common title La *Nouvelle Eve* (Paris: Lethielleux, 1954, 1955, 1956, 1957).

those whose life was enclosed in the life of the Savior. Thus we are mystically called the children of Mary and she is the mother of us all.

This spiritual motherhood of the Blessed Virgin Mary was consummated on Calvary by her compassion, in total dependence upon the redemptive sufferings of her Son. As St. Pius X also writes: "Through this communion of sufferings and of will between Mary and Christ, she merited to become the reparatrix of the lost world, and hence the dispenser of all the gifts that Jesus won for us by his death and his Blood." It is true, as St. Pius X makes clear, that "this distribution of graces belongs strictly to Christ, who alone obtained them by his death." He is by right the Mediator between God and men. However, through this communion of sufferings and prayers of the mother and Son, the august Virgin obtained (as Pope Pius IX says) "to be by the side of her only Son the powerful Mediatrix and Reconciler of the whole world."[16] Christ is the source, and "of his fullness we have all received" (John 1:16). But Mary, as St. Bernard remarks, "is the aqueduct" through which the life-giving flood of graces flows from Christ into our souls.

How can we translate the role of Marian meditation and express it in terms that befit the doctrine of the Mystical Body? What place are we to assign to Mary in the organism of the total Christ? This place must be the first after Christ's. Mary must be the most noble organ, the one having the greatest influence on the life of the whole, after the Head. In the Mystical Body Mary is the heart.

In our analogy the heart best represents the relationship between the Blessed Virgin and Christ the Head, and the relationship between his members. The role of the heart is subordinate to that of the head, and its beats are regulated by the governing activity of the head. The heart contracts or dilates in response to the nature of the object that the senses or the intellect offer to its affections. In addition, the heart quickens the entire organism. Its influence is not limited to a single part of the body but extends to all its members. This twofold relationship of the heart with the head and of the heart with the members symbolizes very well the supernatural relationship of Mary to Jesus and to the members of his Mystical Body.

Mary is full of grace, but her fullness is a participation in the fullness of Christ. Jesus possessed all graces in their absolute fullness from the first instant of the hypostatic union, and this totality excluded any possibility of growth. Mary received a relative fullness of grace, in keeping with her

---

[16] Bull *Ineffabilis Deus.*

eminent dignity. Proportioned to the various stages of her life, this fullness of grace was in a state of perpetual progress.

Mary was full of grace from the instant of her Immaculate Conception through an anticipated application of the merits of Christ the Redeemer: "*intuitu meritorum Jesu Christi Salvatoris*"—"by reason of the merits of Christ the Savior," to use the words of Pope Pius IX in his Bull *Ineffabilis Deus*.

When the Angel greeted Mary at the Annunciation as "full of grace," her perfection had reached a degree that made her worthy of sheltering the Word of God within her virginal womb.

But the Incarnation immediately increased this plenitude in an ineffable measure, through the life-giving influence of the Humanity of Christ present in her virginal womb. And what of the abundance of graces she received at the foot of the cross, the principle of all supernatural life, for it was then that her compassion made her our Co-Redemptrix and that Jesus proclaimed her the *mother of all the living*? Finally what can we say of the communications of grace from the Holy Spirit on Pentecost?

Mary was to communicate the superabundance of graces she had received from Christ the Head to the entire family of the redeemed. Indeed, she received a superabundance only so that she might be, as we have just said, the mother of all the living. Placed between the Head and the members of the total Christ, Mary is thus in very truth the heart of the Mystical Body, the spiritual reservoir into which Jesus pours the infinite riches of his Redemption in order to transfuse them into all his members.

Since the time of St. Bernardine of Siena the role of Mary in the Mystical Body has been compared to the neck which links the head to the rest of the body. St. Pius X himself, in the passage cited above from the Encyclical *Ad diem illum* has applied this analogy to Mary. Mary, he says, is the *aqueduct*, or again the *neck* that links the body to the head, and by which the Head exercises his power and virtue upon his Body. In this connection he quotes a text from St. Bernardine.

This symbolism expresses very well the idea of the mediation of Mary, who is placed between the Head and the members. However, it does not imply the idea of a vital influence, the notion of subordinate causality by means of which the Most Blessed Virgin Mary, dependent upon Christ, sanctifies and vivifies our souls.

Moreover it should be noted that the symbolism of the neck is but a simple adaptation without any basis in Holy Scripture. While Scripture points out in precise terms the analogy of the Body and the place and the role of Christ as the Head of the mystical organism, it makes no similar determination regarding the mediative function of Mary. Besides, there is nothing to keep us from choosing if need be some other symbol, a more expressive and fitting symbol, to signify this role of the Blessed Virgin Mary in the unity of the Mystical Body.

The symbol of the heart is remarkably appropriate. The heart is a life-giving organ, and yet dependent in its functions on the influences of the head, whose every perception causes a mysterious change in its pulsations. The heart is a reservoir of life, it first receives within itself the riches it afterwards distributes to the whole organism. As such it is a striking image of Mary, who is the Mediatrix subordinate to Christ the Head in the transmission of graces.

Thus Father Arintero, in his great work on the development of the life of the Church,[17] after indicating the symbolism of the mystical Neck, which is commonly accepted, proposes another symbol, the Heart, which he prefers to use. He writes:

> If with reference to the Head, Mary is, as it were, the Neck of the Mystical Body,[18] with reference to the soul [namely, the Holy Spirit], she performs the function of the Heart in which life and reparative blood are deposited and then distributed throughout the members and organs. Thus, as the Immaculate Spouse of the Holy Spirit, always intimately united to him and completely obedient to his influences, impulsions, and inspirations, she was always filled with divine life and grace in ever-increasing abundance, so that she might pour them out upon all men, to form and perfect them in Christ?[19]

Already in the last century, Scheeben, a well-known German theologian, justified the analogy of the heart as applied to the Blessed Virgin Mary in the unity of the Mystical Body:

> The relationship of Mary as the maternal Spouse of the Word finds its perfect analogy in the reciprocal organic relationships that exist between the central organ of the animal body, namely the heart, and the head of this body. Here the head is nourished by the heart by means of the blood it receives from it, and thereby owes its material existence to the heart

---

[17] *Desenvolvimiento y vitalidad de la Iglesia*, Volume I, Book 1, par. 7.

[18] We have already seen that even with reference to the Head the symbolism of Mary, *Heart* of the total Christ, remains true.

[19] *Op. cit*, Volume 1, Book I, par. 37.

[analogy with the role of Mary the Mother of God with reference to the human life of Christ]; whereas the head for its part transmits its spirit of life to the heart through the nerves that originate in it"[20] [analogy with the spiritual life that Mary receives from Christ and transmits to the faithful].[21]

From still another point of view the heart shows particular aptitude for symbolizing the role of Mary in the Mystical Body: it differs from the head in being a hidden organ whose secret action is not immediately manifest outwardly. A more recent author has developed this thought as follows:

> Mary has no place in the exterior, social organism of the Church. . . . Her cooperation is rather of a silent, hidden nature. But she nonetheless shares in the most intimate function of the Mystical Body, in the communication of life to the members. . . . Do not the functions of the heart condition and sustain in many ways the influence of the head over the other members? Just as the heart functions secretly but in an uninterrupted manner, so it is with Mary, the invisible and tireless Mediatrix of intercession.[22]

To this is added the fact that the power of loving and of compassionating, traditionally attributed to the heart, is eminently suited to the Virgin Mother.[23] Abbé Geslin writes:

> Jesus entrusts to Mary in the Church the role of goodness and mercy. . . . Jesus loves all men to draw them to himself and present them to God. But he does not want to love them alone and, as it were, by himself. He establishes in Mary the seat of his goodness and of his mercy, the throne of his tenderness and of his compassion. From this point of view, is not Mary also the heart of the Church, just as Jesus is its Head? Jesus allows himself to be touched by Mary and in Mary, and souls go to Jesus through Mary the universal Mediatrix."[24]

---

[20] *Handbuch der Dogmatik,* Vol. III, n. 1612.

[21] We can better understand this symbolism of the heart as applied to Mary, if we note that the heart presides over the very formation of the living being in its evolution. This is a striking picture of the role of the Blessed Virgin Mary united to Jesus in order to form the primitive Church under the impulsion of the Holy Spirit. Thus Father Arintero says in the passage already cited that Mary "the true Heart of the Mystical Body is the *primum vivens* which from the first instant begins to beat and to set in movement the vital elements for the quickening and development of the whole organism."

[22] Feckes, *Das Mysterium der Kirche,* Part II, Chapter 2, par. 5.

[23] Even if the heart is not strictly speaking the organ of sensible love, the fact that through its physiological link with the central nervous system, all the affections of the sensitive appetite find repercussions in it, suffices to justify the universally accepted symbolism of the heart as the seat of love. Cf. Terrien, *La dévotion au Sacré-Coeur de Jésus,* Book I.

[24] "Excursus" on Mary, the Heart of the Church, in his *Commentary* on the Epistle to the Ephesians, p. 54–55.

This function of the heart, the seat of love, quite naturally evokes the maternal role of Mary. The proper function of a mother is to love; all her other functions flow from love. Whereas man the head of the family acts primarily under the command of reason, the mother more easily obeys the impulsions of her heart. Nature herself has fashioned her to love. Thus the symbolism of the heart is closely linked to the spiritual maternity of Mary. In every family the mother is the heart of the home, and Mary is the mother of the great Christian family.

Everything, therefore, induces us to reserve for Mary the analogy of the heart of the Mystical Christ. Let us add that this image also is preferred because the very beauty and nobility of its symbolism far surpasses the symbolism of the neck. There is something heavy about the symbol of the neck that adapts itself well enough to the severity of Latin, but to which our modern languages adapt themselves very poorly. Father Feckes, cited above, does not fear to say in this connection: "Certainly the image [of the neck] is not beautiful. It seems more appropriate to the symbolism as well as more beautiful to call Mary, as do Scheeben and others, the heart of the Mystical Body."[25]

All these reasons induce us to salute Mary as "the center of souls and the heart of the Church."[26]

St. Joseph

Next in importance immediately after the Blessed Virgin Mary is her most chaste spouse, St. Joseph. In the Mystical Body, rank is determined in terms of proximity to the divine Head of the whole Christ. In this respect, the illustrious descendant of David has a place very close to his virginal spouse. His incomparable mission at the side of Jesus, the Word made flesh, his ineffable union with the Virgin Mother, do not allow us to leave him in a secondary rank.

Joseph's paternity with regard to the Son of God made man is a very real one, although of a unique and spiritual nature. He is the virginal father of Jesus. Jesus, the son of Mary, is also child of Joseph. He is the fruit of the virginity of Mary, but the Blessed Virgin was the spouse of St. Joseph. She

---

[25] Feckes, *op. cit.*

[26] "Geslin, *op. cit,* p. 56. This symbolism of Mary, the Heart of the total Christ, is likewise proposed and defended in the work of Derckx, *Psychologie der Vrouwe,* Part III, Chapter 8. Moreover, the late Father Gillet, former Master General of the Dominican Order, called Mary the Heart of the Mystical Body at the Marian Congress of Rheims in 1934.

and her divine fruit belonged to him by a right based on the sacred contract that united them. Jesus willed to have a family on earth, and St. Joseph was the head of this family. Because of this, Joseph was also the father of Jesus. Did not Mary say to her divine Son: "*Ecce pater tuus et ego . . .*"—"Behold, in sorrow thy father and I have been seeking thee" (Luke 2:48).

In consequence of his close bond with our divine Head and with Mary his virginal mother, St. Joseph has a dominant role to play with regard to the other members of the Mystical Body.

When he became the father of the Holy Family he naturally became the official protector of the larger family that is the Church. When the Vicar of Christ proclaimed St. Joseph the Patron of the Universal Church, he was merely recognizing a title and a function that God himself, in the plan of his providence, had attributed to the glorious Patriarch.

Here is the way, with great theological precision, a pious author expresses Joseph's place in the Church:

> The same divine relationship that makes Mary the Mother of all Christians and of the whole Church makes Joseph the Protector of Holy Church: The Church is as it were an extension of Mary, the most pure Virgin; as the guardian of Mary, Joseph is by that very fact the Patron of the Church.
>
> As the adopted Father of Jesus, the paternity of the great Patriarch embraces the members of Jesus and his whole Mystical Body which is the Church."[27]

The role of St. Joseph with relation to the Church, his title as her universal Protector, thus finds its ultimate reason in the doctrine of the Mystical Body. Joseph remains forever the guardian and foster father of Christ in his childhood. Now Christ is prolonged in his Church. The child of Bethlehem, exiled in Egypt and then hidden in Nazareth until the day of his manifestation in Israel is also the whole Church, weak and persecuted, growing up in exile, hidden and ignored until the great day of her manifestation in the fullness of time.

The mystical Christ, carried in Mary's arms and nourished with the milk of her tenderness, finds in St. Joseph a protector, a foster father, a father. The holy Patriarch watches over the mysterious growth of the Church, he foresees the unleashing of the persecutions that new Herods will raise up against her throughout her earthly existence. He foils the hypocritical plots

---

[27] Dom B. Marchaux, O.S.B., *Elévations sur saint Joseph*, Elevation 30.

they unceasingly hatch against her divine life. His paternity wraps the frail members of the Body of Christ in his protective mantle.

As the foster father of Jesus, St. Joseph continues to sustain the divine Child in all those who form his mystical complement. Are not the granaries of Egypt entrusted to him, as to Joseph of old? And did not the virginal father of Jesus receive the guardianship and administration of the divine wheat that nourishes souls in the Eucharist? Just as the holy Curé of Ars said in his pictorial style that the tabernacle is the larder of the Church,[28] so we must say that Nazareth was the first larder of humanity, the first tabernacle where the food destined to feed the whole world spiritually was reserved. Is this not what St. Bernard of Clairvaux tells us in equivalent terms? *"Iste Panem vivum e coelo servandum accepit, tam sibi quam omni populo"*—"[St. Joseph] received in his care the living Bread of heaven, for himself and for all the people."[29]

Is this an ingenious adaptation or a pious exaggeration? Neither; it is doctrinal harmony perfectly founded on the dogma of the whole Christ. The mysteries of the life of Jesus are reproduced in the life of the Church, and everything that happens to the mystical Head is found in his members. The mission of St. Joseph to be by Christ's side is understood in all its scope only if we follow, through faith, its prolongation in those who are the fullness of Christ.[30]

For this reason also the poor and those who labor are entrusted in a special way to the solicitude of the glorious father of Jesus. Do they not resemble more closely the One who "although the Creator of the universe, did not disdain to embrace the condition and the labors of an artisan"?[31]

Virginal souls can rightfully claim the patronage and the devoted love of Joseph who surrounded the most Pure Lily, the Queen of Virgins, with his vigilant care. Finally, the Church calls St. Joseph the hope of the sick and the patron of the dying.[32] Is not he who breathed his last on the heart of

---

[28] Monin, *Esprit du Curé d'Ars*, Part I, Chapter 9.

[29] Homily 2 on the *Missus est.*

[30] Analogously the role of St. Joseph is compared to the mission of the priest in the prayer in his honor inserted at the end of the Breviary, in preparation for Mass. He who treated the Body of Christ, "the virginal fruit of Mary." with so much reverence is proposed as the model of the priest in the respect he should have for the holy mysteries. It goes without saying, however, that we must avoid any exaggeration that would give the virginal father of Jesus a strictly priestly role. His dignity lies on another plane, that of the Incarnation, and by this fact, without implying any priestly character whatever, it nonetheless relates to the priesthood of Christ and receives from it a reflection of glory.

[31] Letter of Pope Pius XI to Cardinal Van Roey, August 19, 1935:

[32] Cf. the Litany of St. Joseph, whose beautiful invocations might suggest more than one analogous application of the doctrine of the Mystical Body to the plenary mission of the virginal father of Jesus.

Jesus and in the arms of Mary the first-fruits of those who die in the Lord's embrace? This help that Christ and Mary gave to Joseph is also a mystery which, like all mysteries, contains a corresponding grace.

St. Joseph assures the benefit of it to those who pray to him for it, and it is through his mediation that incorporation into the whole Christ of heaven is realized at the hour of death.

Clearly the place of St. Joseph in the unity of the Mystical Body is in the very front rank. Even among the angelic choirs it seems impossible to conceive a rank that is higher or even equal to his. St. Michael, the prince of the heavenly host, is simply the defender of the Church and gives honor to the one who is her universal Patron.

That is why especially during the past century all the popes have insisted on affirming the primary role that belongs to the virginal father of Jesus in the life of the Church, and have entrusted to him the most momentous interests of Christendom. Without speaking of Pius IX who declared him the Patron of the Universal Church, we can quote Leo XIII, who said in his Encyclical *Quamquam pluries* of August 15, 1889: "This divine house that Joseph governed as if with the authority of a father contained the first-fruits of the Church. . . . It is, therefore, natural and worthy of Blessed Joseph that he, who once provided for all the needs of the Family of Nazareth and protected it in a holy manner, should cover with his heavenly protection and defend the Church of Jesus Christ."

Most recent is the gesture of His Holiness Pope John XXIII, who entrusted to the holy Patriarch the patronage of the Second Vatican Council. Speaking of St. Joseph, Pope John wrote: "If there is a heavenly protector, appointed to obtain from above during the preparation of the next Council and during the course of its sessions the *virtus divina*, thanks to which it is destined to be epoch-making in the history of the contemporary Church, this mission cannot be conferred to any other saint in the same way as to St. Joseph, the august head of the Family of Nazareth and the Protector of Holy Mother Church" (*Apostolic Letter* of March 19, 1961).

There is no reason to be surprised at the obscurity in which the glory of St. Joseph has remained for so long despite his eminent rank. This obscurity stems from the very nature of his mission by the side of Jesus and Mary. He is certainly the father of Jesus, but only by reason of his virginity. He is the true spouse of Mary Immaculate, but a virginal spouse. His mission was to protect the purity of Mary and the privilege of the miraculous conception of Jesus, during his life and even after his death. During his life his role was to shield Mary and her divine fruit from any suspicion and calumny; after his death his role was to fade into the background so that the mystery of the virginal Motherhood might shine forth in a more brilliant light. For the virginally fruitful Flower was so delicate that even the glory of Joseph might, in the beginning, have jeopardized her integrity in the minds of the faithful. Thus God willed that for many long centuries the incomparable dignity of this great saint should remain in the shade, until faith in the virginal conception was deeply rooted in the hearts of the faithful.

Today this belief is firmly established. However, even now it seems that the love and worship of St. Joseph and intimate knowledge of the sublime prerogatives of the glorious Patriarch are the privilege of interior souls who are better able to discern his true greatness under the appearances of a hidden role. Such souls are less likely to distort the notion of his glorious paternity, which is so delicate and absolutely unique. Thus we can understand why God reserved for the great mystic Teresa of Avila the honor of propagating in the Church the worship of St. Joseph, the virginal father of Jesus.

St. John the Baptist

From earliest times the Church rendered very special honor to St. John the Baptist, which was based on the deep understanding that she always had of the Precursor's mission. "Thus it was by virtue of a design of Providence, as surprising as it is admirable, that the Church of Rome honored the birth of John the Baptist long before solemnizing the birth of the noblest of all creatures who is the mother of God."[33]

This privileged worship derives from the unique place and role of St. John the Baptist in the life of the Mystical Body.

> Too many souls forget that John still is, by reason of a divine decree, the Precursor of Christ and his indispensable witness: *Hic venit . . . ut omnes crederent per illum.* However, the role of prime importance that St. John

---

[33] Dom Flicoteaux, *Le Culte du Saint Précurseur* (Esschen, Belgium: Imprimerie S. Alph, 1924), Chapter 1. This valuable tract brings out the dignity and the sanctity of St. John the Baptist as well as the privileged worship he once received from the faithful. Cf. also a Note published by the same author in *Les Questions liturg. et paroiss.* (1931), 324–26.

The early honor given to St. John the Baptist can be explained because of the fact that the visible and official role of John the Baptist begins at his birth and even before, with the angel's announcement to Zachary, whereas the conception and birth of Mary, incomparably more holy in themselves and much more important to us, are not conspicuous in sacred history and remain for a time the secret of God and of Mary. However, this fact suggests an opportune reflection: we must beware of relying too exclusively on the liturgical argument when there is a question of comparing the merit of the saints and the excellence of their mission.

the Baptist played historically at the time of the Incarnation will be prolonged through the centuries as long as the work of the Redemption has not been completely consummated, and until the Mystical Body has definitely attained its full stature.[34]

Such is the exceptional grandeur of the mission reserved for the friend of the Bridegroom (cf. John 3:29), whose coming was announced by several prophets in the Old Testament. Isaias predicted "the voice of one crying in the desert: Prepare ye the way of the Lord" (Is. 40:3).[35] The prophet Malachias pointed in advance in the person of the Precursor to the angel who would prepare the way before the face of the Lord (cf. Mal. 3:1; Matt. 11:10). Finally Elias, the prophet of burning soul and consuming zeal, was himself only a prefiguration of the one whom Jesus (cf. Matt. 11:14), after the Angel Gabriel (cf. Luke 1:14), was to glorify as the new Elias (cf. Mal. 4:5), the bright and burning torch for the people of God (cf. John 5:35).

God honored the holy Precursor so much that in many respects he treated him as he did Christ himself. Like Jesus, John had his annunciation, and the same archangel who announced the Incarnation of the Word to Mary predicted the birth of John the Baptist to Zachary. His name, like that of Jesus, was brought from heaven. From the womb of his mother he received through Mary the life-giving influences of Christ, and from that moment began to proclaim the coming of the Son of God. His birth, like that of the Savior, was the cause of great heavenly joy. And like Bethlehem, the home of Elizabeth was made famous by remarkable prodigies. In a prophetic inspiration his father Zachary confirmed all the ancient oracles in his regard, tracing in advance the picture of the entire messianic work for which this wonderful child was preparing the way (cf. Luke 1:1–80).

This was only the prelude, but what a glorious one, of the greatness of Elizabeth's son. His mission, his glory would be to live at the juncture of the two Testaments, at the culminating point of the Old Law which would go forth to meet the Messias in his person and finally receive the effect of God's promises. He, the greatest among the children of men produced under the Mosaic dispensation (cf. Matt. 11:11), the last and most eminent of the prophets— indeed more than a prophet (cf. Matt. 11:9–10)—was to lead the Spouse to the divine Bridegroom by preparing her for him through baptism and penance. This is the Spouse, of course, that Christ came to earth

---

[34] *Le culte du saint Précurseur*, Introduction, 8.
[35] Cf. also Matt. 3:3.

to find (cf. John 3:29), that he was to purify in the bath of his divine Blood (cf. Eph. 5:26; Apoc. 7:14), and in the baptism of the Holy Spirit (cf. Mark 1:8). John the Baptist was the best man of the mystical Covenant, which is really the substance of the mystery of the total Christ, the mystery of the union of Jesus Christ and his Church. In this respect the Precursor carried out an official mission that was both singular and unique in the building of the Mystical Body.

To prepare the Spouse, then to reveal to her the divine Bridegroom who seeks her, is the twofold aspect of John's vocation. To prepare the Spouse: *"parare Domino plebem perfectam"*—"to prepare for the Lord a perfect people" (Luke 1:17)—the Angel Gabriel had already announced this as being the role of John the Baptist. The whole of God's providence for Israel had had as its end the preparing of the chosen people for the coming of the Messias. But in the fullness of time that everyone believed to have arrived,[36] there was need of a more immediate preparation, a more complete and more spiritual purification. That is the reason for the confession of sins and the baptism in the Jordan, to which the Jews submitted in throngs under the powerful force of St. John's words (cf. Mark 1:5).

> As it was, the baptism of John was indeed what he wanted it to be: a symbol of penance, signifying that all those who received it needed spiritual renewal, a pledge of purity, permitting the neophytes to hope that their sins would be forgiven them; a rite of initiation into the kingdom of God, conferring rights to this kingdom as well as to the benevolent attention of the Messias. In this way the Baptist was already exercising his ministry as Precursor. He was walking before the face of the Lord, preparing his ways, communicating to his people the science of salvation and obtaining the remission of sins. He walked in the spirit and the power of Elias, re-establishing peace in homes, reorganizing social life on foundations of justice and piety—in a word, preparing a perfect people for the Lord.[37]

The revelation of Christ, Son of God and Savior of the world, constitutes the second aspect of the Precursor's mission. It was also the most noble and excellent part of it. From the moment of his first meeting with the Savior, John realized, through the Father's voice, that he was the Son of God-made-man for our salvation. In this he was far ahead of the apostles, who, despite their constant association with Jesus, only gradually understood Christ and the kingdom of God.

---

[36] Cf. Buzy, *Saint Jean-Baptiste,* Part II, Chapter 2, 149 ff.
[37] Ibid., 146.

At his baptism in the Jordan, Jesus humbly bowed beneath the hand of the baptizer, thus taking upon himself, by an ineffable and merciful substitution, the sins of the first man and of his entire posterity. He declared himself the new Adam and the Head of the new human race. But it was as Son of God that he was accredited before the Father to pay off our debt and to merit for us the good will of our God: "Thou art my beloved Son, in thee I am well pleased" (Luke 3:22). Only John the Baptist witnessed this lofty manifestation; on his testimony the faith of the first disciples of Christ was established. It was he who proclaimed Jesus the Messias and Savior. And in the sublime prologue of his Gospel, which affirms the eternal generation of the Word, St.

John the Apostle took care to relate his own doctrine to the testimony of the Precursor: "There was a man, one sent from God" (John 1:6). This envoy, this apostle "came as a witness, to bear witness concerning the light, that all might believe through him" (John 1:7–8).

What was his testimony? A few days after his baptism, Jesus passed through the desert of John the Baptist and went again to his Precursor. In a holy ecstasy the friend of the Bridegroom recognized the Savior (cf. John 1:29), and cried out to the Jews surrounding him in search of forgiveness: "Behold, the lamb of God, who takes away the sin of the world" (John 1:29; 35–36).

The Lamb of God! He is the Victim of the sacrifice, he is the host for sin, the ransom of the world. The whole mystery of the cross is unveiled in the words of John the Baptist; Calvary appears as the principle of our new life and of our incorporation into Christ who died and rose again.

> At the moment John gave his testimony, he already had all the light on the mystery of Christ the Redeemer that St. Paul was later to receive directly from God in order to spread it over the world. That is why St. John's gaze, like St. Paul's, does not rest exclusively on the person of Jesus. He knows that Jesus is not the whole Christ, but that he must be completed by the successive development of the members of the Church. Anticipating the Apostle of the Gentiles, the Precursor sees the whole human race without distinction (cf. Matt. 3:9)[38] called to constitute the Mystical Body whose growth is to come entirely from Jesus its Head.[39]

---

[38] To the Jews who prided themselves on being sons of Abraham, John was already saying: "God is able out of these stones to raise up children to Abraham."

[39] Dom Flicoteaux, *Le culte du saint Précurseur*, Chapter 2, par. 2.

This was the incomparable mission of the Angel who was sent before the face of Christ (cf. Mal. 3:1), to prepare his ways and to lead the sons of Israel to the threshold of the Messianic kingdom. All the burning supplications and sighs that men had sent heavenward for more than forty centuries were condensed and personified in this last of the Prophets. The *Rorate coeli* of earlier generations was finally heard, and John the Baptist himself, who had been filled with his grace through the virginal womb of his mother and who had lived like the ancients in an immense yearning to appear before the Bridegroom, was finally able to thrill at his voice (cf. John 3:29), to gaze upon his divine beauty, and to proclaim the coming of the Savior to the sons of Jacob.

The Church is still filled with the great trepidation of the dying Law in the person of the Precursor, and has willed to perpetuate the memory of it in her liturgy. During the four weeks that prepare us for the feast of Christmas and that make us relive the days of long expectation, it is the voice of John the Baptist that she makes ring out in the ears of her faithful, to make them hope for the renewal of graces that won for us the birth of the Emmanuel.

In many parts of her official prayer, and every day at Mass, in the confession she requires of her ministers,[40] as well as in the offering of the divine sacrifice,[41] Holy Church recommends herself to the mission and to the merits of the Precursor, of the one who was the first to teach her to do penance for sins committed, who also was the first to show her the Lamb of the eternal sacrifice.

Christian piety should pattern itself readily on the piety of Holy Mother Church and on the order of the pre-eminences established by God in the distribution of graces and of prerogatives.

Then it will eagerly return to the fervent worship that the centuries of faith rendered to the Friend of the Bridegroom. This devotion will give us a deeper understanding of the mystery of Christ that the holy Precursor was sent to manifest to souls and that his prayers are still able to develop within us.

The Angels

"*The Mystical Body of Christ which is the Church*"—this is the way Pius XII expresses himself at the beginning of his encyclical on the Mystical Body.[42] In fact, even though this denomination of the Mystical Body has

---

[40] At the *Confiteor*.
[41] At the Offertory, "*Suscipe sancta Trinitas . . .*"
[42] *Mystici Corporis*, June 29, 1943.

been used through the centuries in a broader sense,[43] it must be understood today, at least since the issuance of the above-mentioned encyclical, in a more rigorous and limited acceptation to mean the supernatural society of men redeemed by Christ and actually incorporated into the Church founded upon Peter.

This society that will continue to grow and to expand upon earth until it attains its full stature at the end of time, is complemented and prolonged in the next world by the Church Triumphant, which is the completion in glory of the Church Militant. By this very fact Holy Mother Church incorporates into herself all those who have already fallen asleep in Christ (cf. 1 Thess. 4:14), but who are still retained in a state of painful purification to make them worthy of presenting themselves "holy and without blemish" (Eph. 1:4) before the face of God.

Do the angels belong to one of the three parts of ecclesial society that is called the Church Militant, the Church Suffering, and the Church Triumphant? Inasmuch as they do not belong to the human family that Christ came to redeem and from which he has made up his Mystical Body, they are not members of the Church in the strict sense. And yet they belong to it in the over-all divine plan that embraces men and angels. The angels belong to the Church *quasi ab extra*, by a twofold right: first, because they too benefit from the divine influences of Christ the Redeemer; secondly, because their ministry dedicates them to the protection and support of the members of Christ who are the redeemed.

According to the more probable sentiment of theologians, which is the view of St. Thomas, the grace and glory of the angels are not the fruit of the Redemption. They have been granted to these heavenly spirits independently of the merits of Christ. And yet the same Angelic Doctor does not hesitate to say that Christ is the Head of the angels[44] in a broader sense. To back up his affirmation, he appeals to the doctrine of St. Paul addressed to the Ephesians: "[God the Father raised Christ from the dead], setting him at his right hand . . . above every Principality and Power and Virtue and Domination. . . . And all things he made subject under his feet, and him he gave as head over all the Church, which indeed is his body, the completion of him who fills all with all" (Eph. 1:20–23; cf. Col. 1:16).

Thus Christ has power and hence influence over the angelic spirits not only as God but as man, since we are speaking here of the risen Christ, the

---

[43] Cf. Tromp, *Corpus Christi quod est Ecclesia*, Volume 1.
[44] Cf. *Summa*, IIIa, q. 8, a. 3.

Head of the Church. Such is clearly the meaning of this passage from the Epistle to the Ephesians.

True, Father Prat found it possible to write with regard to this passage:

> The difference of relation between the angels, *made subject by God to Christ,* and the Church, *which is the Body of Christ* and of which Christ is the Head, is quite clearly indicated in this phrase. . . . Christ is not in the same way Head of men and Head of the angels. As the latter form part of his kingdom, he can well be called their Head, but he does not communicate to them vital nourishment, because they do not belong to his Mystical Body.[45]

And yet Christ's royal power in the kingdom of grace and glory, to which the angels belong inevitably, has many supernatural influences both of an illuminating and life-giving nature, especially in view of making them collaborate in the work of the sanctification of men. The Angelic Doctor, in the passage cited above, says explicitly: "Christ is not only the Head of men, but of angels."[46]

The role of the guardian angels in particular, which both Scripture and Jesus himself affirm (cf. Matt. 18:10), cannot be conceived unless Christ the Head, who vivifies men as the members of his Mystical Body, communicates graces of light and of love to those whom he charges with watching over the life of his members, and with defending and promoting this life until it reaches its full stature. Is this not the foundation of the spiritual brotherhood in Christ that the angels have with us (cf. Apoc. 22:9)?

What is the nature of the influence of Christ upon the angelic spirits? It is of the same order as that which he exercises over men. St. Thomas writes: "The Humanity of Christ, by the virtue of the spiritual nature, that is, the Divine, can cause something not only in the spirits of men, but also in the spirits of angels."[47] While it does not communicate essential grace and beatitude to them, at least it communicates to them a complement of happiness, of accidental grace, of supernatural knowledge. It manifests to them admirable secrets on the hidden depths of God, on the plans of God concerning the Church, concerning her development through the centuries, and finally concerning her ultimate triumph.

In his first epistle, St. Peter says that the "angels desire to look" upon the Christian mystery, the grace destined for the disciples of Christ, whose time

---

[45] *The Theology of Saint Paul* (Westminster, Md.: The Newman Press, 1952), I, 294.
[46] *Summa*, IIIa, q. 8, a. 4.
[47] Ibid., ad 4.

and circumstances "the prophets foretold" (cf. 1 Pet. 1:10–12). For his part, the Apostle of the Gentiles, speaking to the Ephesians of "the dispensation of the mystery which has been hidden from eternity in God, declares that he has been commissioned to announce it to the Gentiles "in order that through the Church there be made known to the Principalities and the Powers in the heavens the manifold wisdom of God" (Eph. 3:8–10).

There is no doubt, therefore, that the angels participate in the mystery of Christ and receive from it graces and treasures of beatifying knowledge in abundant measure. Otherwise how could they fill the function that the Epistle to the Hebrews attributes to them as "ministering spirits, sent for service, for the sake of those who shall inherit salvation" (Heb. 1:14)? Could they really govern and serve the heirs of the kingdom, the members of the Word Incarnate, if they did not receive from Christ himself the necessary directives in the way of light, impulsions of love, and the most diverse graces?

All these reasons led St. Thomas to attribute to the angels the knowledge of the mysteries of grace stemming from the Incarnation of the Word,[48] And he makes his own the teaching of Pseudo-Denys, according to which the angels "interrogate Jesus, receive the knowledge of what he accomplishes for us, Jesus being their teacher without any intermediary."[49]

When we take these things into consideration we have a better understanding of the words of St. Paul, already cited, which tell us that God has restored and re-ordered all things in his Christ, not only the visible world and things of earth, but also invisible and heavenly things (cf. Eph. 1:10). Thus the whole kingdom of heaven was in a certain sense reorganized by the work of the Redemption and by the entrance into glory of Jesus and his triumphal escort.

By his ascension Christ rose above the nine angelic choirs, above the angels, the archangels, and the thrones; above the dominations, the principalities, and the powers; above the virtues, the cherubim, and the seraphim, up to the very throne of God. His Father handed him the scepter of the eternal kingdom. The entire heavenly militia acclaimed its King with ineffable joy, and St. John echoes this angelic jubilation in his Apocalypse: "And I beheld, and I heard a voice of many angels round about the throne . . . saying with a loud voice, Worthy is the Lamb who was slain to receive power and divinity and wisdom and strength and honor and glory and blessing . . . forever and ever" (Apoc. 5:11–14).

---

[48] Cf. ibid., Ia, q. 57, a. 5.
[49] *Coel. Hier.*, VII, quoted in *Summa*, Ia, q. 57, a. 5.

The Saints in Heaven

Having suffered with Christ and shared his works in this valley of tears, the saints born of the human family resemble their divine Head more completely than do the pure spirits. Jesus took on human nature, not angelic nature: "for it is not angels that he is succoring" (Heb. 2:16). Christ chose to resemble the sons of Adam in all things, in order to become their merciful Pontiff, having experienced all their infirmities: "Wherefore it was right that he should in all things be made like unto his brethren . . ." (Heb. 2:17–18).

We shall show the place of the saints in the unity of the Mystical Body by explaining their relationship with Jesus, their Head, as well as with the members of the Church Militant.

When considered in their relationship to Christ the Head, the saints in heaven appear to us as the reflection of his glory and as the fullness, the ultimate flowering of his redemptive grace. In the saints the power of Christ's divine mysteries is revealed and deployed in all its splendor. In them, the limitless power of his Redemption is poured out and unfolded to its fullest extent. "This is because," a pious writer once remarked very aptly, "holiness is but the fulfillment of the evangelical light, a pouring out of the Spirit of Jesus into his saints."[50]

The light of the sun is too strong and too penetrating to allow our weak eyes to gaze fixedly at it, but it is poured out and distributed on the various objects that it encounters, giving them a reflection of its own rays. In the same way, the fullness of holiness that Jesus possesses in his Humanity is poured out and distributed among the great variety of the saints, revealing in each one of them a particular aspect of its incomparable riches.[51] Our weak intellect can thus more easily measure, without ever exhausting its powers, the immensity of life, the superabundance of grace contained in the Person of our divine Savior.

Monsieur Olier brings out this truth in speaking of All Saints' Day:

> This feast makes manifest the life hidden in him [that is, in Christ]. . . . His life was formerly contained within himself alone, his interior was known only to him and to his Father, and the scope of his heart and soul was not revealed or made manifest outwardly. But on this day of All Saints, his interior life is revealed. He explicates[52] himself to the fullest extent. He

---

[50] The Very Reverend Jean-Léon Le Prevost, Founder of the Brothers of St. Vincent de Paul, in a letter dated July 13, 1866. Cf. *Vie*, Volume II, 258.

[51] Cf. *Summa*, IIa-IIae, q. 183, a. 2.

[52] In the Latin sense of the word, that is, he deploys himself.

reveals and unfolds himself in them, and the divine perfumes once enclosed in his bosom and whose fragrance was not known, are poured out in the whole Church and wafted up even to the throne of God where they rise as an odor of sweetness.[53]

As long as the saints remain on earth, the life of Christ in them is, as it were, veiled under the appearances of their earthly existence. Precious as it may be, it is not revealed to our faith. In the words of the Apostle, it is "hidden with Christ in God" (Col. 3:3). For here on earth we live under the dispensation of faith (cf. 2 Cor. 5:7). But in heaven where Christ appears in all his glory, he causes to shine forth in all his saints the fullness of life and glory that he communicates to them: "Your life is hidden with Christ in God. When Christ, *your life*, shall appear, then you too will appear with him in glory" (Col. 3:3–4).

As members of Christ in their ultimate state of perfection, the saints in heaven do not simply remain united to their divine Head to manifest his glory; they also remain in close communion with the Church here on earth. How could they cease to be interested in her? They remember with gratitude that it is she who brought them forth to the divine life. They know it is she who, like a tender mother, carried them on her bosom throughout their earthly life and brought them forth to glory on the day of their death, which was the day of their birth in heaven. It is she who continues, by her spiritual fruitfulness, to people the heavenly Jerusalem, thus increasing the happiness of the blessed with each passing day.

The union that binds the saints in heaven to the faithful on earth is based on their common incorporation in Christ Jesus. One divine life, which is the life of grace, flows from Christ into all his members, whether they be already clothed in glory or still subject to the trials of this life. This is the Communion of Saints in its widest extent. Triumphant with their Head, the glorious members of Christ experience a fraternal sympathy for those whom they see exposed to the risks of battle, and this compassion seeks to express itself in devotion, in efficacious and fruitful help.

What a joy and blessing it is to sense that we are loved by the saints, fraternally supported by them before the Majesty of God! In the temporal order, many make use of powerful friends to obtain easy access to the great of this world! We, the sons of the heavenly kingdom, have no reason to

---

[53] Letter n. 235, Migne, cols. 1050–51.

envy them. At the court of the divine King we have friends whose influence never wanes.

God could no doubt do without these intermediaries in dispensing his graces. But he finds it is to his glory to make the saints serve in increasing his kingdom and in accomplishing his plans for us. St. Thomas remarks, following the author of the *Heavenly Hierarchy*:[54]

> The order established by God among things is that the last should be led to God by those that are midway between. Wherefore, since the saints who are in heaven are nearest to God, the order of the divine law requires that we, who while we remain in the body are pilgrims from the Lord, should be brought back to God by the saints who are between us and him: and this happens when the divine Goodness pours forth its effect into us through them. And since our return to God should correspond to the outflow of his boons upon us, just as the divine favors reach us by means of the saints' intercession, so should we, by their means, be brought back to God, that we may receive his favors again. Hence it is that we make them our intercessors with God, and our mediators as it were, when we ask them to pray for us.[55]

Do we depreciate the power of God when we have recourse to the mediation of his friends? On the contrary, we recognize and glorify his divine wisdom by revealing the admirable order he has established in his kingdom. We are honoring his goodness that is communicated to his saints to the point of making them, in dependence upon him, instruments of his grace and channels of his mercy. We are glorifying the supreme mediation of Christ, to whom all the saints must have recourse, and from whom alone they hold their influence and their merits.

The Church of Christ, guided by his Spirit, has never known the vain scruples that have troubled the disciples of Luther. Her entire liturgy is full of her invocations to the saints and of her trust in their intercession. When she suggests to her children that they make a humble acknowledgment of their sins in the *Confiteor*, she has them do this in the presence of all the blessed in heaven, in order to obtain an added right to their intercession before God: *Ideo precor beatam Mariam, semper Virginem . . . et omnes Sanctos orare pro me!*

In the very offering of the sacrifice of the Mass, whose divine power gives her every reason for confidence, the Church also wants to arm herself with the help of her glorious sons whose

---

[54] Dionysius, *Eccl. Hier.*, V.
[55] *Summa*, Suppl., q. 73, a. 2.

"merits and prayers"[56] give her reason to hope for more abundant graces. The solemn litanies to which the Church has had recourse since earliest times, under grave circumstances, at the ordination of her ministers, or in public calamities, are a stirring testimony of her faith in the influence and mediation of the saints. The Litany of the Saints, in which the Church evokes the names of her most illustrious sons and daughters one after the other, is a very striking expression of the beautiful dogma of the Communion of Saints.

Together with their prayers, the blessed in heaven present their merits to God. The value of their holy actions, of their love and sacrifices is something that exists here and now, that is always before the eyes of God. The Angelic Doctor calls this an interpretative intercession. That is to say, God considers the presentation of the good works of the saints as an endlessly repeated prayer from their lips: "The saints are said to pray for us ... by interpretive prayer, namely by their merits which, being known to God, avail not only them unto glory, but also us as suffrages and prayers."[57]

Sustained by the intercession of the saints in heaven, the Church Militant offers in return the homage of a worship of profound and devout veneration. She lovingly exalts those in whom she contemplates the image of a Christ who is without stain or blemish. With maternal pride she recalls their heroic deeds, which she proposes for the imitation of her children and which she recounts in the celebration of her divine office. With religious respect she honors their precious remains, their venerable relics, which her sons kiss devoutly in testimony of their Christian brotherhood. And it is a very great honor for the martyrs of Christ that the Church has made it a rule to offer the Sacrifice of the Lamb without blemish only over the relics of the saints, especially of those who were immolated with him to bear witness to their faith.

Not only our worship and our prayers, but also our very life contributes to the increase in the glory of the saints. Our works quickened by grace, our efforts to advance in virtue, our progress toward union with Jesus, the whole supernatural capital that increases the treasure of the Church adds to the joy of the blessed. This is called "accidental glory," by contrast with the substance of the beatific vision, which is unchanging. But these joys, added to their essential happiness, are no less ineffably sweet and delightful. They are, as it were, the echo in the depths of each glorified soul of the beautiful dogma of the Communion of Saints lived in its fullness, which permits each

---

[56] Cf. the *Communicantes* of the Canon of the Mass.
[57] *Summa*, Suppl., q. 72, a. 3.

of the blessed to say with the Psalmist: "I am the friend of all who fear thee" (Ps. 118:63). That is to say, I share in the riches of all who fear the Lord.

All who live here on earth united to Christ by faith and holy hope aspire toward the plenitude of happiness, the completion of Christ in his members. So too do all those who, having terminated their period of trial on earth, are retained for a while in the place of supreme purification to prepare themselves for their encounter with infinite Purity.

CHAPTER XVII

The Members of the Mystical Body:
The Church Suffering

Those "who are gone hence before us, marked with the sign of faith, and sleep the sleep of peace"[1] are without any doubt members of Christ just like the blessed in heaven who have already attained eternal glory. As suffering members of the Mystical Body these souls are still united to Christ by the bonds that attached them to him while they were on earth. Are these not the believing and loving souls of whom St. Paul spoke to the Corinthians (cf. 1 Cor. 3:10–15), who built the structure of their spiritual life on the solid foundation laid by the Apostle, the foundation that can be none other than Christ Jesus?

We too are united to these souls by the bond of Christian solidarity that makes of us all a single body with Christ our Head. And this holy union must make our hearts beat with immense compassion for the distress in which these friends of Jesus find themselves.

The whole Church Militant takes an interest in those who just yesterday were her children and who now await the succor of her maternal charity so that they may enter into possession of the supreme Good. The beautiful liturgy of the dead as well as all the prayers that the Church offers to God for her deceased sons deserve our close attention. This will help us to understand the strong bonds that unite her to the saints who are still in debt before divine Justice.

If we want a more complete view of this mystery of Christ, we must look at the kingdom of expiatory suffering with the eyes of faith. This will show us both the fate, worthy at once of pity and of envy, of these suffering souls, and the bonds that unite them to the other members of the total Christ.

---

[1] Memento of the dead in the Canon of the Mass.

The Condition of the Suffering Souls

The condition of the poor souls, debtors to divine Justice, is of the greatest interest to our doctrine of the total Christ. It is important that we should not ignore this large portion of the Mystical Body, or forget the profound distress of these members, who are in the most urgent need of our fraternal aid. We shall therefore set forth the essential facts concerning them.

The fate of souls undergoing expiation presents itself to us under two aspects, which at first sight may seem contradictory. One is consoling and full of hope, the other is terrifying and of a nature to inspire us with salutary fear. Purgatory is a sojourn of holiness and of supernatural joy for these exiles already securely in possession of their passport to heaven. But it is also a place of suffering and of painful purification for those whose blemishes still render them unworthy to appear before subsistent Purity. We would not have an exact understanding of the condition of these suffering members of Christ if we did not consider this twofold state of the saints in purgatory.

Saints! Indeed, that is what these poor prisoners of love are, established forever in grace and in divine friendship. Although they deserve our warmest supernatural compassion for the immensity of their suffering, they are, nonetheless, most worthy of envy and must be the objects of our worship, respect, and love.

These souls are established for all eternity in goodness. They cleave definitively to God by a charity that nothing can impede. They are irrevocably incorporated into Christ, and reveal excellently the life-giving power of his sacred passion and the efficacy of his grace, which makes of them rightful citizens of heaven and members of the elect, henceforth inscribed in the rosters of the heavenly City.

St. Catherine of Genoa, in her admirable *Treatise on Purgatory*, which St. Francis de Sales held in such high esteem, gives us a very exact and very theological idea of this state of holiness in which the expiating souls are established. "Immutably established in charity, and henceforth incapable of deviating from it by any actual imperfection, they can only will and desire the pure will of pure Charity. In this fire of purgatory, they are in the divine order which is pure charity, and hence they cannot stray from it in any way, granted that it is also just as impossible for them to sin or to merit in any way" (Chapter 1).

The acceptance of the divine order enables the souls in purgatory to experience a real and profound joy. St. Catherine of Genoa says: "They feel such great joy in seeing themselves in the order of God who accomplishes in them everything he pleases that no thought can enter their minds to increase their sufferings. They contemplate solely the operation of the goodness of God, and the ineffable mercy that he shows man by making purgatory the path that leads to him" *(ibid.).*

The joy of the souls in purgatory surprises us at first. It is hard for us to reconcile the reality of deep sufferings with the sentiment of intense joy. St. Catherine, however, speaks from experience, for she herself endured the sufferings of these poor souls during her earthly life. Thus she repeats several times insistently: "I do not believe that after the happiness of the saints in heaven there can exist a joy[2] comparable to that of the souls in purgatory. A ceaseless communication of God makes their joy greater from day to day, and this communication of God becomes more and more intense as it consumes the obstacle that it finds in them" (Chapter 2).

Theologically considered, the joy of the suffering souls should not surprise us. Joy results from union with the object beloved, union with the good capable of filling our soul.[3] Divine charity unites us to the supreme Good, which is capable of satisfying every desire. This is the teaching of the Angelic Doctor, who says: "Joy is caused by love . . . through the presence of the thing loved. . . . Now charity is love of God, whose good is unchangeable, since he is his goodness, and from the very fact that he is loved, he is in those who love him by his most excellent effect, according to I John 4:16: 'He that abideth in charity, abideth in God, and God in him.' Therefore spiritual joy, which is about God, is caused by charity."[4]

Who can know the intensity of love for God that consumes the holy souls in purgatory, for the one whom they know as their most loving Father and their one and infinite Good? They are no longer hindered from surrendering to this love because of the fascination of sensible goods. Their love is all the more intense inasmuch as their knowledge of God has become more perfect.

> The soul then sees, without being able to forget it for a single minute, that it is made for God, and having freely accepted to obey him, it will go to him, it will be united to him, it will possess him. It loves this God with a continual love, not through successive acts, but by a single, uninterrupted act. At the same time, it feels an unquenchable need of God. All other tendencies have disappeared. This one has taken their place. It is irresistible; it is so vehement and so compelling that it leaves room for no other.[5]

[2] The Italian word is *contentezza*, signifying contentment, joy.
[3] Cf. *Summa*, Ia-IIae, q. 3, a. 4; q. 25, a. 2.
[4] Ibid., IIa-IIae, q. 28, a. 1.
[5] Msgr. Saudreau, article in *La Vie Spirituelle* (November, 1934), 142.

At the same time that they perceive the immensity of God's goodness, the exiled souls understand the supereminent charity of Christ, who loved them even to death, to the death of the cross. They feel powerfully drawn toward him by a reciprocal love, as toward the Head, who will soon complete the work of his divine Redemption in them. With such a love of God and of Jesus, how could the suffering souls fail to experience an immense joy: the joy of loving and of knowing they are loved, even amid these sufferings that are restoring their spiritual beauty?

It is this love and this joy which make the principal difference between purgatory and hell. Hell is the place *where no one loves*. It is the kingdom of hatred of God and of unmixed suffering. Hell is the "unquenchable fire" into which the dead wood, the sterile branches cut off from the mystical Vine are cast. In purgatory, on the contrary, there is life, intense life, flowing through branches which are forever united to the Vine, and almost ready to produce their fruit for the eternal marriage feast.

After this description of the joys of purgatory, some may imagine that its torments are not as terrible as they are generally said to be. Let us make no mistake about it. Intense as the sentiment of joy may be in purgatory, it does not exclude the reality of pain, indeed the most excruciating pain in the spiritual soul. The mutual exclusion of these two sentiments is verified only in the case of sensible or corporeal joys and sufferings. Such feelings require the concurrence of an organ, of a material faculty whose power of operation is very limited and is modified in various ways in its fundamental disposition by pleasant impressions or by painful sensations. When one or more of our senses dilate and flourish under the sentiment of joy, they cannot at the same time experience a profound impression of pain, which tends on the contrary to contract the organs and emotive faculties.

The same does not apply in the higher region of the spiritual soul. The intellect and the will, nonmaterial faculties, can turn to all sorts of objects without ever exhausting their capacity for knowing or loving. There is nothing to prevent the soul from knowing diverse objects simultaneously; the soul can know God and his great love for it, at the same time that it knows its own sins and their opposition to infinite Holiness. Each of these forms of knowledge arouses in the will a movement in relation to its object. The former will inspire in the soul a lively sentiment of joy and of love, whereas the latter produces sadness and unspeakable regret.

This is precisely the condition of the souls in purgatory. And if their burning love of God fills them with consolation, the clear vision of his supreme Goodness and of the exigencies of his infinite Purity that can suffer no blemish in its presence causes them torment beyond anything we can conceive.

St. Catherine of Genoa says: "The suffering soul endures such extreme sorrow that no tongue can recount it, that no mind can even understand the slightest spark of the fire that consumes it, unless God reveals it through a special grace. He has deigned by his grace to show me one of these sparks, but I do not have words to express it" (Chapter 2).

The principal cause of the torment of the expiating souls is their remoteness from God, the delay in the blessed union for which they yearn with every shred of their will, avid for the infinite. This is not because there remains even the slightest sin in them. Every sin, as far as guilt is concerned, has been fully retracted and wiped out in the first instant after death. These souls are now in the light, and through grace have adhered totally to God their sovereign Good from the instant of their exit from this world. Hence, they completely retract any slight attachments and self-satisfactions they may still have held during their mortal life. The limitations in the total gift to God that we call venial sins, the often unconscious twists of the will that we call imperfections are incompatible with the vision of God's infinite goodness that is granted the souls in purgatory immediately after death.

Nevertheless, after the remission of guilt, of the offense against the divine Majesty, these souls must still pay the debt contracted by them against the justice of God. They must still expiate the temporal punishment that re-establishes the divine order which has been disturbed by sin. This debt keeps them far from God. It keeps them from rising to the heart of light and of beatitude. As long as these souls have not satisfied divine Justice, they still bear, as it were, the stigmata of sin, the terrible debt that makes them the debtors of infinite Holiness.

St. Catherine of Genoa writes on this subject: "Inasmuch as the souls in purgatory are free from the guilt of sin, there is no other impediment between God and them than this punishment that has held them back, so that the instinct [of beatitude] has been unable to attain its perfection" *(loc. cit.).*

The purification of the suffering souls, therefore, is simply the expiation of the punishment they must still pay. Every vicious tendency, every cleaving to evil has been rectified from the instant of death. St. Thomas says this clearly, in answer to the following objection against prayer for the deceased: Souls are said to be held in purgatory so that they may be purified. Now these suffrages do not produce anything in them that effects this purification; therefore they are useless. To which he answers: "The purifying of the soul by the punishment of purgatory is nothing else than the expiation of the guilt that hinders it from obtaining glory."[6]

Therefore, when we speak of the stains that disfigure the suffering souls, we must not understand this to refer to guilt. For guilt is remitted the instant the soul leaves earthly life, insofar as any unforgiven venial sins are concerned. Nor do the souls in purgatory suffer any privation of grace, which is the stain of sin in the strict sense. These souls already possess forever all the grace that will adorn them in heaven. But there still remain the vestiges of sin, the required expiation known as *reatus poenae*. Actually this expiation bears a necessary relation to the evil acts committed.[7] Whence it is that the unpaid debt stains and dishonors the soul, giving it a mark of infamy akin to the nature of the sin that remains to be expiated. It is somewhat the way chains impress upon prisoners of human justice the dishonoring character of the evil act for which they are a punishment.

Kept away from God for a time as a punishment for its sins, the soul suffers a burning thirst, similar to the punishment of damnation suffered in hell, although without the despair and hatred of God that prevails among the damned. With the Psalmist, the soul repeats these words: "My soul thirsts for God, the living God: when shall I come and behold the face of God?" (Ps. 41:3).

This unceasing desire, however, is continually frustrated. The mysterious suffering of the suffering souls has this particular aspect that their very love for God nourishes and activates it; so much so that the holy joy they feel and the extreme suffering they endure are both fed from the same source. For, says St. Catherine of Genoa, "the fire of charity that burns them impresses upon them such an irresistible impulsion toward their last end that they consider it an intolerable torture to feel within themselves an obstacle that halts their soaring toward God. And the more light they receive, the more extreme is their torment" (Chapter 3).

However, this is not the only suffering endured by the souls in purgatory. To the punishment of being deprived of God that torments these

---

[6] *Summa*, Suppl., q. 71, a. 6 ad 3.

[7] This relationship is proportional in the same way that privation of grace is related to the voluntary act which gives it its particular mark of sinfulness.

poor exiles, is added, according to the gravity of their sins, other afflictive punishments, and notably the punishment of fire, which, like that of hell, is experienced by these souls in a mysterious but very real way. St. Paul reveals the existence of a purifying fire that will make known the worth of the work raised up by each one on the foundation which is Christ: "If anyone builds upon this foundation, gold, silver, precious stones, [or else] wood, hay, straw—the work of each will be made manifest, for the day of the Lord [that is, the judgment of God] will declare it, since the day is to be revealed in fire. The fire will assay the quality of everyone's work: ... if his work burns he will lose his reward, but himself will be saved, yet so as through fire" (1 Cor. 3:12–15).

Obviously this passage does not speak of the eternal fire of hell, for the unfortunate ones who fall into hell have not built upon Christ. The Apostle is speaking of the faithful Christians who remain united to Jesus through grace and build upon this foundation the divine edifice of their perfection. Many of the parts that make it up are formed of precious metals, that is, they are sanctified by love of God. Many others, alas, are made of lowly materials, spoiled by self-love and self-seeking. All this will have to be eliminated, and not without pain, in the fire of expiation.

Many revelations of the saints, whose worth and authenticity it would be rash to question, confirm our belief in these purifying flames. Everybody knows the zeal of St. Margaret Mary in succoring her "dear suffering friends," and what she has told us of the punishments they suffer. St. Gertrude also reports facts that can well give the indifferent cause for reflection, and arouse our affectionate compassion for the poor souls, with a view to helping them.[8]

Indeed, it is possible for us to hold out a brotherly hand to these prisoners of love. For even though their distress is such that they can no longer do anything for themselves, they are not abandoned. The dogma of the Communion of Saints is efficacious and beneficial for them, assuring them of help from the other members of the Mystical Body.

Communion with the Souls in Purgatory

In the work of completing and purifying the total Christ that goes on in purgatory, the Church Militant brings fraternal aid to the Church Suffering.

---

[8] Cf. also *Le Purgatoire d'après les révélations des Saints*, by Abbé Louvel. Speaking of purgatory and its fire, St. Thomas used the formula: "Consonat magis Sanctorum dictis, et revelationi factae multis ..." (Suppl., Appendix II, a. 2).

And here is another admirable manifestation of the Communion of Saints uniting the members of Christ for their mutual good.

The Church of this earth cannot abandon those of her children who have died, many of whom she knows remain in debt to God. There is nothing more beautiful or touching than the sight of the maternal charity she displays in favor of the saints of the Church Suffering. This includes her urgent prayers, alms and penances, numerous indulgences, and above all the uninterrupted succession of Masses which she offers up for the redemption of the poor captives in purgatory.

Charity is at the root of this beneficent activity of the Church in favor of the deceased. St. Thomas tells us that "charity is the bond that unites the members of the Church.[9] Now this bond does not extend only to the living, but also to the dead who depart in a state of charity. Charity does not cease with the life of the body; . . . and thus the suffrages of the living benefit the de-ceased, because of their union in charity."[10]

The Christian charity that accompanies the dead beyond the grave is revealed in a touching way in the whole liturgy of the deceased. How beautiful are the Church's prayers for her dead!

Eternal rest, light without end, life and immortality are the treasures she begs for her children, hastening the moment of their entrance into heaven by her suffrages. "*Requiem aeternam dona eis, Domine,*" she sings in her offices, and the faithful answer: "*Et lux perpetua luceat eis!*" This magnificent wish has none of the gloomy desolation of hopeless hearts, even though we may lend a note of sadness to these beautiful texts by the outward panoply of mourning. These verses of the sacred liturgy are truly an expression of a hope that is at the service of charity.

The prayers and suffrages of the Church touch the heart of her divine Spouse, inducing him to yield to his love for these suffering souls and to place them in possession of eternal beatitude.

His justice has, so to speak, bound the hands of his mercy, constraining him to demand rigorous payment for every debt not remitted here on earth. But we, the exiles of earth, *who are still under the dispensation of mercy,* have the blessed power to modify the decrees of divine justice. Evidently our satisfactory works are far inferior to the demands of rigorous expiation in the next life. Because of the fact that they are voluntary and inspired by

---

[9] It is the formal principle of this union, as we have shown in Chapter VIII above.
[10] *Commentary on the Sentences*, Book IV, d. 45, q. 2, a. 2, q. 2.

love, however, we can, since we are still capable of gaining merit, greatly shorten the duration of the terrible trial.

Above and beyond our personal works, we possess the unique treasure which is the Sacrifice of the Mass. The Blood of the holy Victim is poured out on the souls who are being consumed by the fire of divine justice. The immaculate Lamb is the Host of propitiation who expiates all sins, and whose power gives efficacy to our own expiations. For this reason Holy Mother Church frequently offers the Eucharistic Sacrifice for the souls in purgatory; indeed the faithful cannot exercise more efficacious charity toward their dear ones than by having the Mass celebrated for them.

St. Thomas, who always likes to give the underlying reason for everything, also relates the efficacy of the Mass for the succor of the suffering souls to the dogma of the Communion of Saints. He says:

> The suffrages of the living are profitable to the deceased in the measure that the latter are united to the living in charity. . . . Thus, the works that are most helpful for the dead are those that are most closely related to this communion of charity. . . . Now the sacrament of the Eucharist is more closely related to the order of charity than any other thing, since it is the sacrament of ecclesiastical unity and contains him in whom the whole Church is unified and strengthened: Christ.[11]

Generous souls gladly join to the sacrifice of the altar their own sacrifices, fasts, and mortifications. United to the immolation of the sacred Victim, works of penance are of great value for expiation. The same is true of every form of alms, for, according to the Book of Sirach, "Water quenches a flaming fire, and alms atone for sins" (Sir. 3:9). Finally, every good action performed in the state of grace possesses a satisfactory value, and many of the faithful like to apply the fruit of these actions to the relief of the suffering souls.

Furthermore, the indulgences applicable to the deceased place at our disposal the riches of all the saints and the merits of all their good works, which, united to those of Christ, constitute an inexhaustible spiritual capital.[12] The faithful should use indulgences with a zeal that is quickened by great charity.[13]

---

[11] Ibid., d. 45. q. 2, a. 3. q. 1

[12] Cf. Chapter VIII above.

[13] That is to say, not merely with the *quantitative* concern of gaining the most indulgences possible, but with the attempt to increase the *qualitative* element, the desire to accomplish to perfection the work required and to place oneself in the required dispositions for gaining totally the indulgence granted by the church

The Christian charity that leads us to help the suffering souls does not profit only the deceased. It is equally advantageous for those who practice it; this is another consoling aspect of the Communion of Saints. The solicitude to come to the rescue of unfortunate souls is an eminent work of spiritual mercy, and hence a very efficacious means of progressing in the love of God. Did not our Lord set up the practice of fraternal charity as the sign of our love of God?

In addition, devotion to the souls in purgatory and the habitual remembrance of their great distress is supremely salutary for the living. It makes them more attentive to the demands of infinite Holiness, more vigilant to avoid many daily sins and negligences for which rigorous punishment is suffered in purgatory. For example, who can remain unmoved by the revelations of St. Margaret Mary, that great confidant of the Sacred Heart, concerning the belated regrets of unmortified Christians, and especially the heartrending cries of priestly and religious souls that remained too indifferent to the perfection of their state during their mortal lives?[14] The zeal we devote to the relief of these poor souls implies an equal concern to spare ourselves similar sufferings through constant fervor in the service of God.

Finally, the souls we shall have succored in purgatory will remember the charity practiced toward them, and return it with interest. For "ingratitude has never entered heaven."[15] The union of love established with them during their time of trial will grow stronger and blossom for us in the grace of holiness after their entrance into glory.

---

for a given work of piety. The disposition required for obtaining full remission of punishment incurred by sin (and the same rule applies proportionally, it would seem, to indulgences gained for the deceased), primarily are an effective and total renouncement of these sins, a pure heart, and a will detached from all affection for evil. Charity accomplishes this detachment. It follows that *concern for perfection* must always accompany our zeal for gaining indulgences. Otherwise, we are in danger of falling into the materialism of some who burden themselves with indulgenced prayers and exercises, without taking the trouble even once to gain a plenary indulgence or to strive in other ways to advance in perfection.

[14] Let us merely quote a few lines from one of the letters in which the seer of Paray-le-Monial has set down what our Lord revealed to her concerning the condition of the suffering souls. Referring to a Visitandine nun who had recently died, she said: "Our poor Sister made me see the pitiable state in which she was, saying: 'Ah! What rigorous torments I am suffering. , . [especially] for having given my body superfluous comforts. . . Ah! How I am paying now for the undue caresses I have given my body!" (Letter n.28, to Mother de Saumaise). Elsewhere she relates in these words the regrets of a religious soul held in purgatory: "Ah! How I wish all souls consecrated to God might see me in this horrible torment! If I could make them feel the severity of my sufferings and those prepared for souls consecrated to God who live negligently in their vocation, no doubt they would walk with greater ardor in exact observance" (biography by her contemporaries, cited in *Doctrine complète de la Bse Marguerite-Marie*, IV, 362).

[15] St. Margaret Mary, Letter n. 21.

The Church Militant is not alone in her fraternal interest in the fate of the souls in purgatory. The saints in heaven are also in intimate communion with these suffering members of Christ. The angels, ministers of divine mercy, welcome the souls that have completed their time of punishment in purgatory. Above all, Mary, the Queen of the angels and saints, extends her motherly influence to the place of suffering, for suffering souls are also her children. To quote Father Faber: "O magnificent region of the Church of God! O lovable portion of Mary's flock! What a spectacle to see this empire consecrated to innocence and at the same time to the most cruel sufferings! . . . The throne of Mary, shining like the moon, casts its sweet light on this region of pain and of unspeakable yearning."[16]

The Mother of Mercy exerts her influence and her power in favor of those who dwell in purgatory, and often delivers her most devoted servants before their time is up. Some may say that since Mary can no longer merit she must let divine justice follow its course. But in addition to the merits of her very holy life, which have limitless scope, Mary, as a sovereign, disposes the countless satisfactory works and suffrages that her children of earth offer to God, and of which many have made her the treasurer. The devout practice taught by St. Louis Mary de Montfort of entrusting to Mary the value of all one's good works in favor of the souls in purgatory is founded on this faith in Mary's power over the kingdom of suffering.

Rich with the gifts that her children offer her, the Mother of Mercy often visits purgatory. The saints tell us that the days on which we celebrate one of her privileges are notable for the greater number of souls that owe their deliverance to her motherly intervention.

Thus the work of the consummation of the saints is completed by the sweet and merciful mediation of our divine Mother. Mary, the glorious Queen of Heaven and of Earth, is also the clement Sovereign of purgatory. Under whatever aspect we consider the admirable reality of the Communion of Saints, we always find Mary at the heart of this mystery, while Jesus, her divine Son, remains its Head and crowning glory.

---

[16] *Purgatory*, Chapter 4

CHAPTER XVIII

The Members of the Mystical Body:
The Church Militant

The saints in heaven, the poor souls in purgatory, and the faithful still battling here on earth make up one Church by reason of their union to their common Head, Christ Jesus. But whereas the saints in heaven cleave to Christ irrevocably and possess God through the beatific vision, the suffering souls and the exiles of this world know him only in the dim light of faith. It is true that the holy souls in purgatory have a decided advantage over the faithful here on earth. No faltering of their will can make them lose the object of their hope. Wayfaring man, on the contrary, regardless of the assurance he has from divine promises, can lose heaven through his infidelity. His union with Christ is not yet definitive, as is that of expiating souls. The latter are incorporated forever in their divine Head, even if in an essentially imperfect manner. Only the blessed in heaven belong to Christ totally and forever.

Let us now pause to consider the Church Militant and the diverse conditions of men living on earth in terms of their incorporation into Christ. First of all, we must observe with St. Thomas that the Mystical Body does not possess all its parts simultaneously as does the natural body.[1] The life of the Body of Christ extends through the centuries, and the Church embraces in her unity men of the past, of the present, and of the future. No one is saved except through the grace of Christ; by cleaving to him through faith the just souls of the Old Testament attained salvation and received divine life.

St. Augustine has said in this regard: "The Body of Christ is the Church; not only the Church in a given place, but the Church spread over the whole earth; not only the Church of the present time, but the Church that extends

[1] Cf. *Summa*, IIIa, q. 8, a. 3

from Abel to those who will be born in the last days and who will believe in Christ."[2] But the holy Bishop asks himself how the saints of the Old Law can belong to Christ. He answers his own question, pushing the analogy of the human body even further, with a certain realism. He says: "Certain members of Christ preceded the Incarnation of Christ, just as, at the birth of a child, the hand sometimes appears before the head, even though the hand is joined to the head. Do not think, Brothers, that the just who suffered persecution, even among those who preceded and announced the coming of the Lord, do not belong among the members of Christ."[3]

Even among those who make up the Mystical Body at a given period of time, all do not belong to it by the same right. St. Thomas tells us that some are members of Christ only in potency, inasmuch as they are deprived of habitual grace.[4] We may add that these souls belong to Christ by right, juridically, although they do not in fact acknowledge this necessary subjection to their divine Redeemer. For some of these, this potency will never be reduced to act, because they will not submit to the beneficent rule of the divine King. Others on the contrary are destined to be incorporated into the Body of Christ in a more effective manner.

Among those actually united to the Head of the Mystical Body, St. Thomas tells us there are three categories. Some are united to him by faith alone, others by grace and charity, and finally, still others through glory.

There are some who no longer cleave to Christ except by faith. Their souls are dead because of sin. They have lost sanctifying grace and divine charity, as well as the other infused virtues. Only faith, like a valuable cargo saved from a shipwreck, still subsists in them, as often supernatural hope does. However, their faith and hope can no longer carry them to the shores of eternal salvation. If death surprises them in this sad state, they lose the little that remains of their supernatural riches and are cut off completely and forever from the Body of Christ.

Others are united to the Savior by grace and charity. They are members of Christ in the full sense of the word. They live by his life; they bear his divine likeness within them; they are quickened by his Spirit, who is the soul of the Mystical Body; they receive all the sanctifying influences of their divine Head.

---

[2] *Enarr.* in *psalmos*, Ps. 90:1, *PL* 37:1159.
[3] Ibid., Ps. 61:4, *PL*, 37:731.
[4] Cf. *Summa*, IIIa, q. 8, a. 3.

The last group mentioned by St. Thomas are the blessed who have already been established in love of God through glory. We have already spoken of them with reference to the Church Triumphant.

In addition to these absolutely essential distinctions made by the Angelic Doctor, however, many others must be clarified, in order to have a more complete and enlightened idea of the harmonious totality of the Mystical Body.

First we shall consider the various degrees among the ministers that the twofold hierarchy of order and jurisdiction sets up in the Body of the Church. Then we shall speak of the noble rank that belongs to the ordinary faithful in the whole Christ. In the next chapter we shall point out the relationships that can exist between the Mystical Body of Jesus Christ and schismatics, heretics, and unbelievers.

The Hierarchy of Order and Jurisdiction

Holy Scripture recounts in 3 Kings that the Queen of Sheba, having come to see Solomon, whose magnificence and wisdom had been told her, was charmed to the point of losing her breath: "*et non habebat ultra spiritum*"—"she had no longer any spirit in her" (3 Kings 10:5). She was struck by the admirable order that the great king, in his wisdom, had established in his palace and in the service of the royal household: the ordering of his table; the disposition of the apartments reserved for the servants; the various gradations of ministers and servants. This magnificent array enraptured her and she said to the king: "The report is true, which I heard in my own country, concerning thy words and concerning thy wisdom. And I did not believe them that told me, till I came myself, and saw with my own eyes, and have found that the half hath not been told me. . . . Blessed are thy men, and blessed are thy servants, who stand before thee always, and hear thy wisdom" (3 Kings 10:6–8).

We do not envy the happiness of the Queen of Sheba, nor that of the servants of the great king of Jerusalem. For we remember the words of our Savior, referring to himself: "Behold, a greater than Solomon is here" (Matt. 12:42). It is Jesus, the true King of Peace, who has set laudable and heavenly order in the organization of his Church; we are the daily witnesses and fortunate beneficiaries of this work of his divine wisdom.

His wisdom shines forth especially in the variety and subordination of the ministers of his spiritual kingdom. A twofold hierarchy, one of order and the other of jurisdiction, assures the government of the Church and the wise administration of the supernatural treasures that her divine Founder has bequeathed her.

THE HIERARCHY OF JURISDICTION

The hierarchy of jurisdiction consists in the attribution of the power to govern, to rule the Body of the Church. It includes two degrees: (1) the sovereign pontiff, and (2) the bishops, who are the pope's brothers and subordinates in the spiritual governance.

The sovereign pontiff, the visible Head of the whole Church, who represents Christ the invisible Head, has received from Christ the fullness of royal power. It must be noted, however, that Jesus possesses a more extensive power than that he gave to Peter, for Christ is the spiritual and temporal King of the whole human race.[5] He has delegated only his spiritual kingship to his Church, leaving the temporal scepter in other hands. But all the power conferred upon the Church is in the hands of Peter and of his successors to the See of Rome. All the branches of supernatural activity converge toward this apostolic See. From the Chair of the Roman pontiff the voice of Peter is heard throughout the world. On that Chair sits the oracle of truth, without which there is no divine life. From it the word which commands in the name of Christ rings out, reaching out all over the world. From this Chair come the words that enlighten and the counsel that inspires. Whoever hears the voice of Peter hears the voice of Jesus himself (cf. Luke 10:16). In the realization of God's works, our Savior's promises apply only to those who are completely obedient to Peter.

Even if the Roman pontiff has power over the whole Church and over each of her members, he cannot govern her alone in every detail. The Lord has given him aides to share his burden and to exercise pastoral authority within specific areas: the bishops. They were instituted in the beginning by our Savior himself. Since then, however, they have been named individually by the supreme pontiff or in his name by those to whom he delegated the power. Thus the bishops receive their authority from Christ, without any diminution of the power of the sovereign Shepherd. What the bishop can do for each of the faithful in his jurisdiction, the pontiff of Rome can also do for all the faithful of the world, without need of any intermediary. Direct and often opportune intervention, however, will never take the place of the role of the individual bishops or render their mission useless. Thus Jesus

---

[5] Cf. encyclical *Quas primas*, December, 1925; cf. also the author's *Le Corps Mystique du Christ*, Volume II, Chapter 7, on the Kingship of Christ.

provided both for the wise guidance of the Church through a multiplicity of pastors, and for the unity of his Mystical Body by the institution of a supreme and universal authority.

Beneath the bishops no ministers have the power of jurisdiction by divine right, even though the supreme pontiff or the bishops can and do habitually delegate a part of their authority to subordinate aides. Thus the pastors of parishes were set up to provide, in the name and place of the bishop, for the welfare of the souls entrusted to their care. Thus too, those religious institutes whose purpose is apostolic usually receive from the Holy See the official mission that authorizes and legitimizes their holy labors in the vineyard of the Lord. These are the chosen workers, less burdened by the worries of the world, who devote their efforts, at the command of the leaders, to the various parts of the sacred field that call for their particular care.

The hierarchy of order consists of the ministers to whom the administration of the sacraments and the celebration of the divine mysteries have been entrusted. It is identified with the highest degree of the hierarchy of jurisdiction, that is, with the episcopacy. It is distinguished from and subordinate to the episcopacy in all the other degrees of priestly power. In this way also the unity of the Mystical Body of the Church is guaranteed.

According to the actual economy of the Church of the Latin Rite, priestly power is divided into seven degrees, including the three major orders and the four minor orders. At the top of this mystical ladder is the priesthood whose sublime functions relate to the Body of Christ in the Holy Sacrifice of the Mass, and to his members, the faithful, as they participate by Holy Communion in this august sacrifice.

The episcopacy, considered as a power of order, is simply the priesthood in its fullness. Although it involves a more extensive power than that of simple priests, it does not constitute a distinct order nor does it confer a new character.[6] It perfects the priestly character and extends its power to new ministerial acts, notably the power to confer sacred ordination. Because of this the bishops are the born leaders of the priesthood and of the entire ecclesiastical hierarchy, and are the principle of its perpetuation.

The other orders are hierarchized according to their more or less direct relationship to the Eucharist. This divine sacrament is the center of all the functions of the priestly ministry and the raison d'être of all the powers

---

[6] The reason is that there is no power of the ministry *above* that of offering the Holy Sacrifice of the Mass, which specifies the priesthood.

of order.[7] The diaconate confers on the minister who receives it the safeguarding of the Eucharist and gives him the right to administer it to the faithful, at least when the priest is unable to do so. In the churches of the Eastern Rite he presents to the communicants the cup containing the precious Blood.

The subdeacon does not have the right to dispense the sacred mysteries, but he is entrusted with the care of all that immediately relates to the Eucharist. He cares for the sacred vessels, he purifies the linens used on the altar, he prepares the bread and the wine for the Holy Sacrifice.

These, then, are the three major or sacred orders, whose bearers are dedicated exclusively to the service of the God of the Host, and form the immediate retinue of the divine Solomon. Hence the Church wants them to consecrate their person to Christ irrevocably by the solemn vow of perpetual chastity, so that they may be worthy ministers of the God of holiness and faithful dispensers of sacred things: *"Be holy because I am holy"* (Lev. 11:44; 19:2).

The minor orders are related also, but in a more remote way, to Eucharistic worship. The acolyte presents the wine and the water for the sacrifice to the sacred ministers, and carries the candle before them, as a symbol of the spiritual light with which he must, by his example and teaching, illumine the minds of the faithful. The exorcist, the lector, and the porter, each according to his special grace, dispose the Christian faithful to participate worthily in the divine mysteries. The porter convokes the faithful to the holy place, and keeps out of the holy assemblage un-believers, excommunicates, and public sinners. The lector teaches the rudiments of the faith and the doctrine of Sacred Scripture to the catechumens, to the neophytes, and to Christian children. The exorcist drives out the spirits of evil who seek to trouble and sully souls by their evil suggestions.

Minor orders, so-called in relation to the sacred orders, are lofty and sublime when considered in absolute terms. They make of their bearers princes of the house of God, eminent members of the Mystical Body. The same is true of simple clerics who, although they have not yet received any orders, have, by their tonsure, become the heritage of the Lord, according to the beautiful name they bear. *Cleric* actually derives from the Greek word χλήρος which means "heritage." Those who are associated with members of the clergy are the chosen portion of the Lord. Separated from the world,

---

[7] Cf. *Summa*, Supple, q. 37, a. 2.

they profess by their very habit the state of death to the world, to which those who live only for God pledge themselves.

The Simple Faithful

Beneath the hierarchy of order and jurisdiction come the *simple faithful*. Among them we must distinguish two different states: the religious state and the lay state. The first is the state of perfection in which generous souls, free from obligations in the world, publicly profess their resolve to follow the way of the evangelical counsels. The second is the way of the faithful who remain in the world and who, while equally obligated to tend toward perfection,[8] do not pledge themselves to pursue it through the observance of the vows of religion.

In the first place let us point out the special place held by *consecrated souls* in the Mystical Body of Christ. Consecrated souls are those whom the Savior invites to a more complete renunciation, so that they can follow him more closely (cf. Matt. 19:12; 16:24). They are the virgins who, as St. Paul says, think only about the things of the Lord, how they may please God (cf. 1 Cor. 7:32–35), and whose hearts are not divided between God and the world. They are the chaste souls whom St. John saw following the Lamb, singing a canticle that they alone can sing (cf. Apoc. 14:1–4). They are the honor of the Church and the adornment of the Mystical Body of Jesus. Our Savior has such a predilection for the state of holy virginity that he chose to come into the world only through it, suspending in its favor the most immutable laws of nature and granting his Blessed Mother the glory of a divine fruitfulness together with the honor of virginal integrity.

The virginal fruitfulness of Mary, the symbol of the spiritual and most pure motherhood of the Church, is honored in various ways by the faithful, some imitating her holy virginity by perfect continence, others honoring her fruitfulness in the state of marriage. St. Augustine writes:

> Mary is the one woman who is mother and virgin at once, not only spiritually but also corporeally. She is not spiritually the mother of our Head, who is the Savior. For spiritually she is born of him, since all who believe in him—and she among them—are rightly called the sons of the Bridegroom. But she is spiritually the mother of his members, whom we are, for she cooperated by her charity in bringing forth the faithful who are his members. The fact remains that corporeally, she is the mother of our Head.

---

[8] Cf. *Summa*, IIa-IIae, q. 184, a. 3.

> Indeed, it was necessary that our Head be born corporeally of a virgin by a wonderful miracle. Only Mary is Mother and Virgin in mind and body, both the mother of Christ and the virgin of Christ. Spiritually, the Church, in the person of the saints called to the kingdom of God, is totally the mother of Christ, totally the virgin of Christ. But corporeally, the Church is not totally one and the other. In some she is the virgin of Christ, and in others she is a mother, but not the mother of Christ.[9]

This beautiful passage, which specifies the role and place of Mary in the Mystical Body of Christ in such a precise and beautiful way, clearly shows the eminent rank of consecrated souls in this spiritual organism. They honor the sacred virginity of Mary, they prolong it, they extend it, and perpetuate it in Holy Mother Church. Mary was the first to raise the banner of virginity. She is the virgin par excellence, the one whom we call by her right name, the Blessed Virgin. After her, drawn by the odor of her virginal purity, virgins consecrate themselves to the heavenly Bridegroom in great numbers. *Adduncentur Regi virgines post eam*. We must repeat to the faithful whom grace invites to this lofty state the words of our Savior: "*Qui potest capere, capiat*"—"Let him accept it who can" (Matt. 19:12). Let him who can, accept for himself this precious heritage.

We would only like to point out that, after virginal chastity, which is the most excellent of all, there is a place for holy widowhood, and for the chastity restored by tears of repentance. But the Lord's preference goes to the souls that have consecrated to him the first-fruits of their life and the flower of their youth.

After religious, we must speak of those who are called the *laity*, the faithful who form the greatest part of the Church taught, those who on the one hand are not called to enter the sacred hierarchy through the reception of holy orders, and who on the other hand do not follow the evangelical counsels which Jesus addresses to everyone in general without obligating anyone in particular.

The word layman, according to the Greek etymology, signifies one who belongs to the people. The laymen in the Church are those who form the Christian people, the holy people, those whom St. Peter calls in his first epistle, "a chosen race . . . a holy nation" (1 Pet. 2:9), a people purchased by Jesus Christ. Therefore the name "layman" is an honorable and glorious one.

[9] St. Augustine, *De sancta Virginitate*, n. 6.

It has nothing in common with the unfavorable sense often attached to the words "secularism" and "secular," used to designate neutral or even atheistic institutions which exclude any profession of religious faith.[10]

In speaking of the faithful who make up the Christian people, the laity, St. Paul uses a term that should make them proud of their state of life. He calls them *saints*.[11] Are they not members of Christ? And even though their rank in the bosom of the Church is outwardly more lowly, they can still be higher in God's eyes, through grace, then the ministers of the Lord. Their greatness and nobility come from the divine life which quickens them, from the adopted sonship that makes them sons of the Father, from the indwelling of the Holy Spirit that pours grace and charity into their souls (cf. Rom. 5:5).

Furthermore, it is for their sake, "in order to perfect the saints" (Eph. 4:12), St. Paul says, that the various ministries of the ecclesiastical ministry were instituted to build up the whole Christ, "the fullness of Christ" (Eph. 4:13). For this reason the elect of the sanctuary should glory less in their precedence, which involves so many serious responsibilities, than in the gift of divine grace that they possess in common with all the faithful and that alone will make them princes in the heavenly city. On the contrary, their dignity and the holy attributions of the sacred ministry belong to the order of graces called gratuitous or *gratis datae*. They are conferred upon them less for their personal advantage than for the spiritual benefit of the entire flock. They are ordered, as to their proper end, to the grace *gratum faciens*, which alone can make them pleasing to God.

In the participation in the divine nature, there are many degrees and measures, according to the gratuitous favors of divine largess and to the way souls respond to the invitations of grace.

What admirable variety exists in the supernatural world; it ranges from the newborn infant emerging from the baptismal fount to souls eminent in virtue and perfected in transforming love.

Hagiography teaches us something about it, constantly revealing wondrous new facets of holiness.

---

[10] According to the Code of Canon Law, the term "laity" sometimes designates in a general way all who are not clerics, that is to say, religious not in holy orders and Christians living in the world. For example, Canon 107: "*Sunt in Ecclesia clerici a laicis distincti.*" Elsewhere it applies to the faithful who have remained in the world, excluding all religious, as in Canon 471, par. I: "*Religiosi praecedunt laicis.*" We are here using the more restricted sense of the word.

[11] Cf. Rom. 1:7, 1 Cor. 1:2; 2 Cor. 9:1, etc.

This diversity is essential to the harmony of the Mystical Body. Even when we make allowance for the negligences and infidelities that prevent many souls from attaining the summit of perfection to which God invites them, all are not called to the same holiness. God, who is the master of his gifts, dispenses them with a wise inequality. No one can accuse the heavenly Father of injustice. Each one has cause to thank him for what he receives gratuitously, and should rejoice in the honorable place he occupies in the Mystical Body of Christ.

Our ultimate place among the saints of God, however, does not depend altogether upon us. It is untrue to say, as some do, that we can decide for ourselves whether we shall attain the holiness of a Thomas Aquinas or of a Francis Xavier. It is up to us to be faithful to our own grace, which is certainly a grace of holiness. Beyond that, God will always answer our desires of perfection with new gifts and increasing largess. Nevertheless, every saint has his own measure fixed in the eternal decrees, and it is not within the scope of our free will to rise to the summit of perfection of the apostles. Jesus said to the sons of Zebedee: "That is not mine to give you, but it belongs to those for whom it has been prepared . . ." (Matt. 20:23). To God alone belongs the right to order the members of Christ in the organism of the Mystical Body, according to the exigencies of the supernatural beauty he intends to give them and to the demands of multiplicity, inequality, and proportion among its various parts. For as Scripture expresses it, God does all things "in measure, and number, and weight" (Wisd. 11:21). It is up to us to lend our support to God's merciful plans by our own fidelity.

Since this is the supereminent grandeur that the gift of grace confers even upon the simple faithful, we understand the terrible evil that poor sinners bring upon themselves when they kill divine life in their souls. They betray their vocation to become saints. "For this is the will of God, your sanctification" (I Thess. 4:3). They received men by ceasing to be inwardly what their outward profession of Christianity makes them seem to be. As withered members of Christ, they are no longer quickened by his Spirit, and receive only rare life-giving influences from their Head.

However, they remain united to the Church, to the Mystical Body of Christ, and this cleaving to their divine Head, imperfect though it be, is still very precious. It will greatly facilitate their return to the life of the Body and their reanimation by the Spirit of grace. Although deprived of supernatural charity, poor sinners still benefit in a reduced measure from the ineffable advantages of the Communion of Saints. The prayers of the faithful, the fruits of the Sacrifice of the Mass, the intercession of the saints, and the infinite merits of Jesus draw divine mercy upon them and keep them immersed in a supernatural current under the wind of grace.

Unless they resist stubbornly, this will reawaken dead love in their souls and restore them to the divine life of the Mystical Christ.

Far more deplorable is the condition of those wretched men who bear the character of Christ engraved in their souls, but are separated from the Mystical Body by schism or heresy. Even more to be pitied are those whom unbelief or idolatry shut off from the life-giving influences of the one who is rightfully their Head, but to whom they have never been incorporated by the sacrament of regeneration. All of these will remain outside the vital unity of the whole Christ, deprived of the many benefits of the Communion of Saints until the day when their aggregation into Catholic unity makes of them members of the true Church, *outside of which there is no salvation.*

CHAPTER XIX

Outside the Church

Is it possible for us to look upon the total Christ and delight in the harmonious unity of his Head and members, without also turning our compassionate attention to the vast multitude of those who are still far from Christ, separated from him by error, discord, or unbelief? Did not Jesus shed all of his Blood for them? They are sheep that follow other shepherds, flocks that have strayed into poisoned pastures, but Christ never tires of calling them. He invites them to come to his one fold, to fall into ranks under his crook, and to recognize him, and him alone, as their one Shepherd (cf. John 10:1 ff.).

The Church, the Spouse of Christ and his mystical perpetuation, shares her Head's loving solicitude for the great erring mass of redeemed men who are still separated from the One who is her life. She holds out her arms to them with motherly charity, she sends her apostles and missionaries to them, she enlightens and instructs them, and every day brings forth a goodly number of them to divine life by incorporating them into Christ the Savior.

In union with the Church our mother, we who are members of Christ the Redeemer must have the most lively supernatural concern and affectionate compassion for all these separated souls, many of whom, in darkness or in the dawn of approaching day, seek Christ, "the true light that enlightens every man who comes into the world" (John 1:9). The doctrine of the Mystical Body, which is the doctrine of the fullness of Christ, wages us in a special way to work for the completion of the whole Christ. The dogma is also a light capable of showing the path of truth to those who, tired of their isolation or starving for the bread of holy doctrine, have set out in search of the kingdom of God.

Among those who are outside the Church, separated from the great unity of the Mystical Body, we must distinguish three principal categories:

1) *Schismatics*—those who, while they retain or think they retain the integral faith, break the bond of ecclesiastical communion.[1] 2) *Heretics*—those who directly contravene the revealed truth proclaimed by the magisterium of the Church, and thereby break the unity of belief. 3) *Unbelievers*—those who have never belonged to the visible unity of the Mystical Body, inasmuch as they have never received the sacrament of incorporation into the Church, namely baptism. We must take a Christian interest in the fate of all of these groups. Let us now consider their diverse attitudes toward Christ and the Church.

The Schismatics

Jesus founded his Church on unity, and he willed that she should form a single Body of which he was to be the Head. "That they may be one, even as we are one" (John 17:22), was his prayer to his Father the night before he died. The question here is not one of an invisible unity such as certain heretics have imagined. Jesus asks a grace of unity for all those who belong to him which is, by reason of its miraculous nature, a visible and manifest sign to the world of the Church's divine origin and mission: ". . . even as thou, Father, in me and I in thee; that they also may be one in us, that the world may believe that thou hast sent me" (John 17:21).

But how would the world believe if the sign Christ requested, namely the unity of his Church, were not a patent fact visible to all eyes? Jesus asks perfect union for his disciples: *"ut sint consummati in unum"*—"that they may be perfected in unity" (John 17:23). But could it be called a perfect union if the members of his supposedly invisible Church were mutually unaware of each other? There must be not only unity of Spirit, but also unity of Body: UNUM CORPUS, UNUM SPIRITUS (Eph. 4:4). This is the adequate formula given us by St. Paul.

As we have already seen, many of the elements, including the most valuable element of ecclesiastical unity, are interior and hidden. The secret action of the Head in all his members, the influence of the Holy Spirit who quickens the organism of the Church, the supernatural gifts which are poured into the souls of all the faithful from the moment of their baptism—all these things remain secret and are visible only to the eye of faith. They all reside, however, in a visible Body, which is made up of members known as

---

[1] Actually, schism can no longer exist without also being a heresy, by reason of the negation it implies of the primacy of Peter, now a defined dogma of faith.

such and governed by an equally manifest head, in dependence upon the Head who is Christ. This twofold character of ecclesiastical unity, at once interior and exterior, visible in some respects and hidden in others, enables the Church to reproduce and to represent in some manner the theandric unity of Christ, God and man, who is visible in his Humanity, invisible in his Godhead.

To quote the words of Pope Leo XIII: "Just as Christ, the Head and Exemplar of the Church, is not complete if we consider in him only his human and visible nature, following the error of the Photinians and the Nestorians, or if we consider only his divine and invisible nature, as do the Eutychians, and as we must on the contrary consider him as one in two natures, one visible and the other invisible; so his Mystical Body constitutes the true Church only because her visible elements have also a supernatural power and life. . . ."[2]

Jesus himself has marked out the generative principles of this exterior and visible unity. Neither baptism alone, the exterior sign of aggregation to the Church and the necessary condition of salvation, nor the profession of a common faith could assure the perfect unity of the Church of Christ. There is need of a principle essential to every truly unified society: unity of government, the authority of a single Head whom all obey. Jesus must have been thinking of this when he said to the Prince of the apostolic college: "Thou art Peter, and upon this rock I will build my Church" (Matt. 16:18).

From this follows a rigorous and ineluctable conclusion: anyone who withdraws from the authority of Peter, who breaks away from the communion of the universal pontiff, incurs the stigma of being *schismatic*.[3] He is separated; he has ceased to belong to the Body of Christ. This inevitable conclusion is painful for anyone who realizes that it is the condition of the great number of baptized souls who have been separated by discord from Catholic unity.

Some may say that all recognize Christ as their Head, and are thus united in a superior, invisible, and mystical unity. This is the view of a number of

---

[2] Encyclical *Satis cognitum*, June 19, 1896.
[3] Theoretically there are two ways of becoming a schismatic: either by refusing to acknowledge the authority of the successor of Peter; or by breaking away from any part of the Catholic Church. Fundamentally, however, the second mode implies the first, for the refusal to be in communion with a particular Church involves schism only because a particular Church is part of the universal Church, although only by its submission to the apostolic Chair. That is why Pope Leo XIII wrote in his encyclical on the unity of the Church (*Satis cognitum*, June 29, 1896): "Just as the unity of the Church, inasmuch as it is the assembly of the faithful, requires unity of faith, so, inasmuch as it is a divinely instituted society, it demands by divine right the unity of government that includes and creates unity of communion."

our separated brethren, who found consolation from the division even yesterday. Today, however, there are many for whom this spiritual unity no longer suffices. Indeed, this is a sign of progress. For union with Christ and in Christ, without membership in the visible Body established by Christ, can be only an illusion. Jesus tells us that it is useless for us to appeal to our faith in him, and to cry out "Lord, Lord!" if we do not conform to his will. Christ will say he does not know us (cf. Matt. 7:21). The will of Jesus is clear; if we are to obey him, we must submit to his Church: "He who hears you, hears me; and he who rejects you, rejects me" (Luke 10:16). Only one Church of Christ exists, the one he calls *his* Church: *Ecclesiam meam*—the Church that he built on Peter for all eternity.

By renouncing visible unity, the benefit of invisible unity is lost. In fleeing from the crook of Peter, whom Jesus named the shepherd of his lambs and of his sheep (cf. John 21:15–17), a man also flees from the one who called himself the Good Shepherd and who wants all of us to be gathered together in his one sheepfold (cf. ibid., 10:11–16). Our vital union to Christ is conditioned upon our incorporation into the Church. This is according to divine order, and we cannot modify it. To remain outside the divine order is to remain outside the Church, and outside of Christ. To cleave to Christ by a sincere and efficacious love is to cleave to all the members of Christ. True love excludes schism, just as schism excludes authentic love. Thus St. Augustine was able to say, in commenting on the First Epistle of St. John:

> Spread your charity over the whole earth if you want to love Christ. For the members of Christ are spread out over the earth. If you love only one part, you are divided. If you are divided, you are not in the Body. If you are not in the Body, you do not cleave to the Head. What good does it do you to believe, if you blaspheme? You adore Christ in his head and you blaspheme him in his Body. He loves his Body. Even though you break away from his Body, he cannot separate himself from his Body. "It is vain for you to honor me, you speak foolish things, for you honor me without my Body." It is as if someone wanted to kiss your head while he crushed your feet. Would you not, amid such protestations of honor, cry out: "What are you doing? You are crushing my feet." You would not say: "Trample my head," while he honored it, and yet the head would cry out more for its trampled members than for itself overwhelmed with honor.[4]

Hence those whom schism has separated from the Body of the Church no longer cleave to the Head, Christ. They belong to him by right, for they

---

[4] *In I Joan. V*, tract. 10.

are his conquest by the right of Redemption. Even more, they bear, engraved in their souls, the baptismal character that indicates their belonging to the divine Shepherd. But they are sheep separated from the faithful flock, who cannot listen docilely to the voice of the Good Shepherd. "Those who do not have the Church as their mother, cannot have God as their Father."[5]

Does this mean that in the vast multitude of separated Christians there are none who possess grace and charity, and who by reason of this fact are vitally united to Christ, the Head of the Mystical Body? Certainly not. For when these recalcitrants left the true Church, they took with them precious relics of their ancient riches. They kept the divine oracles, the treasure of revealed truths, which is the wellspring of light and of life for souls of good will.

Simple schismatics, for the most part, have taken with them, along with the sacrament of orders, the wellspring of sacramental graces. The invaluable riches of the Church, especially the Holy Eucharist and the Eucharistic Sacrifice, are not sterile for all schismatics.

Admittedly our separated brothers hold these treasures illegitimately. Admittedly the sacraments, valid though they may be, confer grace only upon well-disposed souls. It is true also that the sin of schism, which excludes charity, is opposed to the fruitful reception of the divine mysteries. The fact remains that among our separated brothers many are in good faith, having been separated through the fault of their fathers and forefathers. Many schismatic laymen have never fully understood the state of schism in which they find themselves. Others, even when they study the painful problem, do not grasp the truth all at once. All of them benefit provisionally—and this, in the case of the first case mentioned at least, can last a lifetime—from the privilege of their good faith which, because it leaves them with the conviction that they are in the path of truth, exempts them from formal sin and enables them to receive the sacraments of the Church fruitfully.[6]

Even when good faith excuses them from the sin of schism and allows charity and divine life to subsist in them, separated Christians do not belong effectively to the Body of the Church. They belong to it in desire, *in voto*,[7] according to the teaching of Pope Pius XII in his Encyclical *Mystici*

---

[5] St. Cyprian, *De unit. Ecclesiae*, Chapter 6.

[6] As a rule we must make exception of the sacrament of penance, which requires for its validity not only the power of order but also the power of jurisdiction. Since jurisdiction resides only in legitimate pastors, it follows that schismatics are habitually deprived of it and cannot absolve validly except in danger of death, when the Church grants jurisdiction to all priests.

[7] Every soul in the state of grace has at least the implicit desire to belong to the true church. For true charity implies the will to conform in all things to the order willed of God.

Corporis: ". . . by an unconscious desire and longing they have a certain relationship to the Mystical Body of the Redeemer" (par. 103). And this desire, implicit in every act of supernatural charity, already places them under the life-giving influences of Christ the Head, and of the Holy Spirit the soul of the Church. But juridically, effectively, they do not belong to the Church because they retain an attitude of declared opposition to the principle of unity proclaimed by Christ, which is union to the visible Head of the Church.[8] This is also what the above-mentioned encyclical also teaches: "Actually only those are to be included as members of the Church who have been baptized and profess the true faith, and have not been so unfortunate as to separate themselves from the unity of the Body, or been excluded by legitimate authority for grave faults committed" (par. 22).

The fact remains that there are—and this point has too often been over-looked— even among the schismatics as well as among the heretics who validly administer baptism many subjects who are Catholics by right and in fact. They are the baptized children who have not yet reached the age of reason. Baptism belongs by right to the Catholic Church alone. Whether the minister who confers it is a schismatic, a heretic, or even an unbeliever, he affiliates the baptized person to the Catholic Church, and this incorporation remains intact as long as the subject in question has not, through a personal profession of schism or heresy, broken the exterior bond that unites him to the true Church. It follows from this that, in calculating the number of Catholics now alive, in order to make a strict count, we would have to add all the very young children who have been baptized in schismatic or heretical lands. They are all, even visibly, members of the Mystical Body of Jesus Christ and benefit from the life-giving influences that come to us from the Head.

Doubtless many, in fact most of them, when they reach the age of discretion, will fall from this condition outwardly, even while retaining inwardly, at least for a time, the privilege of good faith of which we have just spoken. But many die before having reached this age, and they die as visible members of the Mystical Body, in the Catholic Communion, in the Church into which their baptism incorporated them.

---

[8] Can we say that they belong to the soul of the Church? We have already remarked (cf. p. 134) that it is dangerous to differentiate the soul and the Body of the Church to the point of separating them. According to the doctrine of St. Augustine, we can be vivified by the spirit of Christ only by belonging in some manner to the Body of Christ. Concerning belonging to the Body of Christ, which is the Church, it remains imperfect and the implicit desire for it conceived by a soul of good will but incompletely enlightened of the Mystery of Christ may not attain its realization and normal fruition.

However this thought does not suffice to console the Church for the vast multitude of faithful that schism has snatched from her. She grieves and weeps over her separated sons. She addresses to God her fervent supplications that his divine Goodness may deign to enlighten their minds, touch their hearts, and finally bring them back to Catholic unity. Speaking the language of the heart, which is born of a burning charity, she urges them to return to the Church of their forefathers, to the Church of Rome that the Fathers and the councils of the East as well as of the West, have recognized as the mother and teacher of all the Churches, whom they have honored as the oracle of truth, and invoked as the born-arbiter of all dogmatic and religious controversies.

Borrowing the words of St. Paul, she says to them: "*Os nostrum patet ad vos*"—"Our words are addressed to all of you" who belong to the Greek rite or to any other Eastern rite separated from the Catholic Church. May it please God to listen graciously to your own supplications:

> Grant, Lord, that there may be an end to the schisms of the Churches. Gather together those who are dispersed, bring back those who are lost, and unite them to your holy, Catholic, and Apostolic Church! May you thus be restored to this one and holy faith that has been transmitted from the earliest times to us as well as to you; this faith that your fathers and forefathers have preserved inviolably; that has been given luster by the splendor of their virtue, the greatness of their genius, and the excellence of their doctrine—by Athanasius, Basil, Gregory of Nazianzen, John Chrysostom, the two Cyrils, and other great personages whose glory belongs both to the East and to the West as a common heritage![9]

What Christian heart could fail to make its own the hopes expressed in this appeal by Pope Leo XIII, hopes that our Holy Father John XXIII held and revived with the burning flame of his own universal charity. This he made known on the feast of Pentecost, 1960, in St. Peter's Basilica. Pointing to the tombs, close by, of two great Doctors of the Greek Church— St. Gregory Nazianzen and St. John Chrysostom—placed there, he said, as if "to implore the return of the Eastern Churches to the bosom of the one, holy, Catholic and Apostolic Church." And he added:

> Oh! what a prodigious event it would be, what a flower at once of human and heavenly charity, would be this beginning toward the reunion of the separated brothers of the East and of the West within the one fold

---

[9] Apostolic letter *Praeclara*, of Pope Leo XIII, June 20, 1894.

of Christ the eternal Shepherd! This should be one of the most precious fruits of the forthcoming Second Ecumenical Council of the Vatican, for the glory of the Lord on earth and in heaven, amid universal rejoicing over the consummation of the mystery of the Communion of Saints (*Allocution* of May 21, 1960, on the forthcoming Council, *Acta Apos. Sed.,* 1960, 526).

The Heretics

The obligation to believe the whole of revealed truth is the fundamental command that our Lord gave his apostles when he was about to ascend into heaven: "He who believes and is baptized shall be saved, but he who does not believe shall be condemned" (Mark 16:16).

Thus, from the beginnings of the Church the attention of the apostles and preachers of the Gospel has been centered on the transmission of an unchanged deposit entrusted to their watchful care.[10] Whence every adulteration of the faith received the name that it still retains as a sign of reprobation: *heresy.*[11]

Heresy like schism, and even more than schism, is contrary to the unity of the Mystical Body. However, it does not destroy this unity. It simply excludes itself from it, and by that very fact allows the full unanimity of the faithful to subsist in the matter of the profession of faith. Heresy could not possibly destroy the undivided unity of the Mystical Body, which survives, often stronger and, as it were, with renewed vigor, all the shocks and painful amputations to which the heresiarchs subject it. The latter, together with their followers, break away from the total Christ, taking with them fragments of the truth, like the soldiers who divided our Savior's garments among themselves at the foot of the Cross but who were powerless against the seamless tunic that has remained undivided and has been preserved by divine decree for the Catholic Church alone.

St. Augustine asks: "What is this tunic if not charity that no one can divide? What is this tunic, if not unity? Lots are cast upon it, but no one divides it. The heretics have been able to divide the sacraments among themselves, but they did not divide charity.[12] And because they were unable to

---

[10] Cf. I Tim. 1:18–20; 4:1–7; 6:20–21, II Tim. 1:13–14; 3 to 4:6; I John 4:1–2: Il John 7–11; Jude 3 ff.

[11] That is to say, a choice, an arbitrary division of the integral truth, which, by rejecting a part of Revelation, destroys the very principle of the faith, namely, unconditional submission to the authority of the divine testimony.

[12] Charity, as used in the passage of St. Augustine, who broadens its meaning, becomes the synonym of the unity of the Mystical Body considered integrally, because, according to the holy Doctor, it is one of the most essential principles of this unity.

divide it, they with-drew. But charity remains whole. . . . He who possesses it is secure. No one will snatch him away from the Catholic Church."[13]

Heresy is the expression of a private judgment that contradicts a truth revealed by God. And this revealed principle must be one that is universally recognized as such by the teaching authority,[14] whether it be the object of a conciliar or pontifical definition, or whether it be commonly taught by the ordinary magisterium, that is to say, by the entire body of bishops spread out over the world.[15]

To renounce this rule of faith is to renounce the unity of the Mystical Body and to cut oneself off from the Communion of Saints whose foundation and guarantee it is. Holy Scripture remains of course, but it too must be interpreted in its true meaning as guaranteed by the doctrinal authority of the Church. St. Augustine said to the heretics of his century and of every century: "Holy Scripture itself, if you do not understand it correctly, profits you nothing. All the heretics who accept its authority are convinced that they are cleaving to the truth, whereas they are pursuing their own errors. It is not because they scorn Holy Scripture but because they misinterpret it that they are heretics."[16]

These remarkable words could have been addressed to the disciples of Luther and Calvin, and are calculated to give pause to those who, although outside the Catholic Church, still claim to be followers of Jesus Christ. As the Doctor of Africa so cogently says: "In name only, Christ is found among certain heretics who want to be called Christians. In reality, he is no longer among them."[17] In truth, union with Christ is accomplished by charity, and charity is founded on truth. In vain do some who are Christians in name only assert their baptism. They have renounced their Mother who gave them life. "A single word, a single sacrament brought you forth. But you will not attain the heritage of life if you do not return to the Catholic Church."[18]

---

[13] *In Psalm, XXI, enarr.* IIa, verse 19, *PL* 36:176.

[14] There are other truths taught by the Church that do not belong directly to the deposit of Revelation, although they are quite closely related to it. These include, for example, the theological conclusions that follow from revealed premises. They also include historical data, dogmatic facts concerning the virtue of a servant of God proposed to the worship of the faithful, the meaning of an author or of a book, or the worth of a scriptural translation. These are all matters that concern dogma itself in a more or less direct way. In these questions the Church also has the authority to make decisions and to impose an obligatory rule upon the faithful. However she cannot transform these related truths into dogmas of faith. He who deviates from them, although he sins seriously, does not become a heretic because of it.

[15] On the nature of the Magisterium of the Church, cf. the author's *Le Corps Mystique du Christ*, Volume II, Chapter 23.

[16] *Epist, 120*, n. 13, *PL* 33:459.

[17] *Enchiridion*, n. 1.

[18] St. Augustine, *Sermon 3, PL* 38–33

St. Augustine's solemn words remain true for every generation. There is but one Ark to save us from the waters of the flood. In order not to be cast out of it, we must hold fast to the rule of faith, without which "it is impossible to please God" (Heb. 11:6). Many of those whose forefathers left the Church some four-hundred years ago feel the need to return to one Church. Some among them, the more sincere and more generous, take the saving step and return to the Church of their fathers; others would like to reconstitute the unity of the Church without going so far, by what they call the union of the Churches. Alas! however laudable their intentions, they are pursuing an unrealizable goal. For if the Church is one, she can be so only through the oneness of her Creed. How can souls who do not profess the same dogmas be united in Christ? In the words of His Holiness Pope Pius XI: "How could charity turn to the detriment of faith?"[19] How can there be molded into one Body those who adore Christ present in the Blessed Sacrament of the altar and those who see in the Eucharist merely a sign of the absent Christ?

Some have attempted to restore the unity of faith by the common profession of what they call "the fundamental articles." When God has spoken, however, his creatures may not distinguish between what they will believe and what they will reject. Pope Pius XI also says: "The virtue of faith has as its motive the authority of God the Revealer, who does not brook any distinction of this sort."[20] Besides, among the articles set aside would be one of the most important, the primacy of Peter and of his infallible Magisterium, which necessarily condemns those attempts at a false unity in opposition to the will of the divine Founder of the Church.

Under the circumstances all we can do is pray to God that his goodness may bring back "to the port of truth and to the unity of faith" those whom discord and error have snatched from the bosom of the Church. "Oh! May our divine Savior, he who wills that all men be saved and attain to the recognition of truth, deign to hear our fervent prayers and bring back all who err to the unity of the Church."[21] May our separated brothers also, if they sincerely desire the great treasure of unity, beg in humble prayer for light and grace from above, and take to heart the words that St. Francis de Sales addressed to the heretics of his own time: "I adjure you, in the name of God, to take time and leisure to set your judgment aright, and pray to

---

[19] Encyclical, *Mortalium animos*, January 6, 1928.
[20] *Loc. cit.*
[21] Ibid., conclusion.

God that he may help you through his Holy Spirit in a judgment of such great moment, so that it may lead you to salvation. But above all, I pray you, let no passion enter your minds but that of our Savior and Master Jesus Christ."[22]

The Unbelievers

As we consider the mystery of the whole Christ, to whom it is our good fortune to be incorporated, at a moment when the entire Church, under the impulsion of the Holy Spirit, is penetrated with a new flame of zeal to bring the precious gift of faith to all the nations, can we remain indifferent to the fate of the countless multitudes of men who live outside the vital unity of the Mystical Body, many of whom do not even know the name of our divine Savior, or if they do know it, use it only to curse or to persecute true worshippers?

THE JEWS

The sons of Israel have rejected the Messias promised to their fathers; the followers of Mohammed rank Christ merely as one of their prophets and deny his divinity and his redemptive mission; idolaters of every name and belief are spread over the earth. All these unbelievers are still deprived of the light of the Gospel and are habitually excluded from the current of grace that flows so abundantly within the bosom of the Catholic Church.

And yet we must not imagine the condition of all of these unbelievers to be the same with respect to the means of salvation and the possibility of entering the Church. St. Thomas long ago distinguished the unbelief of the Jews from the unbelief of the pagans. To his mind, the former have already received the faith germinally in the figures of the Old Testament, whereas the latter have not received it in any form.[23] Even though the former are closer to evangelical truth, whose basic elements they possess in a certain respect in the prophetic Books of the Old Law, however, their case is also more serious and their guilt greater than that of the Gentile because of their stubbornness in denying and in persecuting their Savior and their Christ.

The Church, however, does not despair "of the children of this people once the most favored" of God. In her prayers she frequently implores divine mercy in their favor, "that upon them also may descend, but this time in

---

[22] *Book of Controversies*, Dedication.
[23] Cf. *Summa*, IIa-IIae, q. 10, a. 5.

the baptism of life and redemption, the blood that they once called down upon their own heads."

Words of great hope have been bequeathed to the Church concerning the sons of Jacob: "For the gifts and the call of God are without repentance" (Rom. 11:29). If God has permitted a few branches of the ungrafted tree to be cut off so that the branches of the wild olive might be engrafted upon its trunk, the day will come when the branches that have been cut away will again be joined to the tree which originally gave them life (cf. Rom. 12:11–14). The mystical Spouse of Christ lives in this hope. Each year, in her solemn prayers on Good Friday, she begs God to finally remove the veil from the eyes of this people so that, in renouncing their blindness, they too may recognize Jesus Christ our Lord in the light of truth. "For to this day," says St. Paul, "when the Old Testament is read to them, the selfsame veil remains, not being lifted to disclose the Christ in whom it is made void" (1 Cor. 3:14), and in whom the spiritual content of the Mosaic Law is revealed. "Yes, down to this very day, when Moses is read, the veil covers their hearts; but when they turn in repentance to God, the veil shall be taken away" (2 Cor. 3:15–16; cf. 3:7–18).

Until the general return of Israel, which will bring the Mystical Christ to fullness at the end of time, individual Jews, many of them chosen souls, will continue to enter the Church from the bosom of this mysterious people. They are still a divine sign in the face of the world because they remain unchanged in the midst of other peoples; they mingle without ever losing their identity. The Jews will be witnesses of Christ by their very denials of him, until the day they become his glorious conquest.

THE MOHAMMEDANS

Outside the descendants of Abraham, who hold a place apart among the unbelievers, the disciples of the Koran likewise make up an almost impenetrable mass whose fanaticism shuts them out from the light of divine Revelation. The incomparable Francis of Assisi once dreamed of bringing them the torch of faith, or at least of winning the palm of martyrdom on their soil which was so impervious to the sowing of the seed of the Gospel. His virtue was great enough to make these rebellious spirits venerate his own person, but not enough to make them accept the law of Jesus. And the great Lover of Christ was obliged to turn back without the apostolic conquests of which he dreamed or the glorious death to which he aspired.

The military power of the Crescent was for a long time a threat to the Christian kingdoms. Divine Providence, however, which makes all things work to the good of his elect (cf. Rom. 8:28), made use of these perils to bring to the East valiant phalanxes of crusaders determined to regain possession of the Holy Places. Thus the crusaders were made confessors of the faith and martyrs of Christ.[24]

But what is the fate, from the point of view of eternal salvation, of the millions of unbelievers who follow Mohammed? Do not souls of good will among them have some chance of attaining to the truth and being saved by cleaving to Christ? We know that God never turns away anyone of good will, and that "in every nation he who fears him and does what is right is acceptable to him" (Acts 10:35).

Assuredly in order to be saved under the present dispensation of the supernatural order, it does not suffice to know the one God, as is the case of Islam, solely in the light of natural reason. It is necessary to cleave through faith to the God of Revelation.[25] And yet fragments of revealed truths can be found here and there even in the Koran. And these fragments, seen in a special light of the Holy Spirit, will allow a few souls of good will and eager for God to attain to salvation through Christ, until such time as the compact mass of Islam lets itself be penetrated by the leaven of the Gospel.

THE PAGANS

After the sect of Mohammed, a great variety of forms of unbelief present themselves among the many peoples of the earth. And the parcels of truth hidden under the grossest errors become increasingly rare as we descend the ladder of civilization to the most degenerate tribes of the human family. All of these men, according to the powerful words of Scripture, "sit in darkness and in the shadow of death" (Luke 1:79). The great majority of them are completely ignorant of supernatural truths, and many do not have even a confused knowledge of the essential truths concerning God and the life to come which unaided natural reason enables us to discover. Moral degradation and servitude to the material life have, as it were, clouded the capacity of these uncultivated souls to grasp even the most fundamental philosophical concepts.

Even from their extreme spiritual poverty, that deserves the greatest compassion, however, it is still possible for these men to attain salvation.

---

[24] Cf. *Summa*, IIa-IIae, q. 124, a. 5 ad 3.

[25] Cf. Letter of the Holy Office of August 8, 1949, on the axiom: "Outside the Church there is no salvation," with reference to the controversy between Boston College and St. Benedict's Center.

Even for them, the Apostle's words remain true: "God... wishes all men to be saved and to come to the knowledge of the truth" (1 Tim. 2:4). By mysterious ways that escape our powers of investigation, the God of goodness and mercy knows how to insinuate himself into these rough and ignorant souls to remind them at least of the necessity of being faithful to the observance of the natural law. For every man, even if he has only a most rudimentary concept of God, knows through natural law his duty of submission to him, and has some conception of the just judgment the Supreme Arbiter will give on good or evil acts.[26]

Certainly, the observance of the natural law does not suffice for salvation, which is of the supernatural order. To be saved it is necessary to know God through faith and to love him with a love of charity, which presupposes a certain knowledge of Revelation. But fidelity in observing the natural law, with the help of the grace that God places at the disposal of all, prepares the soul for new graces and for the gift of faith. God has a thousand means by which to lead well-disposed souls to faith, and we must hold it certain that no one is deprived of faith except by his own fault, for not having responded to the first advances of grace.

It is not for us to search into these secret ways of God's saving providence, whose Wisdom is never hampered in its merciful designs by any human obstacle. But we know St. Thomas' statement that if a savage in the forest proved himself faithful in observing the natural law as he knew it, God would see to it that he be informed, through an angel if need be, of the elements of Revelation indispensable to salvation.

The account of the Martyrs of Uganda, who were beatified in 1922, contains an interesting note that illustrates in a remarkable way the above assertion by the Angelic Doctor. The father of one of these martyrs, who died

---

[26] There is no doubt that the idea of moral good, with the obligation incumbent upon us to accomplish it, presupposes the knowledge of God. God is indeed the term of this relationship of dependence that we call obligation. And moral good, according to St. Thomas, exists only as a function of our submission to the will of God. "Every created will has rectitude of act so far only as it is regulated according to the divine will, to which the last end is referred: as every desire of a subordinate ought to be regulated by the will of his superior" (*Summa*, Ia, q. 63, a. 1).

In consequence, in order to know this relationship of dependence we must of absolute necessity know the Superior, namely God, whose will is our rule, and toward whom we are obligated. All the more does the natural law present itself to us as an order of right reason. Now reason is a perceptive faculty which must see what it imposes. It cannot impose upon man a law whose constitutive element it does not know, namely the formal element of moral obligation, the duty of dependence upon God. This fundamental concept of the moral order has sometimes been forgotten in efforts to demonstrate inversely the existence of God by the existence of the law. According to St. Thomas, there is no moral rectitude without the formal conformity of our will to that of God, and hence without a knowledge of God's will as such Cf. *Summa*, Ia-IIae, q. 19, a. 10; Ibid., aa. 4 and 9; articles by Cardinal Billot in *les Etudes*, (1923), on "La Providence de Dieu dans le salut des infidèles."

before the preachers of the Gospel came to that region, had announced to his son on his deathbed the approaching arrival of the missionaries. In substance he said to him: "White men will come who will announce the knowledge of the true God and the manner of honoring him. You will follow them and you will do what they teach you." One after the other, Mohammedan Arabs and Protestant ministers came into the country. The young man, believing he recognized in them heralds of the true God announced by his father, took instructions from them and became successively Mohammedan and Protestant. Nevertheless, an indefinable something was missing to give his soul perfect tranquility until the White Fathers finally arrived in Uganda. Manifestly these were the missionaries whose coming his father had announced. From them the young man obtained, together with the true faith, the Christian courage that made a martyr of him. But what of his father? Had he not been instructed himself, through an angel, of the elements of Christianity and of the means of saving his soul?

Such possibilities of salvation in pagan lands are of course extremely limited. While they suffice to allay the doubts that some might conceive on the justice and goodness of God toward all redeemed souls, they should not lessen the zeal that every member of the Mystical Body should have to bring succor, according to his means, to so many souls in distress. Our love for God, if it is sincere, obligates us to this apostolic collaboration.

In his encyclical on the missions, His Holiness Pope Pius XI declares:

> The duty of our charity toward God demands that we strive to increase the number of those who know him and adore him in spirit and in truth, and that we try to bring the greatest possible number of subjects under the dominion of our most loving Redeemer. . . . What greater charity can we exercise toward our neighbor than by laboring to snatch him from the darkness of superstition in order to obtain for him the possession of the true faith of Christ?[27]

---

[27] Encyclical *Rerum Ecclesiae*, February 28, 1926.

Conclusion

QUI MANET IN ME ... HIC FERT FRUCTUM MULTUM"—"HE WHO ABIDES IN ME . . . HE BEARS MUCH FRUIT" (JOHN 15:5).

To abide in Christ and to act in Christ are two complementary aspects of the mystery we are studying. To abide in Christ is to belong to the Mystical Body in its constitution, in its being. To act, to bear fruit in Christ, is to share in the operations of the Mystical Body. To be and to act are two mutually completive activities. Of what use is it to be rich, to be learned, if we do not turn these talents to advantage, if we do not make them bear fruit for ourselves and for the good of society? Likewise in the Mystical Body, of what use is it to be engrafted upon Christ, to possess Christian grace, to be quickened by the Holy Spirit, if this divine wealth remains unproductive? Does this not lay one open to the Lord's curse, like the sterile fig tree of the Gospel? Christ himself has said: "In this is my Father glorified, that you may bear very much fruit, and [thus prove that you have become] my disciples" (John 15:8).

In the present study we have devoted ourselves to a presentation of the Mystical Body in its static state—*secundum esse*, as the philosophers say. Our work, however, remains incomplete. It calls for another to explain the Mystical Body in its dynamic aspect—*secundum operari*—the divine and supernatural activity of Christ and of his members.

The supernatural dynamism of the Mystical Body reveals all that is most wonderful in the life of the Church and in the heroic actions of her saints; this life and these actions both springing from the redemptive and sanctifying activity of her divine Head, Christ—King, Priest, and Prophet.

In conclusion, we shall merely give a brief sketch of the holy activity of the Mystical Body in its Head and members. It is our fervent hope that a full presentation of this subject will be made available in an American edition of Volume II of our work *Le Corps Mystique du Christ*.

The Life of the Head

At the end of his earthly existence, our divine Savior raised his eyes to heaven and declared to his Father that he had completed the work for which he had come into this world. "Father . . . I have glorified thee on earth; I have accomplished the work that thou hast given me to do" (John 17:1, 4).

In this sublime prayer the Word made flesh gives us a glimpse into the profound life of his soul before God. It is an adoring and loving life, a life that makes reparation by perfect worship in spirit and in truth (cf. John 4:23, 24) for the crime of revolt committed by man in the very beginning. But from the instant Christ entered the world, as St. Paul testifies, he offered himself up to the Father to accomplish the work of love, to do his holy will: "Therefore, in coming into the world, [Christ] says, 'Sacrifice and oblation thou wouldst not, but a body thou hast fitted to me: in holocausts and sin-offerings thou hast had no pleasure. Then said I, Behold, I come . . . to do thy will, O God'" (Heb. 10:5–7).

Adoration, total submission to the will of the Father, was the dominant note of the interior life of Christ from the moment of his Incarnation—a submission and an adoration beyond any human comprehension. In the words of Dom Marmion: "From the instant the Humanity was joined to the Word, this Humanity, in Jesus, was lost in profound adoration, in self-annihilation, before the divine Majesty of the eternal Word whose infinite perfections it contemplated through the beatific vision."[1]

Christ's interior life was to be, throughout his earthly existence and even after his ascension into heaven, the profound source of his mediatory and redemptive activity as our divine Head. For it was for us and for our salvation that the Son of God descended from heaven.[2] He came to adore his Father for us. He came to glorify him for us. Finally, he came to expiate in our place our sin of revolt, our refusal to obey. Then, when he had completed this expiation amid the pains of Calvary by his death on the cross, he reconciled us with the Father, making us his adopted children and heaping his graces upon us.

---

[1] *Christ in His Mysteries* (St. Louis: B. Herder Book Co., 1931), 82.
[2] The Nicene Creed.

The mediative activity of Christ is one in its source, namely, the grace of the hypostatic union. In its unfolding, however, it takes on three different forms, which constitute the three prerogatives of our Head: he is King, Priest, and Prophet. He himself told us during his life that he was the Way, the Truth, and the Life. Since he is our Way, he guides our steps toward eternal life. The mark of royal authority is to rule and to govern, to lead toward the term. As the Truth of our intellects, he teaches us in the name of God; this is his role as Prophet, the mouthpiece of God. Finally, he is our Life by his priesthood, by obtaining for our souls the sanctifying grace that is a participation in the life of God himself.

Jesus willed that his divine mother should share in this threefold prerogative. Mary is the new Eve who stands by the side of the new Adam, and as such is present everywhere in the activity of the Mystical Body, inwardly associated with the work of her Son. One of the best subjects of contemplation for Christian souls is Mary's role as universal Mediatrix by the side of the one Mediator.

The participated Queenship of Mary, recently proclaimed by His Holiness Pope Pius XII, is of a very special nature and needs to be studied with great care. Even more does her spiritual motherhood, which is associated with the priestly activity of Christ her Son, concern in the highest degree the knowledge of what has been called the Mystery of Mary and of our filial relationship toward the one who is the Mother of Divine Grace.[3]

The Life of the Members

The life of Christ becomes the life of his members. For, as the great Apostle declares: "It is now no longer I that live, but Christ lives in me" (Gal. 2:20). Thus we enter into the analysis of the greatest, richest, and most consoling aspect of Christian life. Dom Marmion, the eminent master of the spiritual life, was well justified in writing to a religious:

> I rejoice to see that the Holy Spirit has made you understand that we have everything in Jesus Christ. For this knowledge is the mustard seed of which our Lord speaks, that is very tiny at first, and then, when it is cultivated, becomes a great tree.
>
> Jesus Christ is infinite holiness: "*Tu solus sanctus, Jesu Christe*. But He is not only holy in himself. He has been given to us in order to be *our*

---

[3] Cf. R. Bernard, O.P, *The Mystery of Mary* (St. Louis: B. Herder Book Co, 1960).

holiness: *Christus factus est nobis sapientia a Deo, et justitia, et sanctificatio, et redemptio.*[4]

This life of Christ Jesus in us begins with baptism, the act which incorporates us into Christ and makes us one of his members. From that moment grace erupts into our soul, and we become the living temples of the Blessed Trinity. In its turn, sanctifying grace deploys its power in us through the action of the three theological virtues, which introduce us to the relationship of close friendship with the Three Divine Persons.

On a lower level, the infused moral virtues sanctify and deify our activity, in dependence upon Christ and in conformity with him, in the most varied manifestations of human life. Thus is fulfilled the Apostle's wish that "every man [may become] perfect in Christ Jesus" (Col. 1:28).

But this life of Christ in regenerated man is not merely the individual life of each Christian (cf. Eph. 3:16); it is also and more excellently the life of the whole Church. The Church, in the image of Mary who is her prototype, participates in the priestly mission of her divine Head. The unfolding of liturgical worship, whose center is the Eucharistic Sacrifice, is the continuation and application in time of the one priesthood of Christ the High Priest. The Church is likewise clothed with the royal power of Christ the King. In his name she rules and governs the Lord's sheep (cf. John 21:15–17); by his power she binds and looses (cf. Matt. 16:19; 18:18); by his authority she judges and condemns (cf. 1 Cor. 5:3–5; 6:2–6). Finally the Church, through her magisterium, exercises the prophetic function of Jesus. For when he was about to return to his Father, he commanded her: "Go, therefore, and make disciples of all nations. . . . I am with you all days, even unto the consummation of the world" (Matt. 28:19–20; cf. also Mark 16:15).

Faithful to his command, the Church has been carrying on for twenty centuries, continually opposed and yet always victorious, through the grace of her Spouse, in the work of conquering and of regenerating the world. From century to century the Mystical Body has continued to grow, to attain perfection, and to extend over new lands and among peoples not yet won over to Christian grace. Meanwhile the enemy rages and organizes his forces against her. Against the City of God, which looks toward heaven, the devil opposes the City of the World, whose vistas are purely of this earth. And while the latter claims to make history without God and against God, the Church pursues the meaning of her divine history—the only real meaning

---

[4] Dom Thibault, *L'Union à Dieu dans le Christ*, Volume II, Chapter 4.

of history because it is centered in God and in his Christ, the immortal King of the centuries (cf. 1 Tim. 1:17). Divine history, whose alpha and omega, whose beginning and end is Christ the Redeemer (cf. Apoc. 1:8; 21:6), began with the Creator's *fiat*, and will reach its term when Christ will have returned the kingdom to God his Father (cf. 1 Cor. 15:24).

It is our task to work, each one according to his grace, for the completion of the Mystical Christ, "in order to perfect the saints . . . until we all attain to the unity of the faith and of the deep knowledge of the Son of God, to perfect manhood, to the mature measure of the fullness of Christ" (Eph. 4:12–13).

May our humble efforts help in this work by revealing to souls the great plan of God for the Mystical Body of Christ.